Simulating Good and Evil

Simulating Good and Evil

The Morality and Politics of Videogames

MARCUS SCHULZKE

Rutgers University Press

New Brunswick, Camden, and Newark, New Jersey, and London

LCCN 2020004543

A British Cataloging-in-Publication record for this book is available from the British Library.

♾ The paper used in this publication meets the requirements of the American National Standard for Information Sciences—Permanence of Paper for Printed Library Materials, ANSI Z39.48-1992.

www.rutgersuniversitypress.org

Manufactured in the United States of America

To PB

Contents

Simulating Good and Evil

Introduction

You step out of an elevator into a crowded airport. There are tourists on their way to remote beaches, businesspeople eager to return home, and families saying their goodbyes. They are huddled together in the security line, waiting to pass through the metal detectors before embarking. You take a position behind the throng and open fire. Bullets spray from your machine gun. Along with three companions, you systematically annihilate the crowd of innocent people. Then you move forward, sweeping through the airport to continue the rampage. Guards try in vain to fight back, but their bullets zing helplessly against your Kevlar vests; they succumb to your heavy weapons. To your right, a woman struggles to pull her wounded husband to safety before he bleeds to death. To your left, a man clutches his stomach to stanch profuse bleeding. You cannot stop the attack. It must proceed. You cannot be the good guy. Any attempt to intervene just causes the other attackers to turn against you. Your only choices are to passively watch the attack unfold or put the victims out of their misery with quick shots to the head.

This is the infamous No Russian mission from *Call of Duty: Modern Warfare 2*. It is among the most controversial moments in videogame history. How could it be otherwise? The scene comes in one of the most commercially successful game franchises ever produced and is calculated to evoke strong responses. The violence recalls the 9/11 attacks with its airport setting, and plays on heightened fears of terrorism. Within a few months after being released, it was blamed for inspiring an attack on Moscow's Domodedovo airport.[1] In a rarity for the genre, No Russian casts players in the role of terrorists, allowing them to make the critical decision of whether to kill innocent people.

1

Books and articles about videogames routinely open with anecdotes like this. They present a lurid description of fighting, torture, or rape then ask readers to imagine themselves in the starring role. The twist is predictable: reveal that the atrocities are actually taking place in a videogame. They look and feel real, but they are simulations designed for entertainment. Read enough about videogames and this way of framing them will feel very familiar. It has become one of the stylistic conventions of gaming commentary. Like No Russian itself (or the myriad other controversial scenes that could be used in its place), the stories are designed to capture the audience's attention by provoking surprise, curiosity, and perhaps disgust. Describing in-game events as though they were real underscores a habitual thesis—that games are important artifacts that *feel real* and that can have an impact far beyond the screen. This style of juxtaposing reality and fantasy sets up readers for arguments that attempt to blur the boundaries between these two domains. The actual twist, it turns out, is not that the vividly described carnage is simulated but that the simulation is real. The deeper question, and the point where commentaries diverge, comes when drawing out the implications of the relationship between reality and simulation.

In many studies, the opening anecdotes of simulated atrocities are used to introduce moral claims and, in particular, to provoke a sense of outrage. No Russian is among the most popular targets, but countless other examples could be used in its place. Since their inception, videogames have been a source of moral controversy. They have been accused of making players stupid, encouraging violence, damaging empathy, distracting players from more important pursuits, promoting war, supporting terrorism, and dozens of other evils that I will discuss throughout the book. A smooth rhetorical transition from what appears to be a real act of violence to the revelation that it is a realistic simulation brings reality and fantasy together in ways that allow moral outrage to slip from actual transgressions to those that are fictional. From here, it is easy to take the next step of suggesting that games are dangerous—that they somehow share in the real horrors they simulate.

I start with this reflection on the anecdotal parallels between videogames and real acts of violence with a different intent. The rhetorical strategy simultaneously shows one of the greatest insights of commentary on the medium and one of its greatest failings. This framing highlights the importance of videogames, and of simulations more broadly, while also suggesting that the actions taken in games are in some sense immoral because of the parallel between reality and fantasy. I agree with the former point, but I will devote this book to refuting the latter. I argue that videogames are morally significant but that they rarely warrant moral condemnation. They are better understood as providing low-risk opportunities for moral reflection. Above all, my goal is to show that realistic simulation of serious moral transgressions in popular videogames is not a bug; it is a feature.

Decisions, Decisions

Let us back up for a moment and think about what is happening on a deeper level when someone plays *Call of Duty* or one of the many other controversial videogames on the market. Games are shocking when they simulate morally significant events. They show terrible atrocities but also great acts of heroism, acts that depend on simulated atrocities that the hero can counteract. More than that, games are shocking because they are participatory. They require players to work through disturbing moral challenges, whether the decision is to pull the trigger, observe passively, or stop playing. Participation is vital because morality is all about making decisions. One of the core assumptions in moral theory is that a person must in some sense *will* an action for it to be evaluated morally. That is to say, actions can only be called "good" or "bad" when they are chosen, not when they happen by chance or coercion. This is true regardless of the evaluative criteria used to judge the decision. If morality is a matter of intentions, as in deontological theories, then goodness or badness lies in the intentions that motivated an action. If morality is judged in terms of outcomes, as it is by consequentialists, then attention shifts to the outcomes resulting from a person's decision to act in a particular way. And if morality is primarily concerned with judging a person's character, as in aretaic/virtue-based theories, then vices or virtues within the actor are paramount.

Our intuitive moral judgments tend to reflect the same sense that actions are only blameworthy if they are chosen. Usually, we do not praise or blame people for doing things that they had no control over or for acting under duress. Even willful actions may be excusable when circumstances compel them. If you rob a bank because you want to buy a nicer house, then you are a criminal and deserve condemnation, but if you are lost in the woods and on the brink of starvation, then you may be forgiven for breaking into a person's house to steal some food. Breaking into a house is ordinarily immoral, but being under the duress of facing a life and death decision forces you to act and diminishes your culpability.[2] We tend to forgive people for accidents, provided there was no negligence involved, and even negligence is more forgivable than an intentional wrong.

What does the moral importance of choice have to do with videogames? It may help to explain why they have been such attractive targets for moral condemnation. Other media receive a share of the blame for corrupting audiences and instigating moral decay. In the aftermath of school shootings or when cultural critics decry the decline of traditional values, films, music, and television stand alongside videogames as regular scapegoats. Audiences make the decision to consume these products, which means that audiences can be blamed for voluntarily exposing themselves to movies, songs, and shows that are thought to have a corrosive influence. Nevertheless, these media are more passive than games insofar as audience members do not directly influence the content of the medium through their own choices. Someone watching a movie does not directly intervene in the decision to shoot one of the characters; such decisions about who to kill are common in games. Watch a film twenty times and you will always see the same events. Play a game twenty times and things could work out differently on each iteration, depending on what choices you make. There are important differences between more and less open-ended games. Videogames impose constraints on players, which require them to act in certain ways to proceed. Yet even the most linear games demand some degree of player intent for simulated acts of violence or other misconduct to take place.

Where videogames stand apart from other media is that players are not only subject to judgment as consumers of the entertainment but are also held partly responsible for what happens within the simulated worlds. Those playing No Russian are apt to be blamed both for buying the game *and* for deciding to shoot the innocent bystanders once they start playing. The overall moral valuation of games and players rests heavily on the assumption that interactivity creates a heightened degree of culpability for what happens within simulations. Player complicity in violence arises again and again in critiques of videogames. It establishes grounds for thinking that games are especially problematic from a moral perspective.

I was struck by the No Russian level when I first played it, because of the reactions of family members who were in the same room while I mowed down hordes of innocent bystanders. My family has no qualms with violent movies and television shows, and they have watched me play violent videogames on many occasions. None of it was particularly shocking to them until that moment when they seemed disgusted by the game and disturbed that I was enjoying it. I wandered through the airport, shooting as many people as I could. There were horrified gasps. Sure, the game could show scenes of violence against civilians, but how, my audience demanded, could I voluntarily pull the trigger? I was quick to resort to the amoralist defense that "it's just a game" (a defense I discuss in detail later). I was not actually shooting anyone. I was just *pretending* to shoot because I was *pretending* to be a terrorist. However, it was clear from the reactions that those watching felt that there was something more significant happening because of my voluntary participation in the killings. The same objection continually arises in scholarly research on games, with commentators questioning the judgment of players who willfully simulate atrocities, especially if players find this enjoyable.

Like morality, videogames are all about decisions. They are a form of interactive entertainment requiring choice. For anything to qualify as a videogame, it must at a minimum give players an opportunity to influence events. And it is not enough to simply act. Being successful demands reflection on the decisions with an eye toward identifying the rules of the game, and prediction about how actions will affect outcomes. Games differ substantially in terms of what decisions they present, how these are framed, how realistic they are, and how much freedom of choice they grant. Game design matters a great deal when it comes to creating these challenges and framing them, as well as in determining what consequences follow from decisions within the game world. There is therefore a natural affinity between moral decision-making and a medium that depends on the same skills.

This in turn raises a host of subordinate questions: Is it wrong to play certain types of games? Are immoral decisions in games *really* immoral, or do they just look that way? Do games harm players? Is it wrong for developers to present certain types of content or to frame issues in particular ways? It is also vital to see that these questions are not merely about morality. They are also political questions about what kind of society we live in, the collective responsibility for the content of entertainment, the permissibility of censorship, and the culpability of videogame developers for what players experience and what they do after encountering a game.

Thesis 1: Videogames Are Not Immoral, but They Are Morally Significant

My first goal in this book is to show that videogames are morally and politically significant but that they are rarely immoral in themselves. The parallels between No Russian and real acts of violence matter, as do the countless instances of simulated violence, sexual deviance, racism, and sexism in other videogames. I aim to demonstrate that there is value in efforts to link videogames to real life, and that this is especially important when it comes to moral and political issues. Videogames are not epiphenomenal fictions separate from the real world. They are influenced by real people, issues, and events, and may in turn influence their players. They are a means of exploring complex issues with the help of abstract models. They are a source of moral and political controversy in their own right, being central to debates over censorship and expression. They are tools of strategic communication that political actors use to persuade, and they are tools for fostering dissent that activists use to propagate counternarratives. By entertaining, informing, and inciting debate, they help to make reality what it is. We would do a serious injustice to videogames and their expressive power were we to deny their importance.

It is imperative to understand the interplay between videogames and the real world, but doing so requires first rejecting misguided attempts to show that videogames are immoral. We must eliminate some of the mistaken assumptions that hinder research on gaming and that inhibit the formulation of stronger theories of games' moral importance. Of particular importance are concerns that videogames promote aggression, degrade empathy, train players to kill, or undermine players' abilities to distinguish reality from simulation. Critics invoke dystopian futures in which people have lost empathy, learned to act violently, or simply ceased caring about morality. Critics imagine that this terrible future is coming within reach as videogames become more popular, more realistic, and more violent. Some even take the radical step of arguing that actions taken in videogames may be inherently immoral. Here they worry that simulated behaviors will become ingrained in players, causing character defects that may not be visible but that are nevertheless real. Concern over the moral implications of videogames has also become a political disagreement over whether censorship should be imposed or sales regulated.

Critics of videogames make some worthwhile points. For one thing, it would be wrong to assume that the decision to play a videogame only affects players themselves. Players are not solitary actors in a vacuum; their entertainment takes place in a broader social context in which there are legitimate concerns about what individuals think and how they behave. Societies have a vested interest in the moral education of their members—not in training people to accept a particular ideology but rather in imparting a basic sense of right and wrong, and fair treatment, that governs interactions with others. It is only possible to preserve good social relations and, by extension, to maintain a stable society that can endure over time if a large majority of members share roughly the same moral sensibilities and are generally committed to following them. Social stability and government functionality depend on a high degree of trust that people will usually play by the rules.[3] Wherever people cannot be reasonably assured that others will generally act morally, the result is a rise in mutual suspicion, hostility, and violence. Around the world, "failed states" are a testament to the myriad adverse consequences of losing this sense of common moral grounding: lower trust in governmental authority, organization devolving into small groups that can preserve a modicum of security, and economic uncertainty.

The shared commitment to acting well is at the basis of the idea of a social contract, which is essentially a belief that moral and/or political guidelines can be established through tacit collective agreement. Social contract theorists since Thomas Hobbes have sought to show that individuals can only become fully human by understanding their rights and responsibilities intersubjectively (in relation to others).[4] Even those who deny the existence of a social contract uniting members must assume that there is some basis for social cohesion. Whether this is national identity, shared participation in the economy, or ethnicity, the result is the same: group life depends on the participation of members, which is to say it depends on individuals' beliefs and actions within the broader social context.[5] Moral decisions by individuals are inherently politicized when they have a collective impact. In fact, it would be fair to say that morality is inherently political because moral decisions only arise during interactions between two or more individuals in which conflicting claims about rights and responsibilities must be reconciled.

The outrage against videogames reaches its apogee in efforts to show that they are responsible for atrocities that directly threaten the fabric of social life. Many psychologists who link games to aggression begin and end their studies with claims that their research demonstrates a connection between videogames and mass shootings.[6] The National Rifle Association (NRA) has repeatedly made the same argument following school shootings to shift attention away from gun control proposals.[7] Russian journalists and politicians blamed No Russian for inciting a real terrorist attack.[8] Opponents of the War on Terror have attempted to show that videogames were essential for building support for military operations abroad.[9] In these instances, critics argue that individuals' entertainment preferences are a political issue that threatens collective security. The critiques politicize gaming and show that questions of morality cannot be neatly contained within games or within a person's mind. They have broad relevance and must be approached as such.

The fear that entertainment could have harmful side effects on individual psychology and political order is a long-standing preoccupation of philosophers that can be traced back to Plato. Throughout his writings, Plato cautions against the potential harms that may be inflicted by the media that defined his epoch, especially poetry and written text.[10] In *The Republic*, he imagines the ideal city of Kallipolis, in which personal justice and public order are secured through civic education and careful control of information that could exert a corrupting influence. Plato warns that some poets are "damaging to those who hear them."[11] The potential for ideas to have a contaminating effect upon contact, without being subject to interpretation or doubt on the part of the audience, remains one of the central messages in media critiques. It is presented as a rationale for banishing potentially harmful media outright to prevent the imagined passive victims from being exposed to a pathogen. Plato is especially concerned about how such messages will affect children. There are echoes of this reasoning in the present, with arguments favoring censorship often focusing on adolescents. The irony of advocating restrictions on immoral influences when Plato's mentor Socrates was put to death for corrupting the youths of Athens seems to be lost on Plato. Later philosophers, including Montesquieu, Rousseau, and Tocqueville, make similar arguments, albeit without the same degree of skepticism.[12] They emphasize the importance of being attentive to what kinds of messages are presented in entertainment and what effects these have on the temperament of citizens.

The critics of videogames therefore stand in a long tradition of attacking the latest form of entertainment. The concerns may be directed at a new medium, but these critics participate in an ongoing quest to understand media influence. Analysis of the morality of videogames continues this long intellectual tradition by extending it into a new domain and recasting the critiques to reflect videogames' unique characteristics. The debate remains as important as ever and has broadened considerably by moving beyond the confines of philosophy to form an interdisciplinary conversation shaped by psychologists, sociologists, political scientists, specialists in game studies, politicians, and activists. With this in mind, I respectfully disagree with those who think that the matter is best left to psychologists.[13] The morality of videogames is a complex issue in which no particular research agenda can cover the entire range of questions that must be answered.

As I will show, the vast majority of arguments that games have an adverse influence on players are illogical, empirically unsupported, or based on more fundamental problems that go much deeper than games themselves. A few of the more modest claims have some merit and provide grounds for thinking carefully about what games are appropriate for children and others who may lack the judgment necessary to separate fantasy from reality. For the most part, the chances of moral corruption induced by videogames are negligible and outweighed by the potential moral benefits. The effort to impugn games mischaracterizes games' significance and has led many who enjoy them to defend themselves by resorting to the misguided argument that games have no real-world implications. The protracted war against videogames has made it seem like the medium either has a harmful influence on players or that it has no effects on the real world at all, foreclosing the possibility that they could have an influence that is largely positive.

I argue that videogames and the actions players take within them are not immoral and that efforts to incite moral outrage against moments like the terrorist attack in No Russian are deeply problematic. I dissect the central charges against videogames to reveal that most are fundamentally flawed and that even those with some plausibility can only be accepted with many caveats that limit their scope and intensity. Simulated actions may feel real and may provide a useful analogue for thinking about real moral challenges. However, verisimilitude does not alter the basic ontological fact that actions taken in videogames are not real in a strict sense. They are simulations without any immediate effect. The victims of No Russian are not real people; they do not suffer, and they lack moral agency. They have been killed thousands of times by thousands of players, without any genuine cost. We do actual victims a disservice if we think that the avatars themselves have moral worth or that players' simulation of an attack will cause them to kill. On the other hand, the virtual attacks against these avatars can help us think more deeply about violence and can therefore have real implications. The actions are morally significant because they simulate human analogues that have moral and political importance, but there is an enormous difference between simulating misconduct and actually engaging in it. The representation carries the negative connotations of the immoral act, but is not immoral itself. On the contrary, the representation of immorality is an invaluable tool through which we can understand wrongful actions without really enacting them.

Thesis 2: Simulated Moral Decisions Are a Form of Low-Cost Experimentation

My second goal is to show that videogames are important sites of moral exploration. They allow us to encounter challenges that we might never experience in real life or to see familiar problems from a different perspective. They may even help us appreciate the consequences of moral decision-making via simulations of the plausible results. The ability to create artificial moral challenges that feel real and that players must solve by exercising their own reasoning skills is one of the distinctive benefits of videogames. Games stand apart from other forms of entertainment by exploring moral questions as participatory experiences. When playing, we cannot passively watch someone else make the decision and evaluate the impact from a disinterested perspective. We must decide for ourselves whether to pull the trigger. Then we must grapple with a game world transformed by our actions.

Particular games differ in terms of how, and the extent to which, they take advantage of this capacity for simulating morality. There are games that lack the narrative depth to do this, such as *Tetris* and *Candy Crush*. Opportunities for moral decision-making are therefore not essential characteristics that could be used to define the medium. At the same time, moral reflection is common and is not restricted to games that explicitly include moral labels or moral choice engines. I will discuss some of the dominant strategies for presenting morality in games, with special attention to their strengths and limitations. I show that there is a widespread tendency to engage with weighty moral issues in thoughtful ways, which is evident even in the most controversial games.

Arguing that videogames are morally significant but that their influence is largely benign or even positive may sound strange. It may seem utopian or contradictory to say that games have important benefits while having negligible adverse consequences. The two dominant schools of thought assert that videogames are either largely self-contained simulations that do not have much of an impact on the real world (this is commonly known as the amoralist position) or that they strongly influence players, usually in harmful ways. My own argument runs counter to both of these perspectives and is apt to attract criticisms for trying to have it both ways—trying to celebrate the positive aspects of gaming without acknowledging the negatives. Such a response would make perfect sense. After all, if videogames can be sites of moral experimentation and even education, it seems logical that they could also be sites of moral corruption. Fortunately, this intuition is misguided.

It is easiest to understand the moral significance of videogames by way of analogy. I contend that the moral challenges introduced in videogames are akin to thought experiments that are commonly used to test intuitions in moral philosophy, only with a vastly greater ability to make the simulated decisions feel real. To evaluate the rightness or wrongness of complex issues such as abortion, euthanasia, torture, and war, philosophers tell stories about simplified cases that highlight the key moral considerations. These stories strip away extraneous details and demand answers based on consistent moral precepts. For example, they might imagine a scenario in which two patients are dying in a hospital and only one can receive assistance, then ask what values should guide the decision about which victim to help. These same kinds of counterfactual scenarios arise across fictional entertainment, but the decisions are all too often left up to other people—the characters we observe from a distance—which makes us work harder at putting ourselves in their position and thinking about the right choice than when we are dropped into the action and forced to choose for ourselves.

Videogames are not literally just thought experiments and are certainly not reducible to the moral puzzles they pose. There is much more going on in videogames beyond moral decisions, yet morality is often a key gameplay mechanic and is the reason why games incite panic. Videogames frequently raise questions in ways that are functionally similar to thought experiments. Thought experiments are used to develop models that can test moral intuitions and explore the consequences of actions. They make it possible to explain theories in simplified terms as well as test them against potential challenges. Videogames likewise model decisions in fictional contexts, test intuitions, and allow us to explore the consequences of different ways of acting. They also offer some important advantages over traditional thought experiments, which are typically conveyed in a narrative form that lacks the ludic elements of a game. Among these advantages are situating moral questions in more complex and engaging contexts, giving them a greater sense of concreteness, and raising the possibility of unanticipated consequences.

Why does the analogy between games and philosophical counterfactuals matter? It reveals a great deal about the benefits of exploring moral issues in simulations, even imagining unspeakable atrocities, and why doing so has few harmful side effects. It is impossible to be evil in a thought experiment. Thought experiments may expose poor moral judgment, yet even the worst choices imagined are merely imaginary. It is also implausible to think that thought experiments cause immoral conduct. They may ask us to think about uncomfortable scenarios involving murder, genocide, rape, and torture, but mere exposure to those actions in theory does not provide training for them or cause desensitization. At the same time, thought experiments can be profoundly beneficial, which is why they are a fixture of moral philosophy. Modeling issues within counterfactuals makes it possible to think about them more clearly and pushes us to reflect on our own reasoning strategies. Counterfactuals can even be responsible for moral sensitization by exposing problems we were previously unaware of. It is possible to miss the point of a thought experiment or to make an imagined decision unreflectively, thereby sacrificing the potential benefits. Nevertheless, this is not evil. The unreflective person is not immoral, only careless or perhaps narrow-minded. In the end, the imaginative moral puzzles that philosophers deal with provide a wealth of opportunities for testing moral intuitions without actually doing anything wrong.

Videogames function the same way. They present moral problems and allow us to simulate both good and bad outcomes, thereby granting the freedom to explore different possibilities without actually doing anything wrong. Regardless of whether players act well or badly in a game, there is something to be gained from playing. Branching moral paths show different dimensions of a choice and the results following from alternative courses of action. Players simulating good and bad actions (or perhaps trying both approaches on successive playthroughs) participate in moral exploration without incurring any real costs. It may seem as though the player who simulates good conduct is morally superior to one who enjoys being evil, but nothing could be further from the truth. When the decisions themselves have no consequences and the possible benefits arise from thoughtful engagement with the fictional world, then good and evil paths can be equally enlightening. In terms of moral development, there is as much to gain from simulating evil as there is from simulating goodness. Deliberately being evil forces players to confront what it means to be evil in a particular context and to self-consciously evaluate decisions with attention to what choices would be considered right and wrong. A player who intends to be evil must map out the moral terrain in the process of doing this. That player must fully engage with the moral implications of the simulated actions and develop a sense of how these actions would be evaluated if they were real. The player intending to be good performs the same operations. Both end up navigating identical moral terrain, and in practice many players take multiple paths to see decisions from different perspectives on subsequent replays.

Even making apparently terrible decisions, such as shooting the Russian civilians I discussed at the outset, is a way of exploring the moral possibilities presented by a particular dilemma. As with thought experiments, there is no such thing as acting well or badly, because there are no real actions. The point is that a greater understanding of real moral problems is attained by working with fictional models. Unreflective players may ignore the dilemmas they encounter and focus narrowly on progressing through the game. When this is the case, their ignorance of moral context is apt to blind them equally to any small adverse influences the game may have. In other words, if some players are only interested in destroying the game environment and killing avatars, without considering what implications this has in the game world, then they will also lack context to judge whether their attacks are justified. From the player's perspective, the simulated actions will be amoral. In this way, the question of whether games have moral content depends heavily on how players engage with fictional challenges.

The possibility of pretending to be good or evil depends on players seeing games through a moral lens. However, games tend to discourage unreflective play in subtle ways. Many titles that are associated with nihilistic destruction, such as those in the *Grand Theft Auto* and *Saints Row* series, do in fact provide strong clues that the actions being simulated are immoral. Run over a pedestrian or shoot a rival gang member and you will be hunted down by the police—a strong signal that the action was wrong. Much of the fun in these games comes from flaunting societal rules, which means tacitly recognizing what these rules are. These games permit us to intentionally simulate evil actions, but they do so while emphasizing that the actions are evil and by extension telling us that we should understand simulated worlds in moral terms. We may enjoy crushing an innocent old lady under a semi in Liberty City or Steelport, but we also know that this is wrong and that we can only enjoy it because it is fictional.

In practice, players' choices usually have no real consequences. Beyond the game itself, in the real world, it does not actually matter whether players decide to kill civilians at an airport. The simulated decision has no bearing on real people and thus cannot be properly judged as being moral or immoral. Thus, players can experience a simulated moral dilemma that encourages them to think critically about what their actions would mean if they were real, but the actions remain safely unreal. This is why it is possible for games to offer a forum for moral experimentation without being sites of moral degeneration.

To be clear, I am not arguing that videogames make people more ethical, that gamers are better people than nongamers, or that videogames should be seen as tools of moral education. Rather, the point is that even when videogames are designed primarily for entertainment, they present challenges that invite players to reflect on moral issues. There is no guarantee that players will take this opportunity, and they are under no requirement to do so. There is nothing wrong with engaging in unreflective play that does not consider moral implications. Sometimes players just need to shoot some zombies or Nazis without having to delve into the philosophical implications of doing so. However, many players seize opportunities to read their games' moral meanings, and doing this is a great way to get more out of a game. Developers may likewise find that emphasizing the moral challenges helps to make games more engaging than they would be otherwise. In games like *Life Is Strange* and *Darkest Dungeon*, moral decision-making is central to play, albeit in much different ways. It is doubtful that these games would have been as successful if they had avoided moral questions; in fact, it is hard to imagine them existing at all. Enjoyment and enlightenment can therefore be complementary goals.

Thesis 3: Persuasive Games Function as Arguments

My third goal is to provide a framework for thinking about the moral implications of using videogames to spread ideas or influence attitudes at a collective level. This is important because the debate over the morality of videogames has shifted somewhat over the past two decades. Many of the arguments that I explore when talking about the possibility of being immoral in a game or of games having harmful cognitive effects on players first emerged during the 1980s and 1990s and focused primarily on players as lone actors. In many cases, the research is strongly individualistic, such as when critics talk about the possibility of games inspiring alienated teens to shoot their classmates. Although these fears continue to inform commentaries on games, the scope of critique has expanded to include moral concerns having more to do with what effect gaming has on groups. Here there are concerns over how violent institutions such as the U.S. military produce games in an effort to attract new recruits, the use of games to spread political influence, whether games perpetuate harmful stereotypes, and how games violate social taboos.

Critiques directed at the collective level transform the moral objections relating to individual cognition into objections having to do with social and political relationships. The group-centric critiques therefore have affinities with the individual-centric critiques and often rely on the same basic reasoning. For example, group-centric claims that the U.S. military is using games to train soldiers to participate in aggressive wars depend on individual-centric claims that games can teach players to kill. Similarly, group-centric claims that videogames are being used to produce quiescent citizens who are disengaged from foreign policy decisions embody the same reasoning as individual-centric claims that videogames cause desensitization to violence. The difference between these two approaches to challenging the morality of videogames arises when we look at where the blame is laid and whether the emphasis is on political violence such as war or the more individualistic criminal violence of domestic life.

The shift in the locus of critique is important for three reasons. First, whereas the individual-centric critiques come primarily from social conservatives interested in protecting family values or shifting attention away from gun control, the group-centric critiques have come from academia and often take a more progressive standpoint. This shows that, despite adopting different critical strategies and being informed by different interests, these two perspectives share much in common when describing fears that entertainment can have a corrupting influence. Second, whereas the individual-centric critiques tend to focus more on individual morality and on the impact of aggressive individuals on society, the group-centric critiques look more at causation going in the opposite direction. They are concerned with the conduct of institutions as producers of strategic communication and the values of populations affected by that entertainment. This makes these critiques more overtly political. Looking at the continuities between the two critical strategies helps to expose the continuity between the moral and political issues they raise. Finally, the group-centric critiques focus much less on behavior and more on perceptions. Their concerns are primarily about how games influence attitudes, perceptions, and beliefs. This means that the claims cannot be tested in laboratories. They instead call for a broader perspective on how we judge the influence of gaming.

Despite these parallels, the group-centric critiques raise some unique concerns that are more plausible than those coming from the individual-centric research. For one thing, videogame developers often have persuasive intent. These goals are sometimes clear from institutional interests, but are often stated explicitly. *America's Army* openly affirms its goal of giving players a positive view of what it is like to be an American soldier. Its incentives for presenting a stylized image of the U.S. military could not be clearer. At other times, developers may not have an explicit goal but nevertheless produce games that show evidence of bias based on what information is included, how issues are framed, and what options players are afforded. The military first-person shooter genre beyond *America's Army* provides many examples of this. Games routinely privilege the viewpoint of Western (usually American and British) armed forces. Few attempt to show alternative points of view.

Concern over how games spread ideas is plausible because games do have some power to expose us to new perspectives. At the most basic level, the moral choices simulated and the evaluations issued by games reflect assumptions buried in the code. Developers create the moral challenges that players will experience and can frame them to make tacit arguments. They manufacture moral issues and assign costs and benefits to different courses of action. Some games explicitly label players, calling them good or evil based on how the challenges are resolved. Others may refrain from passing such clear judgments but nevertheless structure game worlds according to morally and ideologically charged presuppositions that are conveyed throughout the game. This makes it possible for developers to set up challenges and rewards that urge players toward a particular perspective.

Games deserve moral scrutiny, and may even be condemnable, based on what messages they implicitly or explicitly advance. Nevertheless, we must tread carefully and see that controversial games can also be valuable. Shocking scenes are essential for posing big questions and prodding players to become more reflective. Game design raises questions about the actors responsible for the games. Is there something morally problematic about militaries creating games to help their public image? Is it wrong to produce games with sexualized representations of women or to invoke racial stereotypes? Are deeply offensive games that deal with real events, such as mass shootings and genocides, immoral? I contend that many attempts to answer these kinds of questions are too heavily informed by the same sense of moral outrage that impedes the individual-centric research on videogames. We need to rethink how we evaluate ideologically charged games and how we understand games that present offensive content.

I expose a problematic tendency among academic commentators and members of the media to dismiss persuasive games and games with ideological biases as being mere propaganda that is intentionally misleading. Such a sweeping indictment of game developers suggests that the ideas that appear in persuasive games are vacuous, serving no other function than to indoctrinate. I recommend taking an alternative approach that is more open to the many different perspectives videogames offer. Games certainly present problematic information and attitudes, but identifying them first requires us to engage with controversial games and the ideas they present. We should approach persuasive games not as blatant lies or as propaganda to unmask but instead as arguments. Games that have strong ideological biases can be enjoyable and even informative. They offer insight into alternative perspectives, which is particularly useful when it comes to understanding how members of specific groups and institutions see themselves and their goals. These games can and should be critiqued, yet critique needs to arise from a very different sensibility that starts by treating the games as communicative acts that are more substantive than mere propaganda. Above all, we must abandon the assumption that exposure to ideas contaminates players and recognize that players navigate videogames with existing beliefs and attitudes that reconfigure games' messages and shape their reception.

Two powerful critical strategies remain open when we read ideologically charged games as arguments instead of lies. The first is what I call an external critique, based on looking at a game's mimetic accuracy. Simulations are models of the real world produced by selecting what information to include and how to frame it. This can lead to factual inaccuracies, the omission of key details, or the mischaracterization of the issues and events being simulated. These choices can be fairly critiqued based on how much they skew the historical record. The second strategy is internal critique, or immanent critique. This approach seeks to expose tensions between ideological assumptions embedded in game narratives or between the game's rules. Both of these investigative strategies depend on approaching games as communicative acts that have more substance than mere deceptions would. Moreover, these strategies only work if we situate games within their social and political context.

I also consider how easily feelings of discomfort can be conflated with genuine moral problems when it comes to games that present upsetting content. Actions in games are not real, but they can still cause discomfort. Virtual murder and rape are not immoral themselves, but they are uncomfortable because they evoke real criminal acts. A simulation of genocide is likewise not real genocide, but it does remind us of the horrific consequences of systematic killings in the real world. The moral panic surrounding games is largely based on a misguided sense that simulated actions are wrong, which draws on feelings of discomfort that critics (and many players, for that matter) experience when engaging in simulations that conjure up difficult subjects. The moral sentiments are understandable, and often praiseworthy, but they are misplaced.

It is vital to distinguish between offensiveness and genuine moral concerns when it comes to games, especially when offensive games are often best suited to challenging our prejudices and encouraging us to see the world from a different viewpoint. Much of the offensive content that draws critics' ire is justifiable when it is put into context. Games based on professional sports leagues or historic events often disproportionately feature white male characters, yet they do this because they attempt to mirror a real world that is marred by exclusion. In some instances, offensiveness is essential for making important points. *Grand Theft Auto* includes upsetting racial stereotypes and violence, but this is vital to the game's satire. Even *Super Columbine Massacre RPG!*, which allows players to carry out a school shooting modeled on real events, tries to make a political statement that gives the offensive content redeeming value.

Games that attempt to incite violence or discrimination are morally condemnable, but such games are rare and have limited success beyond the narrow markets of those who already accept the arguments being made. Critics are right to attack those games, yet they usually pose minimal risk. The games that attract the most vociferous and sustained condemnation are usually popular titles with important messages lying thinly veiled beneath the offensive content. To players' credit, games that advocate blatantly racist, sexist, or militant viewpoints tend to sell poorly and are widely ridiculed. The most important goal is not censoring the rare cases of immoral content but instead protecting games with controversial content from misplaced moral condemnation.

Overview of the Book

Chapter 1 provides a summary of the key concepts that I explore throughout the book and the methods I employ. The distinction I draw between simulation and reality is especially important for setting up subsequent chapters. I aim to show that these categories are neither completely separate (as amoralists argue) nor so intermingled that they can be collapsed into each other (as many critics of videogames maintain). There is a reciprocal link between videogames and the real world. We bring ourselves into videogames, and what we experience during play follows us back out. We may change and grow through our experiences with games, just as we may from other engagements with fiction through books, films, and television shows.

Some interplay between reality and fiction is too often mistaken for unfiltered and uncontrolled spillover between these domains to the extent that simulated actions take on real moral significance or radically transform players. It is misleading to think that visually realistic entertainment causes audiences to lose their sense of what is real and what is not, or to assume that audiences have uniform interpretations of media. People do not encounter entertainment with minds like blank slates. Rather, their interpretations are shaped by existing cognitive frameworks and prior experiences. Games and other types of entertainment do not have a straightforward causal impact such that we could ever say that they cause people to become violent. Psychological research shows that people process information through cognitive filters that moderate external influences and limit their impact, which suggests that the effects of videogames and other media will be slight and always mediated by existing attitudes and values.

Methodologically, I build on insights from ludological and narratological approaches. The field of game studies is moving beyond framing research narrowly in terms of one of these perspectives or the other, but it remains useful to reflect explicitly on these two schools of thought because they can yield different insights. Ludology highlights the importance of game mechanics and interactivity. When applied to moral decisions, it encourages us to think about how problems are constructed and what impact they have on gameplay. Narrative is equally important, as it fills in the details that give decisions a moral character. Narrative contextualizes player interactions with a game to make clicks of a button represent actions and to build a world in which players' decisions matter. I emphasize both dimensions of videogames throughout the book, treating ludology as the structure that makes moral decisions interactive and narrative as the contextual information that allows simulated events to take on moral dimensions.

Chapter 2 discusses the moral panic that has plagued videogames since the 1980s, focusing on arguments about what impact games have on player cognition. Here I consider four of the most pervasive critiques: that videogames train players to kill, increase aggression, cause desensitization, and blur the line between fantasy and reality in problematic ways. This analysis draws on work from psychologists who have developed models of cognition that render the critical claims implausible as well as work psychologists have done to directly refute claims about videogames being a source of moral corruption.[14] I also point out the methodological problems present in many studies charging videogames with immorality and show that they are at odds with sociological facts. I am not a psychologist and acknowledge that more work must be done looking at how videogames influence cognition, yet I contend that the weight of the available evidence provides grounds for rejecting the moral panic about games transforming players' minds for the worse. The paucity of support for these four critiques, combined with the strong counterarguments, should lead us to conclude that the critiques are either wrong in most cases or at least that behavioral changes caused by games are apt to be small and confined to certain audiences who are especially susceptible to media influence (e.g., young children).

In chapter 3, I examine what it means to make moral decisions within simulations. I draw an analogy between the moral challenges created by videogames and narrative thought experiments used by philosophers. Many game theorists resist comparisons between videogames and other media, but here such a comparison is apt because of the close resemblance between these two types of counterfactuals when it comes to how they facilitate the exploration of moral issues. Thought experiments pose moral questions by situating them within fictional hypothetical scenarios. Although these are usually presented using narratives, they are analogous to games insofar as they are interactive and based around rules that dictate what is permissible within a particular scenario. Like a game, a thought experiment must be imaginatively enacted. Computer modeling has even made it possible to transform classic thought experiments from narratives into digital simulations that are indistinguishable from videogames. Moreover, games incorporate myriad counterfactuals that closely mirror famous narrative thought experiments. I contend that the reason for this overlap is that the moral challenges in games have the key attributes of thought experiments along with some distinctive new benefits that arise from enacting moral decisions within digital worlds.

Drawing an analogy between thought experiments and videogames helps to explain the implications of producing moral counterfactuals in spaces that are set apart from the real world. Videogames' convincing graphics may make them feel more real than hypotheticals that are purely narrative in form, but the use of different technologies for building models does not make a morally significant difference. That is, the medium used for creating moral simulations is not itself morally significant. In videogames, as in narrative thought experiments, it is possible to explore serious, and often troubling, dilemmas without incurring real costs. Thought experiments and videogames are alike when it comes to allowing us to imagine good and bad actions without harming others, intending to harm others, or rehearsing real behaviors that might plausibly corrupt our character. On the other hand, imaginatively navigating difficult moral terrain can help us think more carefully about important issues. Simulating moral decision-making therefore presents a win-win scenario in which we cannot cause any real harm but can experiment with different styles of moral thinking.

In chapter 4, I build on the thought experiment analogy to argue that videogames are important tools for confronting serious issues through entertainment. Games immerse us in counterfactuals that ask us to make countless moral decisions and to consider what consequences these decisions might have. They allow us to inhabit worlds that are shaped by alternative moral systems and political ideologies. Just as it is impossible to be truly good or bad in a thought experiment, it is impossible to be truly good or bad in a videogame. Because there are no costs associated with this moral exploration—no harm inflicted in the virtual worlds and little plausible evidence of harm on players themselves—players may pretend to be evil without really being evil. In fact, pretend evil is an important part of mapping out the possible courses of action and thinking about what consequences would follow from them. This shows that videogames are amoral in the sense that there is no wrongness involved in playing them but that they are still morally significant and possibly even beneficial because they facilitate cost-free moral experimentation.

In chapter 5, I evaluate some of the approaches games take to simulating morality. I look at moral choice engines that score players' decisions, games that allow players to choose fixed alignments, reward-based systems, and factional alignment systems, among others. This is not a comprehensive taxonomy but rather an effort to highlight some of the most popular styles of simulating morality. My overall goal is to show the diversity of approaches and how they complement each other by exposing different aspects of real-world moral decision-making. Moreover, the games I discuss demonstrate how morality can become integral to gameplay, simultaneously offering enjoyment and opportunities for moral experimentation. Decisions are integral to videogames and help to make games more fun by heightening players' sense of agency. I also discuss some of the ways that videogames build moral considerations into the background narratives by creating entire worlds based around a particular political ideology, hypothetical future, or imaginary past.

There is no perfect method of presenting moral challenges in videogames. Every approach has advantages and disadvantages. Some, such as reward-based evaluations, tend to be shallower than others, because of the demands of balancing realism and gameplay. Punishing decisions too harshly could hinder enjoyment, so gameplay considerations tend to take precedence. However, I argue that researchers have been too quick to dismiss some morality systems as superficial. Even the routinely maligned unrealistic scenarios and strict good versus evil moral binaries can have some value. Choices may vary in terms of how much player freedom they permit, how closely they resemble real moral decisions, and the extent to which they affect the game. Nevertheless, the value of taking on moral challenges in entertainment supersedes the loss of philosophical rigor. Whether they are sophisticated or simplistic, dilemmas encourage players to think about gaming in terms of moral categories.

In chapter 7, I turn to some additional critiques directed against videogames, this time looking at arguments that games present harmful social and political commentary. Here my concern is not with the cognitive effects that I discussed in chapter 2 but rather with games that critics credit with propagating dangerous ideologies. The ongoing debate over military videogames, especially those produced with military assistance, provides my central case study. I contend that critics are right to challenge the ideas that persuasive games present but that it is vital to avoid falling back on baseless claims that overstate the harms games can inflict or characterizing persuasive games as intentional efforts to dissimulate. Most games with strong ideological biases do not seem to be designed to mislead or indoctrinate. Rather, their creators appear to genuinely believe in the games' messages. Treating persuasive games as mere propaganda lacking any informative content closes us off from understanding ideas that we disagree with and encourages the conceit of seeing such ideas as being wholly without merit.

I attempt to rehabilitate the critique of the ideologies embedded in videogames by treating them as arguments rather than as lies. These arguments help us understand other perspectives, but they can still be challenged and refuted. We can take them seriously without necessarily agreeing with them. I show that there is some value in seeing the world from other perspectives by interrogating persuasive games and thinking about what insight they offer into how others see the world. Much as videogames with morally troubling content can help us think more carefully about morality, playing persuasive games is an important sociological exercise that exposes us to alternative ways of seeing the world. It is fair to challenge persuasive games for factual inaccuracies, biased framing of information, and affirming contradictory values, and it is important for critics to continue uncovering this kind of problematic content. Nevertheless, the overall critical project needs to be reframed with an awareness that critics bring their own biases into games and that the back and forth of ideological disagreement cannot proceed by simply treating alternative viewpoints as fraudulent.

In the book's conclusion, I look beyond ideology and persuasion to assess the moral implications of games that include offensive content, such as sexual deviance, upsetting re-creations of real events, and racial and gender stereotypes.

These games are usually less overtly political than those about war or ideological disagreements, yet they become politicized through their reflection on sensitive events and identity issues. I show the importance of distinguishing between games that are offensive and those that are immoral. It is reasonable to feel uncomfortable about simulations involving offense. However, offense is often essential for making worthwhile points and must therefore be distinguished from immorality. This is particularly important when offensive games convey messages that participate in public debates. For example, videogames about school shootings are offensive, but they can be morally defensible as political speech acts that contribute to ongoing disagreements about gun control. We should only treat games as being morally problematic if they set out to incite violence or promote discrimination. Just as with other speech acts, it is difficult to determine when games cross the line from offense to incitement. This can only be decided on a case-by-case basis, and should be done with an appreciation of the moral and political value of free expression in games.

1

The Conceptual Terrain
of Simulation

The moral issues relating to videogames span multiple academic disciplines, including game studies, philosophy, communications, psychology, sociology, law, and political science, among others. They lead through dozens of intractable debates, such as what it means for media to influence audiences, whether fictional entities are in some sense real, what moral standards we should employ, and what should be covered by free speech protections. The issue is so expansive that it exceeds any single treatment, including this one. I cannot hope to give the definitive last word on all things about videogames, especially when the medium is continually changing. My goal is more modest: to provide an accessible overview of why videogames are morally significant and to make the case for reorienting academic research and popular commentaries away from moral panic. I aim to map out a more constructive approach that recognizes the benefits of the moral exploration made possible by videogames.

This chapter provides an overview of the conceptual terrain. I start by drawing a distinction between videogames and real life, which I continually refer to throughout the book. I acknowledge that videogames influence real life and vice versa; these two domains are irrevocably connected. Any approach to analyzing games must recognize that they exist in the real world and that the ideas they present are real even if simulated actions are not. However, it is still possible to draw a firm line between reality and fiction when it comes to the types of entities they include. Videogames may borrow from real life for inspiration, at times even attempting to mirror it, but they are nevertheless unreal in the sense that any simulated moral transgressions are purely imaginary. To a large extent, efforts to demonize games rest on critics' attempts to bridge the divide between reality and fiction, such as by claiming that games cause players to mistake fantasy for reality or that they provide realistic simulations of violence that can train players to kill. From here, I turn to some of the unique traits that set videogames apart from other media. Above all, videogames are interactive. Player participation is one of their defining characteristics and the key to understanding their moral significance. Players are actors in game worlds. They help to determine what happens, making them ethical agents within the narratives. Players are responsible for causing the fictional events in a way that audiences watching a film or reading a book are not. This makes it possible to judge their *simulated* actions as right or wrong, good or evil, even when there are no real actions that warrant praise or blame.

In the second half of the chapter, I explain the methodological assumptions that guide the analysis. Game studies developed with help from a disagreement between ludological and narratological perspectives. The former emphasizes the importance of gameplay rules and the concept of play, while the latter focuses on narrative elements such as plot and character. Although this disagreement has largely been overcome in recent research attempting to bridge the divide, this distinction provides a useful framework for thinking about different aspects of videogames. Ludological perspectives highlight the importance of game mechanics in structuring moral challenges, determining what options are available, and creating consequences. When approached from this perspective, we can see the moral challenges in terms of what moves they permit and what makes them fun. Narratological perspectives are likewise important, since game narratives imbue otherwise abstract puzzles with a sense of moral significance. The narrative elements of a game make it possible to understand player inputs as influencing fictional worlds.

Polysemy—the possibility of reading a text in different ways—is another key concept informing my analysis. All media are polysemous. The text of a book does not change when different people read it, but each reader can take a different position on what the book means. Some readings may be better or worse when it comes to accounting for the textual evidence provided, but we can never settle on a single definitive interpretation. The entire history of literary analysis, with its constant disagreements over the meaning of great books, provides ample evidence of this indeterminacy of meaning. Polysemy is particularly important when it comes to videogames because they do not offer a consistent experience that is the same for all players. Interactivity multiplies the range of evidence available to formulate divergent interpretations by exposing players to different textual cues.

I devote the final section in this chapter to discussing three of the ethical theories that come up throughout the book: deontological ethics, consequentialism, and virtue ethics/axiological ethics. I will not argue that one of these perspectives is better than the others. Instead, I explore the implications of each when it comes to games. Critics of videogames have launched attacks from each vantage point, often treating these theories as different opportunities for impugning games. However, they have failed to produce convincing arguments that games are wrong according to any of these three dominant traditions of Western ethical theory. There is much to learn from looking at which theories are applied and why. Psychological research and outrage from concerned politicians tends to take a consequentialist approach by attempting to show that gaming has harmful effects on behavior. Philosophers, by contrast, have been more drawn toward deontological and axiological perspectives as ways of showing that games are harmful even if they do not cause behavioral changes.

The Reality of Simulation

Throughout the book, I draw a distinction between the worlds simulated by videogames (which I call digital worlds, simulated worlds, or game worlds interchangeably) and reality. This dichotomy is important to clarify at the outset because it holds a great deal of moral weight. Many commentators who criticize the morality of gaming attempt to collapse this distinction as a way of finding some grounds for saying that simulated actions are in some sense real and therefore capable of being immoral. As I show later, this makes it easier for critics to argue that behaviors learned in digital worlds carry over into the real world. Amoralists take the diametrically opposed position that games are completely self-contained and detached from everyday life. They say that a game is "just a game," with no deeper meaning beyond immediate enjoyment. Here there is a sharp division between reality and fiction, without any intersection between the two and no possibility of games affecting the real world. I take issue with both perspectives and argue that videogames can be significant without treating simulated actions as though they were equivalent with, or even closely akin to, real actions.

Critics of videogames are right to think that there are important connections between the world and digital models of it. Reality shapes the content of videogames by providing events, settings, artifacts, and characters that are incorporated into fictional narratives. And videogames undeniably influence reality, as evidenced by the extent to which moral panic surrounding games has informed policy debates and even been the subject of court cases. There is also overlap between these domains. Gaming is something that we do in the world; it depends on physical objects to provide inputs and outputs, and the code is physically stored on devices. Games are therefore encompassed by the real world. Jesper Juul observes that games are "half real" because they use material artifacts such as machines and lines of code to create fictional worlds.[1] I agree with this point and go one step further by arguing that the fictional elements of videogames are also half real. Just as we may be affected by a film or a book, we may be affected by a compelling videogame. We bring our virtual experiences with us when we turn off games and return to our real lives with memories of what we have seen and done. Critics err by overstating the realness of simulations; amoralists err by thinking that simulations are not real at all.

Establishing connections between the real and the digital is just as essential to my overall thesis about the morally enlightening implications of gaming as it is to critics' efforts to show that there is something wrong with gaming, but for the opposite reason. My argument rests on demonstrating that digital worlds present moral puzzles that are analogous to those we encounter in reality and in other fictional models, and that games therefore provide meaningful spaces of moral exploration. Games have an influence on the real world by serving as spaces to work through moral problems without engaging in any actions that are genuinely immoral. Where I part ways with the critics is when it comes to the nature of this relationship between reality and simulation. I contend that the overlap between these two domains is beneficial rather than being a source of corruption. My effort to distinguish reality from videogames does not preclude some overlap between the two. Such an overlap exists and can help to account for how games affect us, yet it does not make the actions in videogames real in the sense that they warrant moral praise or blame. That is, there is mutual influence, but it does not undercut the clear separation between simulation and reality.

The continuum between the real world and the fictional events of digital worlds is *epistemic*—it is a transfer of *information*. Players take virtual experiences into the real world and are therefore influenced by those experiences. However, the continuum between reality and fiction in games is the same one that exists with respect to other media, such as films and books. These media sometimes spark controversy, but they are generally treated as having a benign or even positive influence. We may learn from a good book or be moved by it; we may be inspired by what we read or terrified. Our lives are affected by prose, but in nearly all instances *only subtly*. This is why most of us now look back on efforts to ban, censor, or destroy books with derision. Fictional experiences help to make us who we are, but they do so alongside many other influences, including what are usually more important formative experiences that take place in real life. Critics describe videogames as presenting information that is inherently harmful, such that players are akin to drug users or passive victims who lack the same critical faculties that they would bring to a book or film. Throughout the book, I argue that this is an unfair double standard. We can recognize that videogames exert a subtle influence on us, just as other media do, without accepting the sweeping claims that critics make about players being transformed into murderers or sociopaths.

Just as importantly, those who condemn videogames for immorality usually only look for the effects that games have on players and not causation moving in the opposite direction. They focus on one side of an epistemic relationship that goes both ways. Players bring themselves into games. They interpret videogames and interact with them, helping to construct their meaning. Players shape videogames through gameplay choices that alter simulated events and through participation in fan communities where textual interpretations are voiced. They may even substantially alter games through modding (creating game modifications), which may in turn transform how games appear to other players. The epistemic continuum between reality and simulation must be seen as one of mutual exchange, in which players wield much of the power for determining the content and meaning of games.

The disjuncture between the real world and digital worlds is *ontological*; it is a difference between what kinds of entities are contained within each. We need moral constraints in the real world because it is populated by entities that can be adversely affected by decisions. Morality deals with agents who can inflict harm or be harmed. It proscribes certain conduct in the interest of protecting individuals and social order more broadly. It also deals with second-order obligations to promote fair treatment and provide assistance to those who are wronged. By some accounts, only humans can be full moral agents, though there is good reason for thinking that animals also may have moral agency (at least as recipients of harm) and that autonomous machines may one day have to be granted a similar status if they become sufficiently advanced. Objects sometimes enter into our moral calculations as things that can be damaged and that by extension harm moral agents, but objects themselves do not have moral agency. We treat the destruction of property as a moral transgression because this injures owners through deprivation. Destruction of physical things may also threaten the future interests of moral agents, as in the case of environmental degradation. We do not treat the destruction of physical things as being inherently wrong, however. Breaking a stick lying out in the woods is an action that lacks moral significance because it does not inflict substantive harm on a moral agent or a moral agent's interests. The destruction of objects must impose some negative costs on moral agents to warrant censure.

It is possible to inflict harm that is purely digital. Erasing someone's pictures or deleting their homework is clearly harmful. Even if these items have no material existence beyond the computer, they are things that people value and have an interest in. It is likewise possible for goods within videogames to take on moral weight. Players may steal from each other in multiplayer games or manipulate each other in ways that cause harm. Sneaking into someone else's account and deleting saved games or erasing achievements would qualify as digital harm, as would transferring equipment to another account without permission—effectively stealing it. Objects can be digital and yet still ontologically in the class of things that are morally significant because they are akin to physical property in the sense that destroying or stealing them inflicts harm. I therefore make a caveat to my arguments throughout the book that it is possible to act immorally in games when it comes to offenses that are akin to property destruction or theft. In some extreme cases, deliberate destruction of digital property accumulated in a game has even led to prosecution, which is justifiable considering the genuine cost this inflicts.[2]

Theft is possible when there is scarcity of digital goods. Having a rare sword stolen in *World of Warcraft* inflicts harm because it cost time and/or money to obtain and cannot be easily replaced. This scarcity is artificial, but just like digital currencies, maintaining it is essential to preserving the overall sense of value and ensuring that users trust the game's economic system. Stealing another player's sword by hacking their account breaks the game rules, while taking a sword in accordance with the rules after defeating the other player in a consensual battle does not. Game rules establish a kind of moral boundary to govern play, and immoral treatment of other players is only possible when players go beyond those rules to inflict harm. Simulated aggression within the boundaries of game rules is not only expected—it is essential. It is what allows games to function and is something that players tacitly assent to by choosing to play.

The scope for immorality in games is fairly small, and the extent of the damage it causes is usually minimal. The first clue that videogames occupy a distinct ontological space is that transgressions do not match up with their real-world analogues. Cheating to kill another player's avatar is a minor infraction. It is cheating, not murder. Stealing a rare sword from another player's account may be punishable, but probably not to the same extent as stealing physical property like a car. Attacks against avatars and digital goods seem less serious than those against actual people and property because they are confined to a special domain. Virtual attacks primarily affect players within the game and do not follow them into the real world in the same way as the loss of money or material property.

For the most part, videogames simulate harm that is ontologically distinct from the harms we experience in real life. They simulate murder, yet the entities being killed are not moral agents. They are not real in a sense that would make them deserving of moral consideration. Even if the characters can exert some influence epistemically (i.e., by providing experiences that players take out of the game world), they nevertheless remain ontologically unreal. Avatars may appear to die, but they do not really die. They may look injured, but they are never really injured. Moreover, they do not have any value as property, because they are not scarce. They are infinitely reproducible entities that can never be truly destroyed. Any injury inflicted on avatars disappears upon pressing the reset button. Videogames likewise simulate property destruction, but it is not truly property destruction, because it does not inflict any harm on moral agents. There is no loss involved in stealing a car in *Grand Theft Auto* or blowing up a city in *Fallout 3*. No moral agent is affected by these actions. The entities being stolen or destroyed are digital. Moreover, these entities are meant to be infinitely destructible.

The line between reality and simulation is somewhat blurry. There is epistemic exchange between the two domains, and there are some instances in which violence against digital entities can inflict real harm. However, for the most part, game worlds are ontologically separate from the real world, with costs that are safely contained within the simulations. Central to my overall thesis is the contention that none of the actions players perform in single-player videogames are themselves moral or immoral. The same is true for actions in multiplayer games, so long as they do not affect other players in ways they have not explicitly or tacitly consented to. Videogames are simulations; they are not real in the same sense as the activities they represent. Games may have an influence that players take back to the real world, giving gameplay greater significance than amoralists acknowledge, but this does not change the ontological fact that the simulations themselves are not real and that they do not feature any of the harms or intentions to do harm that moral judgments depend on. Judging simulated actions by the same standards as real actions makes a fundamental mistake of attribution and degrades moral precepts through misapplication.

Some philosophers have attempted to deconstruct the boundary between simulation and reality to show that it is illusory or at least fading away with the proliferation of digital media. Poststructuralists such as Jean Baudrillard have spent decades arguing that the line between simulation and reality is blurring to the point that reality itself is unreal.[3] According to Baudrillard, the postmodern reliance on technologies and techniques to mediate experiences of reality allow the representations to supplant reality. Representations become more real than the things they represent as they become increasingly accepted as the new standards by which authenticity is determined. One of Baudrillard's most famous examples is the transformation of war into a media experience. He argues that the real events of the Gulf War were overshadowed by a media spectacle.[4] During that conflict, audiences were given the illusion of direct access into events—direct access into reality—when in fact they only witnessed images cultivated for mass consumption. When taken to an extreme, representations emulate other representations in an endless cycle. Audiences then lose contact with what is real and what is simulation. In the end, real activities like war may be judged as authentic to the extent that they live up to media representations. New media, such as videogames, are central to this process because they sometimes feel more real than the events they purport to mirror. Watch a scene of real-life combat from Iraq, then compare it to *Call of Duty* or the latest war movie. The fictional experiences are designed to give a sense of immersion by conforming to expectations of what war is like, while real events can differ from expectations. Moreover, the simulations rely on dramatic spectacles of violence that may seem more intense than the drawn-out gunfights featured in many real combat videos. This can foster the illusion that they offer better insight into the feeling of war than the lens of a documentarian's camera.

The effort to collapse the boundary between reality and simulation shapes the course of game studies by inspiring a search for instances in which real life resembles a game or in which gaming takes over a domain of real life. The gamification of everyday life is a clear case of this. Gamified fitness trackers allow people to score points for running and lifting weights in much the same way as they score points by collecting rings in *Sonic the Hedgehog*. Augmented reality videogames such as *Pokemon Go* bring gaming out into the world, juxtaposing reality and simulation on the same screen. The other side of this is the popularity of games that emulate real life. *The Sims* makes it possible to build an ideal of domesticity, while countless simulations of everything from flying an airplane to driving a tractor allow us to explore real occupations from the comfort of our living rooms. In some cases, in-game activities become sources of income, such as for those who sell rare items and gold in *World of Warcraft*, and therefore qualify as real work.[5] Summing up these kinds of trends, McKenzie Wark argues that "games are no longer a pastime, outside or alongside life. They are now the very form of life, and death, and time itself."[6] He suggests that games and everyday life are merging on a number of fronts. Mirroring Baudrillard, he argues that war is becoming a game because the controls and visual experiences are becoming more gamelike.

There is a great deal of insight in poststructuralist analyses of the distance we often have from the real world. Baudrillard, Wark, and others are insightful in pointing out the proliferation of computer-mediated activities and showing that the logic of games is colonizing everyday life. They are likewise right in saying that experiences of reality can be impoverished by excessive reliance on simulation. However, the problems they identify are generally extrinsic to videogames and overstated. Videogames are still clearly identifiable as a separate sphere of activity apart from what they simulate. Aside from very young children or people with cognitive difficulties, there is no compelling evidence for thinking that gamers struggle to understand that their simulated actions are not real. This may change in the future with augmented reality, but my focus is on existing game platforms. I will return to this issue in chapter six when I address concerns about realistic games promoting immoral attitudes or behavior.

What Is a Videogame?

It is surprisingly difficult to determine what counts as a videogame. Efforts at demarcation are persistently frustrated by borderline cases, such as videos that only allow minimal player involvement and are similar to films, or text-based simulations that feel like choose your own adventure books. The choice of which characteristic(s) to take as defining games is invariably controversial. Highlighting the importance of a particular characteristic inevitably leaves out other relevant attributes or aggravates the challenge of drawing a precise boundary around the borderline cases. Continual changes in the medium and the regular emergence of new gaming technologies exacerbate definitional disagreements. With more innovations on the horizon, it would be risky to formulate strict definitions that assume a particular class of technologies. I will not attempt to define what counts as a videogame in the strict sense, and because this label is used so inconsistently, I doubt that any precise definition could be formulated. It is based on family resemblances between various media instead of a precise checklist of characteristics. Commentators disagree over precisely what counts as a video-game because "videogame" is not a naturally occurring category that exists apart from efforts to theorize games. It is a social construct open to endless defini-tional argument. The blending into other media types such as film and literature is itself one of the defining features of videogames, which means that working with a loose conception of the medium is an essential precondition for dealing with it in a nonreductive way.

I will use the term *videogame* to refer to digital simulations that permit player interaction with a narrative within the boundaries of established rules and objec-tives. Note that I am *using* the term in this way, not assuming that this is exactly what the term means or asserting how it should be generally understood. This usage helps me focus on the kinds of games that have moral importance but does not preclude other texts from qualifying as videogames or being theoretically important. I am not interested in videogames that lack narrative elements and will not use the term to encompass them, for the simple reason that the lack of narrative leaves the events in these games without any moral weight. I doubt that Pacman's decision to eat yellow dots is one that most players will experience as having a moral dimension, just as there does not seem to be any moral significance attached to stacking *Tetris* blocks. *Pacman* and *Tetris* are clearly videogames, but not the kinds of games that I am referring to when I talk about gaming as a moral choice simulation. The videogames I consider are those that can model actions that we would normally consider morally significant if they were performed in the real world.

My use of the term *videogame* closes off some titles that have minimal narra-tives, but it is far more permissive when it comes to those that include narratives with limited gameplay options. I count minimally interactive titles such as *Heavy Rain* and *Indigo Prophecy (Fahrenheit)* as videogames because they pose moral challenges and permit some degree of player involvement. Interactivity is an essential characteristic because this is what separates the moral challenges presented by videogames from the moral issues that are present in other media. A quick time event may not allow much player control over the narrative, yet it still constitutes a choice over what course of action to take and can therefore transform players into moral decision makers within the game.

To the extent that there can be one defining characteristic of the videogames I discuss, it is that they grant players the ability to make choices. This is an intentionally loose and open-ended conception of what qualifies as a video-game. I will later argue that videogames have important similarities with other types of simulations presenting moral choices. The similarity between video-games and moral thought experiments is especially important, as the latter easily transform into videogames when they are recast from simple narrative descrip-tions into digital simulations. Similarities between choose your own adventure novels or paper and pencil role-playing games are also important to be aware of, as they may present comparable opportunities for moral exploration and experimentation. What is important is the creation of a space within which moral decisions can be simulated without any ontological consequences, which is to say, without any harm or intent to harm.

There are important differences between videogames and virtual worlds when it comes to making moral evaluations. The former tend to be structured around objectives—missions that players have to achieve by themselves or with others. These drive gameplay, with progress toward the objectives often being measured with points, level progression, or reaching the next chapter of a story. Videogames come in myriad forms and are continually developing in ways that reshape the medium, yet they share this characteristic. Virtual worlds, by contrast, are less structured spaces in which multiple players may come together to interact or build. Virtual worlds may incorporate games, but they are not primarily driven by the progression through levels and objectives. They are largely user-driven experiences, often allowing players to generate their own content. Virtual worlds certainly have moral components, but these tend to be less overt and more easily avoided than in videogames that explicitly construct moral choices or that build narratives laden with moral weight.

Based on these definitions, *Grand Theft Auto*, *BioShock*, *HALO*, *Counter-Strike*, and *Red Dead Redemption* would all qualify as videogames. There are vast differences between them, with some being single player and others multiplayer, and some being linear while others are open world, but each follows the pattern of creating specific challenges that players must overcome. By contrast, *Second Life*, *Habbo*, and *Minecraft* would qualify as virtual worlds because they are more open and comparatively unstructured spaces that emphasize association with other players and world building.

My analysis focuses on videogames that present clear moral challenges within spaces that are largely devoid of genuine moral considerations. The lack of strong objectives for players to pursue means that virtual worlds are usually far more open-ended than videogames and that the moral challenges they raise tend to have more to do with interactions between players than with questions posed by game narratives. Because videogames present clear challenges that players have some sense of before they start playing, the simulated transgressions involving multiple players are usually consensual. That is, players are willing participants in the simulations of murder and theft. The same may not always be true of virtual worlds. With an emphasis on property accumulation and social life, virtual worlds may have greater scope for genuine infractions such as theft. When they are extremely open-ended, it may also be possible for players to experience content that they did not anticipate or that they did not in some sense consent to.

Finally, there are important moral differences between single-player and multiplayer games. Single-player games and games played in a single-player mode include few, if any, opportunities to cause harm in a way that could make players' decisions good or bad, simply because there is no interaction with other moral agents. These games are spaces in which to explore serious moral issues without any genuine adverse consequences. Any harm the player inflicts remains entirely digital. Multiplayer videogames pit real people against each other, sometimes permitting simulated violence in which avatars are dismembered and killed. However, player control over the avatars does not itself change the games' moral status. So long as combat, sexual activities, or other simulated behaviors are consensual and take place within the scope of the rules that players tacitly agree to by participating in the game, they have no real moral cost. Multiplayer games are only morally special insofar as they create opportunities for cheating that allow players to go beyond the rules to inflict real harm, such as by depriving other players of special items without their consent. Once again, it is important to note that most genuine infractions occur outside the games themselves, in the sense that they require cheating—play that goes beyond the boundaries of the game rules—or account hacking.

Methods of Studying Games

No study of videogames is complete without making some reference to the ludology versus narratology debate that structured much of the research in this field, especially during its formative stage. To summarize, the former perspective holds that videogames are best understood as systems of rules that structure play. Here the analysis gravitates toward processes of gameplay rather than the narrative elements, such as story and characters. Ludologists tend to pursue this formalist approach because they think that it gets at the essence of what makes videogames unique. As Graeme Kirkpatrick says, "The significance of ludology lies in its assertion that to be understood properly games must be viewed as play that is structured by rules of a certain kind."[7] Some ludologists take a hard stance against attempts to interpret games in terms of narratives.

The ludological approach is attractive. It has the advantage of being able to explain why so many videogames that lack well-developed narratives (or perhaps have no narratives at all) still qualify as videogames. This is a step toward solving that problem of demarcating videogames from other media. Equally important is that ludologists are able to give games their own identity as a distinct medium apart from those that are more narratively driven, and by extension establish game studies as an independent field of research with its own theoretical concerns and methods. It is no accident that ludology had a powerful influence over the development of game studies when it was escaping from other disciplines and building its own identity. The ludological perspective justified this move and presented a barrier against encroachment from researchers studying other types of media.

Despite these strengths, ludology has a problematic tendency toward reductionism. Focusing on gameplay at the expense of the broader narrative context would leave us without a sense of what gameplay actions are supposed to mean. We only understand clicks of the button as killing people or saving them because narratives give these inputs meaning. If narrative were epiphenomenal, then it would be hard to account for why so many games of the same genre exist. First-person shooters are often nearly identical in terms of gameplay; there would be little reason to play more than one of any given generation if not for the different stories they offer. Zeroing in on the unique aspects of videogames may help to define what videogames are, yet it also comes at the high cost of artificially separating games from other media. With so much game content being shaped by other influences and with games generating fan communities beyond the confines of the game rules ludologists prioritize, such a narrow focus would miss the broader context of gaming and hinder the search for deeper meaning in games. This is far too high a price to pay for a convenient definition.

Narratology emphasizes the storytelling elements of games—the character, plot, and settings. Narratologists tend to read videogames in much the same way that they might interpret novels and films. They look for meaning, symbolism, character development, and story. Henry Jenkins correctly points out that many game developers aspire to tell stories. They put considerable time and effort into building characters, settings, and plots. The same is true of players.[8] Critics chide games for having shallow stories, and players seem to be more attracted to those games that build interesting worlds. Some of the most successful games of the past two decades achieved prominence in large part because of their captivating narratives, including *BioShock*, *Red Dead Redemption*, *Mass Effect*, *The Witcher*, and *Silent Hill*. At times, games that tell interesting stories can develop cult followings despite fairly repetitive gameplay. *Spec Ops: The Line* is a notable example of this. Many reviewers and players expressed disappointment at its bland third-person shooter style while praising the game as something akin to a literary masterpiece.

Of course, a purely narratological approach also runs into problems. Extreme narratology is reductionist in its own way, suggesting that there is nothing special about videogames that can mark them as being different from other media. This is perhaps an even more pernicious reductionism than a purely ludological perspective, since endorsing it would transform games into just another storytelling device, downplaying the importance of interactivity and the sense of play. Ironically, this kind of reductionism would even undermine analysis of game narratives. In open-ended games, the narrative is shaped by player decisions, which means that it is impossible to provide an adequate account of the game narrative without looking at how players influence it. And once this influence comes into the analysis, theorists need some way of explaining how the gameplay rules shape the player's role.

The debate between ludologists and narratologists is subsiding, as many commentators now recognize that each element is essential to constituting videogames. Research can be sensitive to gameplay and narrative without losing sight of what distinguishes games from other media or underestimating the importance of narrative when it comes to making a good game. Conversely, it is impossible to account for the nuances of a game's narrative and its construction of characters without devoting some attention to how they are affected by players' choices, the gameplay mechanics, and the overarching rules that structure the experience. Debate between these two camps tends toward reductionism when taken to either extreme and establishes a false dichotomy, but the debate has left a valuable legacy by developing conceptual frameworks that can be applied in concert. Both perspectives inform my analysis of the moral challenges of videogames because ludic and narrative elements jointly create those challenges and structure players' options for resolving them.

When analyzing the morality of videogames, the ludological perspective helps us evaluate the importance of player choice and the rules that determine its scope. Casting moral challenges as an element of gameplay makes them interactive and forces players to consider which course of action to take. Interactivity transforms players from audience members who merely observe fictional interactions into moral agents whose decisions have consequences within the simulations. Even when the choices are made by other characters or are beyond players' personal control, interactivity encourages attentiveness to moral considerations that shape the game world. Gameplay rules provide the overall structure for moral decisions. They dictate whether moral issues will be made explicit with karma or reputation systems, what range of options will be available when players must choose a course of action, and how decisions affect subsequent gameplay. These convey tacit moral messages, as the possibilities they permit signal what actions are sanctioned within the game. As Garry Young puts it, "One may not wish to engage in a given act, but one accepts that it is permitted within this space."[9]

Narrative elements are likewise essential when reading videogames through a moral lens. They give otherwise abstract puzzles moral meaning. They transform button clicks into simulated murder and controller vibrations into a simulation of being attacked. Narrative gives gameplay greater variety by placing the same basic choices within different stories that continually imbue those choices with new life. Narrative elements can also give us the feeling that decisions have an impact. We may get to know characters and mourn their loss or feel guilty about committing transgressions against them. The No Russian mission is shocking because the avatars under attack are framed as innocent people within the narrative. This is what transforms the *Modern Warfare* series' routine violence against evil terrorists into an atrocity that can offend sensibilities even among veteran gamers.

Evaluating Influence

One of the central methodological problems in research on videogames is a tendency to underestimate player agency. Failing to appreciate players' capacities for interpreting and responding to videogame content creates an insidious barrier to understanding the moral implications of gaming. This treatment is evident in the language used to describe players and the cognitive abilities that they are assumed to have. First, those who express concern about the morality of gaming often label players "users," as though they were addicted to drugs.[10] This term evokes a sense of helplessness and an inability to fight against an outside influence. Even when using more neutral language, experimental research tends to neglect player cognition. Studies look at how games raise players' heart rates or activate certain parts of the brain, then take these reactions as proxies for players being influenced in harmful ways without much consideration of what the physiological changes actually mean from the player's perspective.[11] Biological metrics stand in for cognitive processes, even though researchers are usually at pains to explain how physiological responses can offer reliable guidance in the search for how videogames affect thought.

Second, players are often treated as an undifferentiated mass, without much attention to what individual differences could make them more or less susceptible to influence. At most, critics of videogames may make a distinction between adults and children. This leaves far too much unsaid about how individual characteristics influence reception. Players with existing violent tendencies, for example, could plausibly be more accepting of violence in videogames than others. Players who already have high esteem for military service may be more likely to take military videogames as a call to arms supporting real wars. Those who condemn videogame violence likewise come at games from a particular interpretive strategy that is interested in highlighting the most objectionable aspects of a game. This homogenization of the audience is a serious problem. Virtually every study dealing with implicit bias shows that everything from the political ideologies and religious affiliations to the priming experiences encountered just before starting a new task influence the reception of messages. Because games are open to divergent interpretations and can affect audiences in different ways, studies positing a straightforward link between games and increased propensities for antisocial behavior are woefully inadequate.

Behind these two methodological problems is a deeply flawed assumption that Steven Pinker calls the "Standard Social Science Model."[12] This view, which is consistently refuted in studies of cognition, is that people are like blank slates that are imprinted with any information they are given.[13] Audience members are far from passive. They process information through classificatory schemes that help them organize it and make sense of it. This leads to biased processing in which new information is distorted to fit preconceptions.[14] As David Redlawsk, Andrew Civettini, and Karen Emmerson put it, "People are psychologically motivated to maintain and support existing evaluations."[15] Rather than simply accepting new messages, people are inclined to shape information to fit expectations and existing values.

Of course, this assumes that players are adults who have developed the cognitive framework required to be intelligent consumers of new information.

This is not true of all players, especially those who are young or suffer from cognitive impairments. It is reasonable to restrict young children's access to games because they may not have developed the cognitive maps that help them filter new information effectively. It may likewise be necessary to restrict access to videogames among those who have mental challenges that limit their capacity to critically evaluate the messages that games present. However, most people seem to interpret media in terms of existing beliefs rather than uncritically accepting messages like drug users or conforming to a single interpretation. This provides grounds for doubting excessively formulaic models of how games affect audience members.

Third, studies critiquing videogames rarely distinguish between the different strategies that can be used within a particular game and how these affect the information players receive. Many games include options for violence and stealth. *Dishonored* and *Assassin's Creed* are prime examples of this. Some players rush into battle, killing everyone in sight, while others sneak around enemies and reach objectives with minimal conflict. Different gameplay strategies are apt to result in different experiences. More constraining games that require players to use a particular strategy can still be experienced in divergent ways. Much of the pro-war and pro-military rhetoric in military videogames appears during cutscenes, which means that even a seemingly small decision to watch or skip the cutscenes would have an impact on how much ideologically charged messaging players are exposed to. Even if all players were equally susceptible to media influence (which is doubtful), we cannot assume that all gameplay strategies expose players to the same messages.

Finally, there is an unfortunate tendency in popular and scholarly commentaries to give games one particular reading while excluding others. Alternative interpretations are rarely denied explicitly. Rather, they are marginalized or omitted. This gives the impression that the interpretation described is correct and authoritative, and all too often the interpretation that receives the most attention is one that presents the game in a negative light. Thus, *Grand Theft Auto* becomes a murder simulator rather than a driving or exploration simulator, and *Modern Warfare 2* becomes a terrorism simulator rather than a warning about the risks of unquestioningly following orders. Commentators cannot account for every possible interpretation. At the same time, every analysis should acknowledge its own perspectival limitations. Scholars need to be modest and recognize that their own view of a game is not a definitive interpretation; other players may reach different conclusions.

There is no single correct interpretation of a videogame, just as there is no authoritative interpretation of a book or a film. Media are polysemic—capable of supporting multiple interpretations. The process of meaning-making can happen at individual or group levels. John Fiske views polysemy as an individual process by which people reach divergent views through their own efforts to understand a text.[16] This means that a dozen players sitting at home and experiencing the same game could end up with a dozen different interpretations because of their unique backgrounds, biases, and interests. Jenkins treats polysemy as a collective effort—a "process of negotiating over the meaning of the text."[17] In this sense, we would have to look for divergent interpretations emerging as audiences come together in different groups to talk about their experiences. When it comes to videogames, both conceptions of polysemy are at work. During solo play, gamers are left to make sense of events on their own and may reach different interpretations based on their preconceptions and how they navigate the game. Those who play with others or who discuss gaming can join in the collective effort to construct a text's meaning, which is apt to leave multiple different readings, without a clear sense of which one is correct. Steven Jones perfectly captures this when he says that "players make games meaningful, make their meanings, as they play them, talk about them, reconfigure them, and play them again."[18]

This is not to say that all interpretations are equally valid. Readings can be better or worse depending on how effectively they use the available textual evidence. As Fiske says, "This polysemic potential is neither boundless nor structureless: the text delineates the terrain within which meaning may be made and proffers some meanings more vigorously than others."[19] It would be fair to say that a person who reads *Grand Theft Auto IV* as the story of an immigrant struggling with his criminal past is more correct than someone who reads it as an allegory for animal rights. The former player can mobilize far more support from the game narrative than the latter. But even allowing for this, the range of potential interpretations available for any game is vast and never yields a single correct perspective. Interpretive disagreement is part of what helps media endure over time. It provides a sense that there is always more to discover upon a second reading, viewing, or playing. Returning to *Modern Warfare*'s simulation of terrorism, it would be equally plausible to see No Russian's simulation of an American special operative's participation in a terrorist attack as a critique of American military adventurism as it would be to read the mission as an endorsement of terrorism. Both readings could find ample support from the game narrative, leaving us without an authoritative position.

Polysemy is a characteristic of all media, but there are good reasons for thinking that it is especially pronounced for videogames. First, audiences of films, television shows, books, and songs encounter roughly the same text. They see the same words on the page and the same images on-screen. The divergence between readings comes from how a particular stimulus affects different audience members. Videogames, by contrast, do not provide uniform stimuli. Their interactivity ensures that each player will not only interpret the text from their own perspective but also have unique experiences that reflect decisions they make within game worlds. This is especially true of videogames that are more open-ended or that permit a variety of gameplay strategies. Open-world games such as *Skyrim* or *The Witcher* may lead to such radically divergent experiences that an individual may come away with different interpretations upon successive playthroughs.

Even an extremely linear game may yield different content depending on the player. Experiments involving videogames typically offer participants a set amount of time to play. This is often only fifteen or thirty minutes. During this time, a veteran gamer could rack up dozens of kills and start experimenting with different gameplay strategies, while a novice might struggle to figure out the controls before the study ends. The affective reactions are also apt to vary depending on prior skill with videogames. The veteran may end up feeling empowered, the novice frustrated. This would leave them with different evidence from which to draw interpretations and vastly different emotional responses.

Second, much of the content in videogames is optional. Cutscenes tell a story and provide context for the action sequences, yet players who are only interested in the gameplay are usually able to skip them. Games often include dozens of special challenges that are peripheral to the main story, which may change the overall experience depending on which of these challenges players pursue. I can attest to playing all the way through several games with only a vague sense of the overall plot because I did not watch any cutscenes. This is especially easy in first-person shooters. I have also used games to imaginatively enact my own stories. For example, I was once obsessed with the *Fallout* series to the point that I would play other sci-fi games while pretending that they were set in a postapocalyptic future. I doubt I am alone in this kind of deliberate misreading of games to fit my own sense of what is enjoyable. The projection of meaning onto a game further expands the range of meanings available for players. Moreover, these meanings matter for players even if they deviate wildly from anything we might recognize as being supported by the available textual evidence.

Developers can try to provide authoritative interpretations by explaining their intentions and deciding which events are canon. However, they are often reluctant to do this, because it stifles player creativity, and in any case, large development teams may have their own conflicting visions—a polysemy in the development process itself.[20] Add to this the changes that come from modding, and the scope of meaning expands still further. With these many interpretive challenges in mind, we should be wary of any claims that games exert the kinds of straightforward causal influence that would affect players in uniform ways.

Moral Theories in Game Analysis

There are three dominant traditions of Western moral theory: deontological, consequentialist, and axiological. These are likewise the three dominant analytical frameworks used to evaluate the morality of videogames. Academic researchers tend to invoke these theories by name, often in a quest to explicitly map out how different moral traditions would evaluate games.[21] Journalists and those in popular media implicitly rely on the basic reasoning associated with these perspectives without as much concern for the underlying theories. That is, academics tend to have equal interest in moral theory and gaming, whereas other commentators tend to treat theory more as a means to an end. Although the three moral philosophies come in dozens of varieties, with subtle differences that provoke endless debate among philosophers, a brief overview of them should suffice in this context because the different strains of each philosophy generally agree on the core points that are relevant when analyzing videogames. For example, if videogames cause real murders, then they are problematic for all variants of consequentialism. Each school of consequentialist thought accepts the wrongness of murder, so accounting for their subtle variations is unnecessary.[22] Similarly, if games have no significant impact on real-world behavior, then they should pose no problem for consequentialist theories in general. I will return to each perspective throughout the book to offer further details about specific variants within each tradition when these are directly relevant to gaming.

Deontological theories prioritize intentions and rules. According to Kant, the preeminent exponent of this approach, good actions are only possible when they are undertaken with good will. You cannot be accidentally good; true good actions require intent. You have to do the right thing because it is the right thing to do. Kant would say that accidentally saving someone's life by bumping into them and knocking them out of the way of a speeding car would not count as a good deed. It would be more praiseworthy to attempt the rescue and fail. This would at least show that the action was motivated by good will.

Deontological ethics also places a high value on rules. Good will is driven by a respect for moral rules and an intention to act in accordance with them. Kant offers several formulations of an overarching moral rule he calls the categorical imperative, including "act only in accordance with that maxim through which you can at the same time will that it become a universal law"[23] and "so act that you used humanity, whether in your own person or in the person of any other, always at the same time as an end, never merely as a means."[24] The former statement of the categorical imperative is an exhortation for consistency—to follow moral rules that can hold true for all people. By this logic, murder is wrong in every instance because permitting it as a universal norm would cause a total breakdown of social order. Kant thinks that lying is likewise contradictory when generalized, which means that even seemingly innocent "white lies" are wrong. The second formulation of the categorical imperative urges respect for others by avoiding exploitative relationships and treating others as human even when relationships are structured by instrumental goals.

Some commentators, whose work I will discuss later, have criticized videogames on deontological grounds by attempting to show that they involve ill will or a violation of moral rules. If you play a violent game, this reasoning goes, you are intending to commit violent acts. However, I argue that of the three ethical philosophies, this one is the least plausible to deploy as a critique of gaming.

Videogames designed to simulate immoral actions cannot result in the kinds of contradictions that would violate the first formulation of the categorical imperative. Disregarding moral rules within a game simulates immoral action but is not genuinely immoral, because the simulation is not real. It does not include real moral agents. Murder contradicts the categorical imperative in the real world because allowing everyone to commit murder would result in chaos. There is no comparable breakdown of social order within games that simulate murder, because the permissibility of murder is incorporated into the game rules and all the harm can be repaired by pressing the reset button. Unlike real murder, it is perfectly reasonable to think that every person could simulate murder without undermining social order. It does not violate the universalization test.

The second version of the categorical imperative also provides no grounds for criticizing videogames. According to Kant, the issue of good or bad will only arise with respect to moral agents, such as humans or animals. Attacking a character in a videogame does not presuppose any real intent to cause harm to a moral agent; it only involves an intention to harm avatars that look like humans. When simulating murder, a player's intention is probably just to have fun, not to violate a moral norm. Even if a player enjoys simulated violence and revels in the fantasy of committing a real murder, their intent when pushing buttons on the controller is still just to simulate murder. It would only be possible to intend to kill a real person while simulating the killing of an avatar if a player did not grasp the difference between reality and simulation. Someone playing a game with a desire to commit murder at some later time certainly has bad intentions, but the wrongness of the intentions can only be expressed in terms of what they mean in the real world. That is, the immorality of such a player would lie beyond the game, in the desire to commit actual murder, not in the desire to simulate murder.

Consequentialist theories link the rightness or wrongness of actions to the outcomes produced. They disagree with deontological theories' emphasis on intentions and consider them secondary to outcomes, or perhaps irrelevant. Consequentialist theories vary considerably in terms of what consequences they treat as being morally relevant. Utilitarianism, the most theoretically sophisticated variant, strives to maximize "the greatest happiness for the greatest number." Some utilitarians think of happiness in a hedonistic sense, in terms of the total amount of happiness rather than its quality.[25] Others think that there may be higher or lower forms of happiness that should be weighted differently,[26] which essentially means that the pleasures of high culture and philosophy count more than the cheap thrills of reality television and pop music. When it comes to claims that videogames are harmful, the debate over what kind of happiness should be maximized is largely irrelevant, because the potential bad outcomes are ones that all the leading consequentialist theories would consider undesirable. Critics argue that videogames promote violence, sexual assault, antisocial attitudes, and militarism—effects that, if real, would constitute a serious concern for any consequentialist, regardless of the subtle perspectival differences. This means that for the purposes of judging whether games are harmful, all consequentialist theories can be grouped together.

From a utilitarian perspective, morality is not just about avoiding wrongful actions but also about finding happiness. This raises the question of whether the billions of hours of enjoyment derived from games are morally significant and how these should be weighed against any costs that gaming may have. If we take a hedonistic view of utilitarianism, then this massive amount of happiness should count for quite a bit, especially when compared to the paucity of evidence implicating videogames in real acts of violence.[27] I contend that weighing the volume of pleasure that clearly follows from games against uncertain costs establishes good grounds for thinking that games are permissible. On the other hand, if we treat certain highbrow pleasures as being more important than popular entertainment, then the argument depends more heavily on whether games present meaningful content. Here again, I think that there is a strong case for videogames. As I show throughout the book, videogames are a valuable tool for exploring moral issues, presenting different perspectives, and problematizing social issues. There is even good reason to think that some videogames qualify as works of art, which would place them in the pantheon of high culture.[28] This means that even in a stricter conception of utilitarianism that privileges certain types of content, videogames are morally defensible.

One vital point to bear in mind when applying consequentialist moral theories is that actions should not be treated as being bad simply because they have some bad effects. Such an approach to morality would be simplistic, as many activities have inseparable good and bad outcomes. At times, good outcomes can only be brought about by inflicting some harm. For example, it is good to put criminals in prison, though this does cause criminals displeasure. On a more mundane level, it hurts to be stabbed by a needle, but this minor harm is certainly outweighed by the value of being inoculated against a disease. Many critics imply that games are wrong if they can be linked to any adverse consequences at all, but this is an unrealistically high standard that we do not hold for any other social practice. Driving cars, owning weapons, swimming, playing sports, conducting home repairs, and raising animals are among the myriad dangerous activities that are treated as being permissible because the dangers are outweighed by the benefits. Videogames would not violate consequentialist precepts even if there were a few isolated cases in which they clearly cause violence, addiction, or antisocial attitudes. The bad effects would have to be systemic and severe to outweigh the benefits of gaming.

Virtue ethics, or axiological ethics, provides a third lens to complete the trinity of predominant traditions in secular Western moral theory. This viewpoint had been marginalized until fairly recently, when it was rehabilitated by G.E.M. Anscombe[29] then popularized by Alasdair MacIntyre's *After Virtue*.[30] The central ideas can be traced back to Greek and Roman writers, and Aristotle in particular. When virtue ethics is applied to videogames, it is almost always with Aristotle in mind, so I focus on what his ideas can tell us about gaming. Aristotle contends that moral education should not be directed at developing rules or decision procedures. Instead, the goal should be to cultivate good character that can reliably yield good actions in practice. Aristotle is less concerned with the morality of specific actions than with the morality of people themselves. As he sees it, actions follow from character dispositions in fairly predictable ways, so looking at a person's character goes right to the heart of the issue of moral decision-making. It is also at this level of character that we find the best opportunities for moral education that goes beyond simply giving people rules, instead teaching them to work through novel problems independently.[31]

People with good character have *phronesis*, the practical wisdom to evaluate moral dilemmas and resolve them with a great deal more contextual sensitivity than deontological and consequentialist theories can provide. Abstract norms can be difficult to apply and may fail to offer clear guidance in especially challenging situations, but wisdom can always provide direction. Virtues and *phronesis* cannot be taught as though they were rules. They must be cultivated through practice. According to Aristotle, good character must be learned by deliberately practicing good actions until they become habitual. Routinized good conduct transforms a person's character and in doing so makes continual good conduct more natural. The ultimate goal of character education is to produce a good person who is able to recognize and choose the right course of action in any situation simply because of this character disposition and good judgment.

The typical Aristotelian concern commentators raise is that videogames may provide opportunities for the wrong kind of habituation, corrupting players with simulated acts of violence and criminality that become ingrained in their character and may thereafter be enacted in real life.[32] To assess this effort to mobilize Aristotle's theory to critique videogames (usually violent videogames), it is essential to look more deeply at what counts as habituation and how plausible Aristotle's account is when it is applied to a medium that is so far removed from anything he experienced. I will return to these issues and consider Aristotle's ideas in more detail in chapter 4.

Conclusion

This chapter has established the conceptual and methodological framework that I will deploy throughout the rest of the book. I will continually return to the distinction between simulations and reality to emphasize that, despite their considerable interpenetration when it comes to the spread of information, they have distinct moral implications. I rely on the three moral theories presented in this chapter to show that critics of videogames are wrong to think that simulated actions are real enough to qualify as being morally significant in themselves. They are likewise misguided in claiming that the line between fantasy and reality is so blurry that actions and attitudes deployed in the former will transition easily into the latter.

Amoralists are correct in thinking that simulated decisions are morally neutral because they are purely fictional, but we must recognize that entertainment can influence or persuade us. To say that there is nothing morally significant about gaming—that a game is just a game—wrongly implies that videogames are completely separable from real life. Games are shaped by real events and other fictional media; they impart experiences that we take with us back to everyday life. The relationship with the real world can therefore best be characterized as one of epistemic exchange but ontological separation. I develop these issues in more detail in chapter 2, as I refute four of the most common arguments for thinking that videogames are morally problematic.

2

The Moral Panic
Surrounding Videogames

Research on the morality of videogames has for decades focused disproportionately on determining whether violent videogames have some kind of corrupting influence on players. Politicians, parents, academics, and religious leaders have criticized violent videogames for training players to carry out attacks, indoctrinating them with ideological messages, fostering aggressive attitudes, and leading them to become obsessed with gaming to the extent that they lose contact with the real world. The outcry reaches its climax following school shootings in which games are blamed for transforming ordinary children into vicious murderers. Exploring the arguments against violent videogames is essential for refuting misconceptions about the negative effects videogames supposedly have on players and establishing a stronger foundation for future research that overcomes misguided ways of thinking about the medium.

In this chapter, I survey four of the most pervasive critiques of violent videogames. These are claims that videogames train players to kill by giving them the skills needed to enact violence, foster aggression, desensitize players to violence, and blur the boundaries between simulated and real violence. The arguments complement each other and are often made in conjunction, but it is useful to separate them into distinct claims for analytical purposes. Each has its own logic and draws on its own body of faulty inferences. The training thesis rests on the assumption that practice playing a videogame can give players the experience they need to wield real weapons and use them effectively. The aggression thesis draws on research attempting to show that physiological responses to gaming, such as an elevated pulse or increases in the stress hormone cortisol, tell us something about players' hidden feelings about violence. The empathy thesis suggests that simulated violence damages real moral intuitions, making gamers less able to think morally even if they do not actually become more violent. Finally, when it comes to realism, critics are concerned that increasing visual similarity between computer models and real life will shatter the barrier between reality and fiction and result in the violence that was once reserved for videogames being directed at real people. Realism may also aggravate the other three conditions.

If critics are correct in thinking that violent videogames encourage aggression, desensitize players, or train them to kill, then we should expect to see clear adverse effects from playing videogames. If games truly have the power to erode moral sensitivity and incite attacks, then there should be little difficulty in substantiating these effects. Based on the massive popularity of videogames, especially violent games, we would expect to find that gaming correlates with the higher levels of crime that evince social fragmentation, but this has not been the case. Despite decades of research and hundreds of studies purporting to show the harms of gaming, no studies have found clear and compelling evidence that videogames have an adverse influence on players. In particular, research has failed to establish any conclusive links between gaming and violence. Much of the commentary is purely speculative, and even the empirically grounded experimental work has not uncovered a causal link between gaming and substantive behavioral changes. The weak support for critics' claims, combined with methodological errors, logical failings, and contrary evidence, indicates that games have little or any harmful influence on players aside from young children and those who are predisposed to violence for reasons that have nothing to do with videogames.

More important than any of the individual studies that I talk about in this chapter are the flaws in the overall approach that critics of videogames take. They tend to accept what I call the "contagion theory of violence," according to which any exposure to violence is apt to make a person more violent or more accepting of violence. There is little sense of the importance of context in shaping how games are understood (for example, critics rarely consider whether simulated violence is glorified or satirized). This same sense of contagion arises when critics condemn other types of game content, such as ideological messages and sexism. There is likewise limited recognition of how players interpret their experiences and how they may reconfigure or resist messages presented by games. Critics describe games as fixed stimuli that have a fairly predictable effect on attitudes and behavior, which vastly underestimates interactivity and polysemy. The contagion theory of violence constitutes a major impediment to research that has changed shape over time but that continues to exert a powerful influence.

Training Players to Kill

Of all the supposed harmful consequences of playing violent videogames, the most extreme and least plausible is that they actually train players to kill. Depending on who is advancing this thesis, this training effect may be described as videogames imparting a desire to kill, giving players the skills necessary to operate weapons, or both. Ironically, the training argument seems to hold the most sway in the United States, which is also where it is the least plausible. With over 300 million guns in private ownership,[1] Americans have ample opportunity to practice shooting without recourse to videogames. In fact, the popularity of this argument in the United States has much to do with the popularity of guns and attempts to defend them from government regulation. The training argument has become a political weapon in the hands of gun rights advocates such as the National Rifle Association, allowing them to shift the blame for gun violence away from the weapons themselves and onto videogames. It was especially attractive as an explanation for the wave of school shootings that began in the late 1990s, though it has become less influential as mass killings have moved beyond schools to be carried out by older attackers who do not have a gaming background.

The training thesis was popularized by Dave Grossman, who remains the most widely cited proponent of this view. A broad range of commentators who are concerned about the effects of violent videogames turn to Grossman for support,[2] making him a shared reference point across research in psychology, game studies, political science, sociology, communications, and other fields. Grossman is a former U.S. Army soldier who works as a writer and consultant on issues related to violence. He also runs the Killology Research Group.[3] He credits games with providing the cognitive and physical training needed for transforming ordinary people into killers. Like many critics of videogame violence, he is a staunch defender of gun rights who has sought to deflect regulatory efforts aimed at gun control.[4] In 2013, he collaborated with Glenn Beck to produce *Control: Exposing the Truth about Guns.*[5] This background is important to bear in mind, as it fits into an established practice of American gun rights activists shifting the blame for shootings from guns onto videogames and other entertainment media. This is a prime example of how the moral panic surrounding games plays into broader political narratives that have clear policy goals. The condemnation of entertainment not only protects guns but also aligns with a widespread conservative fear over popular culture that leads some of its central leaders to proclaim a "culture war."[6] Grossman's critiques of videogames are sometimes written independently and sometimes in collaboration with like-minded activists, such as Gloria DeGaetano, founder of the Parent Coaching Institute.

Grossman professes to be a master of "killology" and has written widely about the psychology of violence, not only in entertainment but also in military and law enforcement contexts. Much of what he has to say about videogames and desensitization draws on previous work about how soldiers are socialized and prepared for war. Grossman argues that people have a natural aversion to killing and that the history of warfare has been shaped by efforts to suppress this urge.[7] He claims that armed forces have subjected soldiers to more rigorous training regimes, mediated violence with technologies that make killing easier, and dehumanized their enemies. This results in increasingly sophisticated practices of desensitization that yield more reliable killers. Grossman and DeGaetano see the same desensitization processes at work in videogames, which leads them to conclude that these destroy the natural psychological barriers against killing.

Grossman and DeGaetano use Michael Carneal, who shot eight people in a Kentucky high school in 1997, as a case study for how games can directly impart shooting skills. By their estimate, an experienced police officer can only hit a target with around one shot out of five at a distance of seven yards. At the same distance, Carneal was able to shoot eight children with as many bullets, and five of them in the head. They ask: "How did Michael Carneal acquire this kind of killing ability? Simple: practice."[8] Here the authors' argument goes beyond speculation about games' cognitive impact to say that games can teach the physical abilities needed to operate firearms. The comparison between police officers and the teenage killer suggests that videogames not only convey exceptional marksmanship skills but that they are actually more effective training tools than the live fire practice employed by police officers. This assertion that casual gaming is better preparation for a gunfight than a career in law enforcement imbues games with incredible destructive potential.

Grossman's work on the psychology of war is widely cited and has helped to create a narrative about desensitization during war that gives his claims about media desensitization a false sense of plausibility. Although his studies of violence during war are popular, few researchers have attempted to test his assertions, and those who have raise serious methodological problems that should lead us to doubt his conclusions. The bulk of Grossman's evidence is taken from previous studies by S.L.A. Marshall,[9] which have been largely discredited.[10] For example, as evidence of the natural aversion to killing, Grossman cites Marshall's estimates that fewer than half the soldiers involved in World War II and the Korean War actively fought, even though historians investigating these figures find no basis for these estimates. In many instances, it appears that Marshall simply fabricated the numbers he provides and that they were widely accepted as true before they were corroborated. Grossman's own investigations are likewise deeply problematic, because they rely on unsubstantiated stories and a deeply biased reading of events. Robert Engen reaches the opposite conclusion in a study of the Canadian armed forces, finding that they struggle to prevent soldiers from firing excessively and wasting ammunition.[11] These kinds of serious empirical mistakes in Grossman's historical research into the psychology of killing undermine his overall account of how people are conditioned to act violently.

Grossman's claim that socialization has created a world that accepts violence is wildly inaccurate when judged against more systematic research showing that violence is actually in sharp decline.[12] More credible studies that rely on statistical evidence reveal that, if anything, digital media are helping to reduce violence. Even within the military, where Grossman finds most of his evidence of desensitization, there are few signs of this process in action. He argues that desensitization made enormous strides during the latter half of the twentieth century, when in fact the trend in most major militaries was toward stricter ethical regulations and legal oversight.[13] Desensitization is inimical to the work that contemporary militaries do; incidents of misconduct discredit military interventions, compromise efforts to build relations with foreign populations, and provoke international outrage. Contrary to Grossman, military training programs have become far more focused on ethical awareness and cultural respect.[14] Desensitization is real, but it seems to come primarily from direct experiences of violence in combat, not from deliberate inculcation in training.[15]

Even psychological research that forms the theoretical foundation of Grossman's work is problematic. He relies heavily on B. F. Skinner and other behaviorists who developed theories of operant conditioning during the 1940s and 1950s, overlooking the many serious flaws associated with that approach and the far more sophisticated models of cognition that subsequent researchers have developed.[16] More serious problems with this model are evident in research on the relationship between games and aggression that I discuss in the next section.

These issues are enough to cast doubt on the theoretical framework that Grossman builds on throughout his critiques of videogames, but further problems crop up when we look at the game studies in particular. Perhaps the clearest problem is that conjectures about videogames providing adequate preparation for physical skills such as shooting wildly overestimate the similarity between simulations and the physical activities being simulated. Anyone who has played a first-person shooter and fired a real gun can attest that the experiences bear little resemblance. The interfaces are completely different, as are the skills involved. Most gamers fire virtual weapons using a mouse, keyboard, or gamepad. Some consoles have developed game guns that look like pistols, rifles, or rocket launchers. These allow players to point at targets on the screen but do not behave like real weapons. No videogame requires players to control their breathing, absorb recoil, and practice squeezing a trigger so gently that the gun does not jerk. I can say from personal experience as an avid gamer and a former competitive rifle shooter that there is no transference of physical abilities between the two domains. Even the most detailed shooting simulations from games like the *Sniper: Elite* and *Sniper: Ghost Warrior* series only provide a general sense of the skills that would go into marksmanship, without actually teaching them. This is no doubt why armed forces sometimes use videogames to practice tactics but not as a substitute for time on the shooting range.

Few games aspire to accurately mirror the physical activities they simulate. Most developers are far more interested in providing an engaging experience than in advancing pedagogical goals, which leads them to only provide a vague sense of what the simulated activities are really like. Just as hours playing *Guitar Hero* and *Rock Band* leave players with no greater grasp of how to play musical instruments, hours spent with *Call of Duty* and *Counter Strike* do not bring players any closer to mastering firearms. The game guns players use on their home videogame consoles are hardly better suited for training purposes than a water gun would be. The comparison between virtual and real weapons becomes even more attenuated considering that videogames are played in carefully controlled environments, such as players' living rooms, which are unlikely to be like the highly stressful situations one would encounter during a real gunfight. Fear and physical exertion interfere with targeting under real circumstances in ways that gamers could never hope to replicate. In short, there are so many vast differences between the physical activities associated with realistic and simulated violence that Grossman and DeGaetano's argument is implausible.

We can gain greater appreciation for why the training thesis is misguided by revisiting the ludological versus narratological divide. We see actions in games as being simulations of war and murder because of the narrative details overlaid on the game mechanics. Narrative imparts meaning to button clicks and joystick movements that have no inherent meaning. Gaming does improve skills, but not in the sense that critics seem to think. Gamers learn to be better at videogames, which is to say they learn ludic skills. They are not necessarily better at performing the actions being simulated, which exist only in the narrative. This is why gaming skills are usually transferable. Our thumbs and fingers make the same movements whether we are directing Mario through the Mushroom Kingdom, reaching the finish line in a big race, or mowing down hordes of civilians at an airport. When it comes to the equivalents of these activities in real life—running and jumping, driving a car, and killing—the physical movements vary enormously and have little transferability. The impression games offer of becoming better at these skills is a largely illusory effect of how the narratives construct meaning.

Some videogames rely on motion controls, as in Nintendo's Wii or Xbox's Kinect. These allow players to pretend that they are swinging a tennis racket or fencing sword, among dozens of other activities. For the most part, these motion controls have been utilized for nonviolent sporting and dancing games. Furthermore, existing motion control systems remain poorly suited for training purposes. The controls are often temperamental and bear limited resemblance to the actions they re-create. There is also little tactile feedback, which means that players pretending to shoot a gun will not feel its weight or recoil. Most importantly of all, the inputs remain distant from the real activities and largely the same across games. I have used my Kinect to pretend that I am skiing, skydiving, and riding a motorcycle, in each case by providing roughly the same input and without developing any knowledge of how to do these things in real life. Once again, this makes games poorly suited for teaching real-life physical skills.

For games to teach killing, they would have to become far more immersive. They would require different inputs, as players would need devices that accurately simulate the mechanics of real weapons. Although videogames could potentially accomplish this in the future, it is unlikely. At present, the only simulations that seem to have plausible benefits for small arms training are expensive systems developed for police and military purposes, such as VirTra,[17] and even these do not purport to improve accuracy. Rather, they are meant to supplement target shooting with simulations that test reaction time and judgment. The most realistic shooting simulators not only fall short of the claims that Grossman and DeGaetano make about training superkillers but are actually marketed as tools for improving ethical and legal compliance.[18]

If the training argument is implausible, then what should we make of the claims about Carneal's superhuman shooting abilities? For one thing, videogames were not his only entertainment. Victims represented by Jack Thompson filed lawsuits against the makers of several films, including *Natural Born Killers* (1994) and *The Basketball Diaries* (1995), in connection with the shooting, and Carneal was found to be a fan of Stephen King.[19] There was such a rush to find fault for Carneal's terrible crime—and to shift attention away from gun legislation—that the net of blame was cast widely and onto virtually anything in Carneal's life that was even remotely violent. It is revealing that the court adjudicating claims about harmful media influence on Carneal ruled that there was too far an inferential leap to think that videogames and other media had anything to do with the attack.

In Carneal's case, as well as in every other school shooting to date, judges and investigators have ruled out the influence of media as a cause of violence. Lawrence Kutner and Cheryl Olson investigated school shootings in detail and conducted interviews with weapons trainers, which led them to conclude that Carneal and others have been able to shoot their victims not because of simulated training but because of the circumstances under which school shootings take place.[20] Most, including Carneal's, happen at close range, without any armed adversaries, and while the victims are stationary. Under these conditions, even untrained shooters can hit their targets. As they explain in response to Grossman and DeGaetano, "Unlike the situations described in the FBI's statistics, Carneal was not involved in a 'shootout.' He was the only one with a weapon; no one was firing at him. He was also much closer to the other students than seven yards. He simply walked up to them and fired."[21] So the more accurate story is that Carneal had access to real firearms and enough practice with them to hit stationary targets at close range.

Games have more potential for teaching players the intellectual skills associated with fighting, such as small-unit military tactics, the best ways to sneak up on an unsuspecting victim, how different types of weapons can be used, or how to evade the police. Although all these skills have some physical component, they are largely based on having a particular type of technical knowledge, which means that they are skills that might be imparted by a videogame designed to be a training simulator. The possibility that games teach military tactics is probably the most plausible concern of all, as players in military videogames may find themselves working alongside teammates and attempting to outmaneuver opponents.

Despite having a capacity for teaching players tactics, violent games rarely attempt to do so in practice. Popular videogames are designed primarily for entertainment, which means that they typically create battles that look more like action movie scenes than like documentaries or military training manuals. Players typically learn a few of the most basic tactics, such as staying behind cover and shooting at enemies to suppress them, but little beyond this. Any kind of complex tactical maneuvering or detailed instructions on how to perform the simulated actions in real life would probably be disastrous for enjoyable gameplay, which is doubtless why few games attempt to provide it. Even *America's Army*, which simulates U.S. Army training programs, only provides players with the most rudimentary instructions. That game's platform is incorporated into military training simulations, but these are heavily modified and used within a military training context that provides myriad other lessons that extend beyond the videogame simulation.

Succeeding in videogames requires players to do things that would get them killed in the real world. In some multiplayer games, players constantly jump up and down to make themselves harder targets or shoot rocket launchers at the ground to propel themselves into the air. Needless to say, such tactics would be dangerous in practice. And no one could seriously think that stunts like riding a tank off the top of a skyscraper or parachuting from one jet into another— regular events in your average multiplayer war game—are really possible. For every piece of genuine tactical advice players of violent videogames receive, they are apt to experience a dozen bad examples that would be fatal in real life. This means that the tactical training is not only minimal but also subverted by highly stylized fictional violence.

If games become more realistic, to the point that they can impart fighting skills and increase players' proficiency with guns, then there would be cause for reconsidering age and content restrictions. However, realistic games would not be wrong simply because they are realistic. There is nothing intrinsically immoral about teaching players how to operate weapons or how to use military tactics. So long as target shooting is considered a legitimate activity, there cannot be any genuine moral problem with a videogame that teaches players to shoot. The ability to shoot well does not, in itself, have any moral implications. Players could enjoy pretending to fight in games and have no desire ever to act out their fantasies in real life. For this reason, it is not sufficient that videogames train players to shoot for them to be morally harmful. Games would also have to affect players in some way that gives them a desire to act on those abilities. This is no doubt why so many critics describe games as teaching players to kill rather than simply teaching them how to shoot. The case against videogames therefore depends on assumptions about the psychological impact of games—assumptions that turn out to be just as dubious as claims that games impart violent skills.

Increasing Aggression

Few academics make such sweeping and implausible claims as Grossman and DeGaetano. Rather than relying on behavioristic models according to which gaming conditions players for violence and teaches the skills needed for killing, academics more often argue that games cause subtle changes in players' cognition that make them more amenable to violence. The charge against videogames therefore transforms Grossman's causal certainty that videogames will produce violence to a probabilistic claim about building predispositions for violence. The key claim when looking at this line of argument is that videogames make players more aggressive. This developed out of a long tradition of media effects research, which has often been guided by efforts to link new types of media to antisocial behavior. Studies of videogame violence draw inspiration from earlier work on television, music, and films, though often making stronger claims about games' adverse effects because games are interactive.

What this line of argument gains in plausibility over the training thesis's stricter causal models it sacrifices by introducing vagueness. Aggression is a slippery concept. It refers to a mental predisposition rather than a specific act, so it is exceedingly difficult to measure. Moreover, the idea that games incite aggression is inherently suspicious because it vastly oversimplifies cognition. As Pinker points out, "Aggression is not a single motive, let alone a mounting urge. It is the output of several psychological systems that differ in their environmental triggers, their internal logic, their neurobiological basis, and their social distribution."[22] Researchers who link games to aggression err in thinking that aggression is something that builds over time with exposure and that naturally culminates in a violent release, as well as in thinking that aggression is a single, discrete feeling.

Critics linking videogames to aggression must operationalize the concept of aggression by finding some physical manifestation of it. They attempt to identify some relatively simple and easily testable physiological correlate that can serve as a proxy for an increase in violent tendencies, even though none exists. This leaves them wide latitude to describe virtually any response as a sign of heightened aggression. Looking across these studies, it is striking to see how often basic physiological responses to play are taken as evidence that games transform players' cognition in the absence of strong evidence establishing the supposed link.

In one study, Mary Ballard and Rose Wiest divided participants into groups playing *Mortal Kombat*, *Mortal Kombat 2*, and a billiards simulator. They find that those in the former group experienced higher blood pressure, which they interpret as a sign of players having more aggressive thoughts.[23] The inferential leap between blood pressure and violent thoughts is enormous. The jump from blood pressure to an increased propensity to commit or tolerate acts of violence is larger still. The findings are all the more questionable because the study involved only thirty undergraduate students—a small number from which to draw such strong conclusions. In another experiment, Nicholas Carnagey, Craig Anderson, and Brad Bushman test the effects of playing violent videogames by looking at the heart rate and galvanic skin response in two groups of participants watching a ten-minute violent video. One group had played violent videogames for twenty minutes beforehand, the other had not.[24] The gaming group showed a lower response to the violent video according to both metrics. Once again, a physiological response with an unclear relationship to desensitization is used to impugn games. It would be more reasonable to conclude that watching television is simply less stressful than gaming.

Klaus Mathiak and René Weber find that areas of the brain associated with empathy are less active when subjects are playing violent videogames.[25] This study involved a tiny sample size of only thirteen participants, which is far too small for reliable generalizations. On a more fundamental level, this approach suffers from the same limitation as the other studies. As with blood pressure, the causal implications of brain activity are unclear and poorly understood, without a firm link to aggression or desensitization. There is no way of determining whether activation of brain areas associated with aggression has any effect on cognition, and thus far no studies have demonstrated harmful long-term effects of such activation.

Douglas Gentile, Patrick Bender, and Craig Anderson find higher levels of cortisol in the saliva of gamers playing violent games than in those playing non-violent games. Because cortisol is associated with stress and the fight or flight response, the authors argue that the higher cortisol level among those in the violent gaming group is evidence of aggression. They also gave participants word completion tasks in which they could fill in missing letters to make aggressive or nonaggressive answers. "For instance, the fragment 'KI__' could be completed aggressively (e.g., 'KILL') or non-aggressively (e.g., 'KISS')."[26] The design of the study is questionable on many counts. For one thing, Spider-Man for Xbox is used as the example of a violent game and compared against *Finding Nemo*. With the latter being more of an interactive movie without much difficulty, it is predictable that respondents would experience less stress playing it than when playing a game that pushes their abilities further. Even if the study had included different games, it is not clear that these metrics would be useful. As in the other studies, there is reason to doubt whether a physiological response like increased cortisol will increase aggression. After all, similar responses can arise from many different types of stressful experiences. Sports such as rock climbing, skydiving, and rafting are all associated with higher levels of cortisol.[27]

A litany of other studies claiming a link between videogames and physiological arousal could be cited here, but suffice it to say that there is an endemic methodological problem when testing what aggression is and finding physiological indications of changes in aggressive tendencies. Without a stronger basis for thinking that aggression can be reliably measured in laboratory settings, experiments purporting to demonstrate a link between games and violent tendencies have little merit.

Quite a few studies purporting to find a link between violent videogames and real aggression fail to achieve convincing results even by their own standards. Craig Anderson and Karen Dill argue that people develop scripts that dictate automatic behaviors. They think that certain people have aggressive personalities, which means that their scripts predispose them to aggressive and potentially violent responses even when they are confronted with only minor provocations.[28] They believe that videogames and other violent media help to produce these types of scripts, thereby setting their users on course for transferring simulated acts of violence into reality. This sounds plausible, but when it comes to testing, the theory does not fare well. Anderson and Dill only uncover evidence of aggression using one of the four metrics they provide.[29] The authors claim that the results support their contention that games promote aggression, yet a one in four confirmation of this thesis suggests that it is not accurate. Moreover, other researchers were unable to replicate their results using the one test that did indicate heightened aggression.[30]

In another study that is widely cited as evidence of the evils of gaming, Bruce Bartholow and Craig Anderson divided forty-three undergraduate college students into two groups.[31] One group played *Mortal Kombat* and the other played *PGA Tournament Golf*. Players were able to punish their adversary (who was really one of the experimenters) with a noise blast. The authors predicted that those playing the violent game would show their aggression by making more liberal use of this punishment. With volumes ranging from 0 to 10, participants in the *Mortal Kombat* group averaged an intensity of 5.97 and those in the *PGA Tournament Golf* group averaged 4.6. With such a slight difference in the willingness to inflict pain with a noise blast, the authors do not seem to be justified in claiming that their results show that videogames promote violence and are responsible for school shootings. To make matters worse, these results contradicted those of Anderson and Dill's study, by the authors' own admission. Both studies are widely cited by critics attempting to link videogames to violence, even though they employ different metrics of aggression and posit divergent explanations.

One of the most widely cited pieces of evidence supporting the link between videogames and aggression is a meta-analysis from Craig Anderson and Brad Bushman.[32] It promises an authoritative overview of the research that brings thirty-five studies together to reach general conclusions about how videogames cause aggression. The sheer number of studies and of participants included is given as evidence that they are accurate in finding a link between videogames and violence. However, this study suffers from a number of serious shortcomings. First, a meta-analysis can only be as good as the studies it draws from. Bringing many studies together can filter out anomalous results and errors, yet when the experimental research on videogames is already plagued with methodological and logical errors, the sum total of these efforts is unlikely to lead us closer to the truth. Second, although many studies have claimed to show a link between videogames and violence, they do this in divergent ways. As we already saw, some studies take contrary or even contradictory approaches to establishing this hypothesis, which means that they cannot be taken as being complementary for the purposes of a meta-analysis. If anything, the dozens of different strategies for linking games to violence that posit different explanatory mechanisms and yield few compelling results should lead us to doubt their overall conclusions. Finally, the Anderson meta-analysis includes unpublished studies that have not undergone peer review from other researchers. This kind of quality control is essential for giving studies some degree of credibility, and without it we have no indication of whether the studies were properly conducted. It is a cautionary tale of the need to critically evaluate research, which shows that we cannot accept quantity over quality.

Just as important as the methodological problems affecting studies of videogame-induced aggression are the many studies that reach the opposite conclusion.[33] Despite professing an expectation of discovering a clear link between violent videogames and aggression, John Sherry reports that he was only able to see short-term increases in arousal that dissipated with longer exposure to games. Lawrence Kutner and Cheryl Olson produced one of the most comprehensive overviews of research purporting to show a causal link between videogames and violence, ultimately concluding that the evidence is dubious.[34] They discover a pattern of studies using metrics to gauge violent tendencies that have little relation to real-world displays of violence. They also identify a serious publication bias when it comes to publicizing research. Evidence that videogames have some negative impact is more likely to be attractive to high-profile journals and to pass through the rigorous academic peer review process. Studies that fail to find any effect are unattractive to journals and their reviewers, making them poor candidates for publication.[35] Christopher Ferguson finds no evidence that any studies linking violent videogames to real acts of violence have validated their metrics by showing that these really correlate with a heightened propensity to carry out attacks. Moreover, he shows that researchers systematically overstate their findings by magnifying the effect sizes or erroneously concluding that success in triggering stress responses among players is tantamount to finding that games cause aggression.

The aggression thesis is also strongly contradicted by the available evidence about real attacks. With millions of people playing violent videogames, even a subtle increase in aggression should be obvious from crime statistics. Nevertheless, the rate of violent crimes has dropped steadily since the 1990s in North America. Pinker points out that "Hollywood movies are bloodier than ever, unlimited pornography is a mouse-click away, and an entirely new form of violent entertainment, video games, has become a major pastime. Yet as these signs of decadence proliferated in the culture, violence went down in real life."[36] Faced with such a clear drop in violence, it is unclear how videogames (or other media for that matter) could be cause for panic.

If anything, it appears that gaming is associated with lower levels of violence. Michael Ward evaluates the relation between videogames and violence by looking at trends in violence as more videogame stores open.[37] This is an imperfect way of measuring the rate of game sales given the availability of games online. However, the presence of stores does indicate that there is a perceived market on the part of those selling the games, and this calculation is informed by overall trends in consumption, including those from online retailers. This way of gauging games' popularity therefore has some explanatory power even though it is imperfect. Ward's analysis reveals that more game stores correlates with lower overall crime in a particular area. It is difficult to say what can account for this trend, but the results certainly cast doubt on the belief that games cause aggression.

Charlotte Markey, Patrick Markey, and Juliana French similarly find that "annual trends in video game sales for the past 33 years were unrelated to violent crime both concurrently and up to 4 years later" and that the "monthly sales of video games were related to concurrent decreases in aggravated assaults and were unrelated to homicides."[38] Violent crime statistics likewise tend to show that violent crime is lower among the demographics that are more likely to play videogames. The best explanation is that playing videogames keeps people occupied and gives them less time to get into trouble, though it is also possible that playing games could help to release aggression. Faced with the lack of correlation between expressions of aggression and videogames, the aggression thesis is implausible.

It is revealing that critics of violent videogames tend to focus more on a handful of specific incidents of gamers appearing to act aggressively rather than the general trends in violence. They especially like to cite examples of killers who have shown an interest in videogames. As Ferguson points out, "It is not hard to 'link' video game playing with violent acts if one wishes to do so, as one video game playing prevalence study indicated that 98.7% of adolescents play video games to some degree."[39] It is worth repeating that law enforcement investigations into the shootings have found no credible evidence that videogames bear some responsibility. Moreover, some of the favorite examples of school shooters obsessed with games have turned out to be incorrect. This means that the aggression thesis contradicts statistical trends that can be used to gauge violent behavior and that there are good grounds for doubting many of the specific case studies attempting to impugn games.

Even if videogames do increase aggression (and by now it should be clear that this is very doubtful), they might not be morally problematic. Aggression is not in itself immoral. Ferguson rightly points out that aggression is a normal social response; we feel it for a reason. It would be strange for people not to experience some level of aggression when faced with competition, stress, frustration, and other adverse stimuli. Aggression is not deviant or problematic so long as people develop impulse control. Flashes of hostile feelings under certain conditions may reflect a natural temporary response. Under some circumstances, aggression may have a pro-social influence. For example, a person may feel a surge of aggressive impulses when witnessing an assault; if this directs that person to intervene, then the aggression should be praised. The trouble is not with aggression itself but rather with how it is expressed. After more than three decades of media effects research directed at videogames, the absence of evidence that videogames foster harmful aggression should lead us to conclude that there is either no causal relationship or that it is negligible.

Desensitization

At its core, the desensitization thesis holds that videogames desensitize players to a particular experience—usually violence, but possibly sex, racism, or something else—through repetitive exposure. This results in players being comfortable with the experience to the extent that it feels normal and does not provoke moral reflection. The desensitization thesis overlaps with claims that videogames provide training and promote aggression, as desensitization is often described as an outcome of training for violence or as a step toward aggression. It is part of the package of harmful cognitive effects critics attribute to games. Many writers slip between the four arguments I discuss in this chapter without carefully distinguishing them, but it is important to take on desensitization as a separate issue, as it is possible that desensitization could occur without causing any behavioral changes. Desensitization can be part of the broader case against games or it can be treated as an independent evil that would constitute sufficient grounds for thinking that games are immoral.

The desensitization argument is attractive to critics because it shifts the focus away from finding demonstrable harms that fall under the consequentialist moral framework, such as higher rates of violent crime, and toward a deontological perspective where it is intentions that matter. Critics can respond to the lack of conclusive evidence linking games to violence and the counterevidence afforded by crime statistics by saying that games may desensitize players even if they do not cause behavioral changes. Desensitization is a disruption of moral sensibilities that precludes the kind of good will that deontological theories prize. This makes the desensitization thesis a compelling refuge when empirical support is in short supply. This may explain why it has gained traction over time, with some researchers who previously claimed to find a link between games and aggression moving to this more modest position that is difficult to falsify with experiments or statistics.

For example, a 2007 article by Craig Anderson, Douglas Gentile, and Katherine Buckley proposes that videogames may not actually cause violent behavior but that they do trigger an attitudinal shift that is one risk factor among others that may indicate a propensity for violent behavior. They state that "media violence exposure may be able to elevate someone several levels on the risk thermometer, but by itself is not a strong enough effect to move someone from routinely respectful behavior all the way to shooting someone."[40] This conclusion is a prime example of the desensitization thesis coming as a tacit hedge on earlier research, since earlier work from Anderson and his coauthors made more definitive claims that games increase aggression and even incite violence.[41]

Jeanne Funk and her coauthors have produced the most systematic investigations of desensitization, with multiple studies claiming to show that repeated exposure to simulated violence lowers the cognitive and emotional impact of real violence. Most of these studies rely on surveys of young children who are between five and twelve years old. The children are asked to report on their own media viewing habits and complete questionnaires about their attitudes toward violence. The authors find that those who report more contact with violent media tend to be more accepting of violence and weapons, saying that "in violent video games, violence is acceptable because it is not real; therefore, 'victims' do not really suffer. In violent subcultures in the real world, dehumanizing victims is a commonly used technique for minimizing the activation of moral reasoning."[42] They also borrow from Grossman's problematic research on desensitization in the military as evidence to support their reasoning about videogames. They link themselves to Grossman's theory of violence and provide evidence to support his contention that "the steady drip of video game violence throughout kids' days has brainwashed them to enjoy inflicting and reveling in others' pain."[43] Here we can see the overlap between the different arguments directed at violent games, which suggestively links a relatively modest claim about desensitization and the supporting research to more sweeping claims about videogame violence.

Monique Wonderly makes the case for desensitization on philosophical grounds by borrowing from David Hume's work on empathy. As she sees it, violent videogames "may damage our empathetic faculties, and in so doing, they may be directly harming our centers of moral judgment."[44] She hedges this by saying that the loss of empathy may occur even if it is invisible: "An impaired capacity for moral judgment may not immediately or invariably translate into aggressive behavior, but such impairment might, at least initially, only impact one's attitudes towards characters and conduct."[45] If the process is invisible, then the assertion is extremely difficult to test or falsify. In the end, Wonderly considers this to be a valuable approach because it provides an account of why videogames are wrong: "it elucidates a direct connection between playing such games and moral harm," without the recourse to the empirical support that is needed to establish the wrongness of violent videogames on consequentialist grounds.

It is more difficult to evaluate the research on desensitization than the studies of training and aggression, because of this tendency to make claims about cognitive processes that are difficult, or even impossible, to verify or falsify. This thesis also has added plausibility because desensitization is sometimes used to help people overcome fears or cope with posttraumatic stress disorder.[46] Nevertheless, serious methodological problems with the empirical studies and conceptual mistakes in the application of moral theory should lead us to reject this line of argument.

As with the studies of aggression, those of desensitization tend to rest heavily on shaky methodological foundations. These include the publication bias and problematic metrics that I discussed previously and go still further. The bulk of the evidence supporting the desensitization thesis comes from self-reporting in surveys, but self-reporting is notoriously inaccurate. Studies gauging the accuracy of self-reported technology use show large discrepancies between reality and perceptions.[47] Self-reports fluctuate wildly, being both much higher and much lower than real usage figures, which means that even the error in such estimates does not follow a consistent pattern. This suggests that we should not put much faith in respondents' estimates of how much time they spend playing violent games or in surveys that are designed to quantify the extent of a person's desensitization. It is especially questionable to assume that young children will have a good sense of their own media consumption habits. There is also a double standard regarding how self-reporting is incorporated into research on desensitization. Many gamers think that videogames do not have adverse effects,[48] but critics dismiss these assertions. If we trust self-reporting, then we should trust gamers' claims that their play is harmless fun and give such statements the same weight as self-reports of desensitization. It is misleading to disregard self-reporting that attests to a lack of influence while utilizing self-reporting on gameplay and attitudes toward violence as evidence against games.

Another problem is that quite a few of the central claims used to support the desensitization thesis are either misleading or entirely incorrect. For example, Funk et al. claim that the U.S. military uses videogames to desensitize soldiers.[49] This is a shocking point, suggesting that videogames have immense power over our minds. Funk et al. offer no support for this claim and would no doubt have trouble finding any because the U.S. military does not actually do this. Studies of desensitization during war link atrocities to inadequate oversight, unhealthy unit subcultures, and prolonged exposure to real violence—not to videogames.[50] I have not been able to find a single study of wartime misconduct that faults videogames. The most extreme atrocities of the past century were committed before the advent of videogames or in areas where they are not widespread. When work on military socialization mentions videogames, they are usually described as being part of the solution. The U.S. Army used its *America's Army* platform to help soldiers practice resolving moral dilemmas. It has also produced dozens of other simulations to provide moral instruction and practice in correct target identification. The International Red Cross has likewise produced moral training simulations with videogames, which it uses to train armed forces around the world in the Laws of Armed Conflict. Videogames are even being used to treat soldiers who suffer from posttraumatic stress disorder. Far from desensitizing players, the games are used in conjunction with therapy to assist soldiers in developing healthier emotional responses to violence.[51]

Perhaps the most serious empirical error of all is that desensitization research "only examines how violent media desensitizes us to other violent media, not how it affects our sensitivity to real-life violence."[52] In studies that compare gamers' and nongamers' responses to violence to conclude that the former are less affected by it, the violence in question is always simulated. Those who routinely engage in simulated violence might be less upset by it than those who do not, but there is no credible evidence to show that this attitude carries over into the real world. Moreover, many longtime gamers report that they are routinely upset by some of the violent content they encounter in games and that they do not like to play as evil characters, which indicates that even desensitization to simulated violence is limited.[53]

Claims that videogames desensitize players are also dubious on moral grounds. As evidenced by Funk et al.'s link between characters in videogames and real victims of violence, critics tend to downplay the gulf between real and simulated actions. It is counterintuitive to say that nonhuman and noncognizant characters can be moral agents who have victim status when they are attacked. Asserting that these avatars are dehumanized like real victims trivializes genuine atrocities and is implausible unless these avatars are in some way capable of being harmed. Similarly, Wonderly's suggestion that we should feel the same empathy for digital images of people that we do for real people overextends and attenuates moral sensibilities. I doubt that it would be desirable for us to feel the same kind of empathy for fictional characters as we do for real people. Empathy is best directed at genuine moral agents and not spread thinly via a misplaced concern for representations of moral agents.

Losing Reality

The fourth major strategy of critique is an attempt to show that actions taken in game worlds are in some sense real and that they therefore have moral content. In other words, the argument is that events in videogames are either ontologically real or that players accept them as being ontologically real. The key challenge for those who take this position is to collapse the distinction between reality and simulation to show that the two are identical or overlap to a large extent.

Tilo Hartmann and Peter Vorderer offer one of the best accounts of this perspective because they identify several characteristics of realism that might plausibly make games morally problematic.[54] First, they say that videogames encourage players to anthropomorphize characters, who are presented as being real people or as sentient nonhumans. They are modeled as accurately as possible given the current state of technology and are guided by artificial intelligence that makes them act as though they were conscious. Games strive to bring their characters to life by giving them backgrounds, personalities, and aspirations, adding to the sense that they are people. Moreover, the goal of creating convincing characters is usually explicit. Developers regularly promote games by emphasizing their realism. According to Hartmann and Vorderer, characters are so convincing that players learn to associate them with real people. The line between real humans and characters in games blurs to the point that simulated immoral actions against the characters produce the experience of committing real immoral actions against real people.

Second, Hartmann and Vorderer say that many gamers are "believers" and that their "default mode of reception seems to perceive things as real, whereas it takes irritating media cues or motivational efforts to suspend the belief in an 'apparent reality.'"[55] The effects are cumulative, with repeated exposure to games gradually shaping players' sense of what constitutes reality, leading them to accept simulation as being one facet of reality instead of a fictional alternative to it.

Finally, building on their second point, Hartmann and Vorderer maintain that players *willingly* suspend their knowledge that games are simulations and accept them as being real. Players are believers not because they are deceived but because they choose to submit to the fantasy. This suspension of disbelief happens for innocent reasons; it is an effort to make games more engaging and enjoyable. As the authors say, "If users continuously reminded themselves that 'this is just a game,' the game would hardly be enjoyable."[56] By accepting experiences as real, players allow themselves to be taken in by the simulation and make the experiences real. In many ways, this is the most plausible claim, as it is consistent with players actively interpreting games. It recognizes that players are not simply passive dupes, only to then suggest that players are responsible for self-deception.

Other critics have similarly attempted to show that actions in videogames are real and that simulated violence is therefore immoral. Like Hartmann and Vorderer, David Waddington argues that videogames have become so realistic that it is difficult to distinguish between simulated immorality and real immoral conduct. Even though players are able to say that simulated events are fictional, part of the simulated experience seeps into their perceptions of everyday life. Waddington writes, "As video games increase in verisimilitude, and continue to up the ante in terms of violence, it will become increasingly difficult to differentiate between real transgressions (which everyone knows are wrong) and simulated transgressions (which everyone knows are OK). If one cannot differentiate between real transgressions and simulated transgressions, then one has to devalue the idea of wrongness."[57]

It is important to note that the concern expressed in this passage is only justified if gamers lack the ability to distinguish reality from fantasy. Waddington goes on to argue that people have a sense of wrongness that can be devalued when they are routinely exposed to violence, whether simulated or real. To substantiate this, he offers the example of currency. If the sense of wrongness is like money, then violent entertainment is like counterfeit money that devalues the thing it reproduces.

The plausibility of the realism thesis is highly contingent on what games are being discussed and when. Outrage at "realistic" videogame violence has existed since the late 1970s.[58] Throughout the 1980s and 1990s, games that we would now consider to have extremely poor graphics, to the point that the characters are little more than stick figures, were accused of realistically simulating violence. James Newman notes that "using today's standards, '*Pac-Man*' and other early videogames like '*Space Invaders*,' '*Defender*,' and '*Asteroids*' appear relatively nonthreatening; however, in the early 1980s these games were characterized as violent."[59] This has left critics who think that there is something morally questionable about realistic simulations with the problem of continually having to distance themselves from arguments directed at older games while still invoking the same logic against new games that have the power to shock with representations of violence that will themselves look dated in a few years. Any convincing attempt to show that realistic videogames are immoral would have to say when representations cross a certain threshold of realism that reverse-transubstantiates them from amoral representations into morally significant ones. Those who advance this thesis have yet to offer any such criteria, leaving the scope of their arguments poorly defined.

Many who are concerned with realistic violence look to the future with predictions about how improvements in simulation will make the moral concerns more compelling. Grossman and DeGaetano say that "of course, we all realize that the images on video screens are just that, just as they're not real on TV screens; but the sophistication of this technology is making it hard to tell, especially for children whose minds are not fully formed."[60] Such reasoning is deeply problematic. It is fair to say that the future may bring changes that make videogames indistinguishable from real life, but we are certainly not at that point yet and should not bring speculations about future technologies into debates about present conditions. Critics advancing this line of argument like to raise *Ender's Game* as an analogy.[61] That book tells the story of children in a futuristic dystopia playing a war game that turns out to be real, using this fictional story as a case study to impugn existing games. It is possible to imagine such a simulation existing, and it would be morally questionable, but it is far removed from any existing game. Games cannot be blamed for hypothetical futures any more than a person can be blamed for the crimes they might one day commit. Regardless of what the future may hold, the simple fact is that even the most visually convincing games on the market can be easily distinguished from real life by all except the extremely young or those suffering from some kind of cognitive impairment.

The arguments that violent videogames can be immoral because of their level of realism rest on the assumption that anthropomorphizing a representation of a person makes that representation a moral entity such that treating it well or poorly has real moral significance. This is a deeply problematic assertion. Those who make this claim are certainly right in thinking that videogames often strive for verisimilitude and that their characters tend to look more real and more human with each advancement in graphical representation. They are also correct in thinking that people tend to anthropomorphize nonhuman entities, even developing deep attachments to them. However, it is doubtful that realism can elevate videogame characters to a moral status or that anthropomorphization changes moral sentiments related to real people.

To test the strength of this line of critique, it is helpful first to think about how we approach representations of people in other contexts. Movies and television are among the clearest analogues, and are similar to videogames in each of the ways that Hartmann and Vorderer consider significant. Characters in movies and television shows look extremely realistic—usually far more realistic than those in videogames. Viewers frequently accept the pretensions to realism at face value, just as videogame players do, making them "believers" in the sense Hartmann and Vorderer describe. Finally, those who watch movies and television shows tend to become willingly immersed in stories. Viewers can lose themselves in a fantasy world and become totally immersed in it to the extent that the movie and its characters feel real.

The question, then, is whether the critique of realistic videogames can extend to these other media. I doubt that many people would be willing to classify characters in movies as being moral agents even though they are played by real people. The appearance of being real does not impart moral status. We may consider one character's killing of another to be murder in the context of the narrative, but such fictional actions lack moral significance when taken out of that context. This is why we do not issue arrest warrants for movie villains or the actors portraying them.

Of course, the likely response from critics is that videogames are special—that there is something about them that makes their realism morally significant even when realism in other media is not. Hartmann and Vorderer's argument rests heavily on the claim that interactive engagement in the narrative leads players to accept actions in videogames as being real. It is therefore not just realism that is at stake but realism combined with interactivity. The problem is that this is all based on conjecture that is sharply at odds with what empirical research with gamers has uncovered, and it reflects faulty moral reasoning.

In terms of the empirical side of the argument, Hartmann and Vorderer are wrong in assuming that enjoyment of videogames involves a willing suspension of any conception of the real world. As Steven Jones correctly points out, "Playing usually involves remaining simultaneously aware of both the gameworld and of the real world, of yourself and of other players as performing at the boundary of the two, while you go online to search the boards for a helpful 'cheat,' for example, or consult a printed game guide, and then follow up by looking at a fan-authored article in a dedicated wiki."[62] Play is not contained within the simulated world but rather tends to spill out into fan communities and forums. Players may be talking to friends who are also in the game or switching between the game and a strategy guide. Even when players are completely immersed in a single-player campaign with no outside social contact, it is implausible to think that they lose awareness of the line separating reality from simulation. How could players not feel a difference between their ordinary lives and events taking place on a flat screen that they interact with via a keyboard or control pad? Real life and gaming are qualitatively different. It is entirely possible to imagine immersive simulations like *Star Trek: The Next Generation*'s holodeck or *Total Recall*'s memory implants causing disassociation, but these are far removed from current gaming technology. Those fantasies of advanced simulations are alluring precisely because no current technology comes close to a level of realism that can truly bring fiction to life.

Despite their graphical sophistication, videogames often emphasize their fictional status. Some re-create famous scenes from films (few World War II first-person shooter games can resist emulating the Omaha Beach landing sequence from *Saving Private Ryan*), reminding us of other works of fiction. Controversial ultraviolent games like those in the *Grand Theft Auto* series are often heavily satirical in ways that highlight the gap between reality and fiction. Many games are popular because they flaunt physical and social constraints; they allow players to fly, single-handedly defeat hordes of enemies, and recover from life-threatening injuries by picking up a health pack. Games allow us to act in ways that are distinctly *unreal*, which is part of their appeal. Videogame protagonists are more often like superheroes than like realistic representations of ordinary people, and, of course, the reset button is always close at hand after the character dies. It stretches the limits of credulity to think that simply because players become immersed in their play they also lose the capacity to understand that it is fictional.

Those who present the realism critique against videogames like to provide evidence from players who profess being emotionally invested in the characters they create to the point that they feel a deep connection with them. But becoming emotionally invested in a character or a story is not the same as mistaking it for something that is ontologically real. For one thing, players tend to feel invested in characters they create, not in the comparatively empty characters that are the enemies in violent videogames.[63] Moreover, being invested in a character does not give any indication that players are unable to separate fantasy from reality. For example, Waddington quotes one obsessive player as saying that videogames are "where I live . . . more than I do in my dingy dorm room."[64] Here and in other instances, the attachment to simulation exists precisely because it is fictional and offers an escape from reality. Escapism is possible because videogames are epistemically real, in the sense of providing imaginative experiences, without being impeded by the ontological constraints of real life.

The moral reasoning behind the critiques of realistic violent videogames rests heavily on dubious empirical claims. Waddington's theory of moral devaluation depends on the assumption that players are unable to differentiate real violence from simulated violence, just as Hartmann and Vorderer's argument presupposes that players willingly disengage from reality. As I showed, these are doubtful propositions. If they are discarded, the overall arguments fall apart. And such assertions should be discarded, at least until their authors are able to provide compelling evidence that gamers are detached from reality.

Deeper flaws in the moral reasoning undermine the strength of this line of critique even if we set the empirical claims aside. The realism critique draws parallels between real moral agents and simulations based on their visual similarities, which dramatically overstates the role of appearance in constituting moral worth. Images and other representations are not the kinds of things to which we ascribe moral agency. Someone who destroys a portrait of another person is not a murderer. There is a vast difference between a person and an image of that person, and a still greater difference between a real person and the image of a fictional person. Some people may feel a sentimental attachment to pictures, but this has to do with their importance as unique pieces of property and not to any inherent moral worth of the images themselves. The infinitely reproducible characters of videogames only bear superficial resemblance to real people, so they do not warrant a special status beyond that given to other types of images.

People are inclined to anthropomorphize objects and may derive a sense of self-worth from owning cars, clothes, and houses, yet most of us would probably say that this fails to impart moral agency onto those things. Objects take on value for their owners, but they are not moral beings themselves. Moreover, there is a difference between anthropomorphizing nonhuman objects and seriously treating them as moral agents. Does a person who names their car and treats it as a member of the family genuinely fail to recognize that the car is not human? I doubt that this is the case. Does the car become a moral agent simply because someone names it and feels a deep personal attachment toward it? Certainly not. If we do suspect that people who anthropomorphize other objects are unable to distinguish fantasy from reality, and if we do not grant the objects moral status, then consistency demands approaching videogames in the same way.

The realism argument rests heavily on flawed analogies, as evidenced by Waddington's currency analogy. He is right in saying that counterfeit money can devalue real money, but this is because they are both physical objects capable of performing the same functions.[65] The former undermines the latter's value because the two are often indistinguishable in economic transactions. That is, the similarity is not merely *visual*; it is also *functional*. You can spend counterfeit money. Regardless of how realistic it is, videogame violence is, for now, safely contained in television screens and computers. The simulated violence does not mix with actual violence any more than Monopoly money mixes with real currency. No competent person would witness a simulated murder in a game and report it to the police. The reason is simple: the real and simulated actions are not functionally alike. A criminal can spend counterfeit money by using it to function as real money, but a criminal cannot kill a person by simulating murder in a game. Waddington's argument would only be plausible if simulated violence were functionally indistinguishable from real violence. This could be possible in a future of augmented reality, but no existing videogames have such a close functional relationship with the real world.

The realism argument is guilty of doing precisely what it accuses games of doing: diluting important moral categories. We do not devalue our moral sentiments by witnessing simulated violence, yet we would badly devalue them by treating simulated violence as being akin to the real thing. How insulting would it be to real murder victims if dead avatars were likewise accorded victim status? How flawed would our understanding of animal cruelty be if, as Waddington suggests, we treat videogame characters as being like animals insofar as they are analogues to humanity? Conflating simulated moral transgressions with real ones would be a genuine instance of moral counterfeiting. It is a supreme irony of misplaced moral panic that the effort to collapse essential moral distinctions comes more from the critique of violent videogames than from games themselves.

General Problems with Moral Panic

The four critiques of violent videogames I discuss in this chapter suffer from serious shortcomings that should lead us to discard these critiques as grounds for thinking that there is something morally problematic with videogames. The evidence that games foster violence and interfere with moral reasoning is dubious. The results of existing studies are too weak and mixed to support strong claims that videogames harm players. Moreover, the panic surrounding games has shifted attention away from more plausible explanations for crime, such as easy access to guns. Looking at the four antigaming arguments collectively, it is possible to identify seven general problems that should be avoided in analyses of videogames. The strategy for theorizing the moral significance of videogames that I present in subsequent chapters is informed by an effort to reorient analysis on a more solid foundation that avoids these errors.

First, most critiques show a remarkable lack of appreciation for polysemy. Critics tend to treat each game as having a single, consistent meaning for all audiences. And that interpretation is imagined as promoting violence or at least encouraging passive acceptance of it. If this assumption were accurate, we would have to expect every player who encounters the No Russian mission to interpret terrorism as being good and admirable. Of course, many players are disgusted by the mission and see it as a representation of something horrific.[66] Moments like that one are shocking precisely because they simulate actions that are abhorrent and that are capable of provoking a strong response. This shocking mission helped to garner greater attention for the game because it runs contrary to our moral intuitions. If the mission represented something praiseworthy or acceptable, it would have been far less effective in drawing attention. In other words, flouting moral conventions for commercial success depends on our believing in those conventions both as individuals and as societies. It may be fun to simulate such attacks or to participate in games that incorporate shocking scenes, but assuming that this enjoyment counts as tacit acceptance of real violence seriously underestimates players' interpretive power.

Ironically, critics of videogames confirm the multiplicity of interpretations and the prospects of disagreeing with the things videogames represent. They see simulated violence as a representation of something terrible that should not be emulated in real life, yet they assume that they have privileged access to this interpretation and that other players are dupes who lack the ability to distinguish fantasy from reality. Critics play or watch the games to uncover their illicit messages while remaining aloof from the ostensibly harmful effects of gaming, yet they assume that players have no comparable immunity from the same messages. Such conceit should be seen for what it is: an unfair double standard. It may be appropriate to think that adults looking at videogames are in a more suitable position to judge their content than young children who lack developed moral sensibilities or who lack a clear sense of what is real, but it is wholly inappropriate to deny that adults playing these games lack the same capacities for critical reflection as academic commentators. And this double standard is revealing because the tacit admission that games permit multiple interpretations undermines the assumption that all players are affected in the same way.

Second, building on the former point, the studies show little appreciation for the importance of context in structuring simulated decisions and giving them moral weight within game narratives. Funk et al. say of videogames that "violence is presented as justified, without negative consequences, and fun."[67] Although this is sometimes true, it vastly understates the nuances of how videogames represent violence. Again, the No Russian mission is a prime example. The narrative explains that this simulated terrorist attack was orchestrated by an American general, making him the game's central villain. This helps to transform an American officer into an evil enemy, despite the game's incorporation of many pro-American themes. Thus, even within the confines of the game narrative, there may be ample cues that players should not accept the simulated violence as being legitimate and good, especially in extreme cases. I show in subsequent chapters that some of the most shocking scenes of torture, rape, and murder in recent games are embedded in narrative contexts that cast these acts as being immoral. Some games simulate punishments for unjustified violence (going to jail in *Grand Theft Auto*), show negative consequences (the outbreak of World War III after the No Russian attack), and even overtly challenge players to think more carefully about their attitudes toward real and simulated violence (as in the case of *Spec Ops: The Line*). It is disconcerting that so many researchers claiming that videogames are harmful do not show much awareness of the differences between games or the different ways they approach violence. It suggests that researchers are either ignorant of the games or that they set out to create a negative impression.

Third, critics take an opportunistic approach to interactivity, in the sense that they treat player participation in games as an added moral danger that makes games uniquely abhorrent but without acknowledging the problems that interactivity introduces for their own research designs. Because games are interactive, they can yield different experiences depending on player input. This poses significant challenges for research, since it means that no two players come away with the same impression of a game. Those who have no prior experience with games may not be able to make any progress, some may take stealth approaches rather than using violence, and any branching path can take players into different gameplay domains. Without the ability to control what players are exposed to, as is possible when studying films or books, experiments cannot be properly controlled. Much of the research ostensibly showing that videogames are morally problematic depends on experimental techniques that cannot contend with interactivity. Nevertheless, critics use those techniques and sideline the issue of interactivity except when it comes time to argue that interactivity lures players into a morally dangerous identification with the violence they imaginatively participate in.

As Mia Consalvo points out, "Gamers are often seen as actively participating in games, but at the same time being actively (and negatively) affected by the content within the game. Fundamental to such an approach is the negation (or dismissal) of how players constantly make choices about their in-game behavior, as well as consider and frame their game actions relative to other daily situations and contexts."[68] This desire to emphasize interactivity when it comes to promoting a moral panic while downplaying it in research further distances critics from the medium and challenges the fairness of their findings.

Fourth, researchers assume that just because violent games are entertaining and popular, players must support the actions the games simulate. For example, critics read the popularity of the *Grand Theft Auto* series as evidence that the games are making people more supportive of real criminality rather than reading this as evidence that people enjoy fantasizing about criminality. Ethnographic and survey research on gamers reveals that this assumption is inaccurate. Amanda Lange reports that in a survey of 1,067 gamers, "43 percent of participants said they had encountered an act in a game that was vile enough that they refused to commit it. In some games, this would mean ending the playthrough."[69] This suggests that many gamers are attuned to the moral significance of their simulated actions to such an extent that even pretending to be immoral causes discomfort. The No Russian mission was among those that players refused to participate in, as were a torture scene from *Grand Theft Auto V*, harvesting Little Sisters in *BioShock*, and destroying the town of Megaton in *Fallout 3* (I discuss each of these examples in more detail in later chapters). From this, we can conclude that witnessing or even participating in simulated immoral actions does not constitute support for those actions. Players are capable of enjoying games while still objecting to the actions that are simulated.

Fifth, critiques of videogames' harmful effects tend to endorse what I call the "zero acceptable risk" assumption. They assume that videogames are objectionable if there is any risk of players, or society more broadly, experiencing harmful side effects. Even the slightest evidence of an adverse response from players, such as a heightened pulse or a willingness to subject opponents to a slightly louder noise after playing a violent game than after a nonviolent one, is taken as evidence that videogames are dangerous. This is an unreasonably high standard. Few activities are truly risk-free, even when they are just entertainment. Sports such as football, hockey, boxing, and wrestling, among many others, can inflict serious injuries or even kill participants, yet we generally accept that these are worthwhile risks because they are outweighed by our enjoyment. I acknowledge that there may be outlier cases in which violent videogames do have adverse effects on players who are very young, predisposed to violence, or lack the ability to distinguish fantasy from reality. There may be some small risks associated with gaming, yet it would be unfair to take this as evidence of immorality when leeway is granted to the risks associated with other forms of entertainment. In fact, weighing the scant evidence of harm associated with videogames against the harms associated with other activities, such as contact sports like tackle football, shows that the former come off very well. Consistency demands that we judge different types of entertainment by roughly the same standards when determining whether they are acceptable. It is inconsistent to think that the poorly substantiated risks associated with videogames make gaming immoral but that activities with clearly established harms are acceptable. It is likewise inconsistent to think that simulations of violence in a game are somehow more corrupting than sports that involve physical violence.

Finally, there is a pervasive tendency to overstate weak empirical findings or simply accept false information that fits the narrative that games are evil. As I have shown, Dave Grossman's work has had an especially harmful effect on research by providing a body of work on training, aggression, and desensitization that is widely circulated despite suffering from serious faults. Claims about military desensitization involving videogames and the innate desire to avoid violence being overcome with digital training techniques are repeated as truisms, despite being largely fabricated. It is disconcerting that there appears to be so little fact checking in research on violent videogames and that critics readily parrot flimsy research just because it fits their conclusions.

Conclusion

Responding to these four critiques of violent videogames marks an important first step in the project of reorienting the moral analysis of videogames in a way that is methodologically stronger, less prone to misguided panic, and, most importantly of all, sensitive to the potential benefits of playing videogames. Some games may not be appropriate for young children who do not understand that events simulated in games are not real. There may also be legitimate concerns with how players who have severe cognitive impairments or who are predisposed to violence are affected by games, although even in these cases the evidence is inconclusive. It is implausible that the current generation of games trains players in fighting skills or truly interferes with their capacities for distinguishing fantasy from reality, but there is reason to be cautious about developing more advanced simulation technologies in the future. Similarly, the clear distinction between the real world and game worlds could be bridged with augmented reality, and it is possible to imagine a future in which simulated violence is indistinguishable from real violence. We should therefore make prudential calculations about new simulation technologies that could bring us closer to realizing these moral concerns, though with the goal of promoting research and debate rather than panic.

Although I have sought to dispel misguided claims that videogames are immoral, I do not want to suggest that games are amoral. Garry Young says that amoralists, for whom games have no moral implications, appeal to a reductionist strategy, according to which games are just the manipulation of pixels, regardless of what those pixels represent.[70] He rightly counters this perspective by pointing out that amoralists overlook the obvious fact that the pixels are meaningful because they are representative. They produce controversial images that are capable of simulating moral dilemmas and giving rise to the moral concerns that I have discussed. Amoralists are correct in thinking that playing videogames is not immoral because the simulated actions are not real, yet games' power to evoke moral problems through simulation makes them morally significant. In chapter 3, I turn toward a more profitable approach to looking at the moral implications of videogames by drawing analogies between them and other types of simulations.

3

Imaginary Transgressions

Videogame scholarship has gone to great lengths to emphasize games' distinctiveness compared to other media, especially when taking a ludological perspective. This work has uncovered genuinely novel features associated with the medium, such as the high degree of interactivity and the opportunities for modifying content. However, the emphasis on novelty and distinguishing videogames from other media has led to a problem when it comes to understanding the moral implications of videogames. In particular, it has supported the narrative that videogames exercise a peculiar new form of influence that is exceptionally dangerous. It is important to be aware of the unique features of the medium yet equally important to see the parallels between videogames and other types of simulations. Videogames are special, yet they still bear important resemblances to other media, which makes comparison rewarding.

After spending the preceding chapters discussing the distinctive features of videogames, it is now worth turning to characteristics they share with other simulations that deal with moral puzzles. This can help to elucidate the meaning of moral challenges that games introduce and clarify the moral status of players who simulate immoral acts. Throughout the preceding chapters, I have emphasized the ontological distinction between digital worlds and the real world. Videogames may look realistic and may even have real consequences, but the events they represent are not real. Games are digital models of the world or of abstract puzzles. Although I will go on to explore the various ways in which videogames are used with persuasive intent, any degree of influence does not change this fundamental fact that simulated events are not real. Rather, such influence only shows that events need not be real to be persuasive. The same holds true for other types of models and simulations, which may take place across an array of media aside from videogames, such as in written texts, songs, movies, television shows, or even just in the mind. Looking at the moral significance of simulations in general is therefore a useful step toward understanding how simulations work when it comes to videogames in particular.

Thought experiments provide the most helpful analogy. These are fictional models that are designed to test specific philosophical and scientific puzzles that either cannot be subjected to empirical testing or where doing so would impose excessive costs. Thought experiments are a method of exploring immorality without actually being immoral. They allow us to consider the effects of terrible atrocities and even imagine ourselves as murderers, with the goal of clarifying our intuitions and values. These experiments are usually conducted through narration but can be just as effective (perhaps even more effective) when conveyed using computer simulations. Such simulations blur the boundaries of philosophical analysis and gaming in ways that reveal striking similarities between the two.

I devote this chapter to exploring the importance of thought experiments and of their similarities with the moral challenges that arise in games. As Nicholas Rescher points out, "The use of thought experimentation in philosophy is as old as the subject itself."[1] Videogames lack this impressive lineage and are only made possible by digital technologies, so it may be tempting to deny that they can offer enriching encounters with moral challenges. However, beneath the superficial differences, the two are alike in ways that make the comparison a useful heuristic for understanding what it means to simulate assault, murder, war, and the other terrible atrocities that videogames make possible. Both create fictional models of problems, are structured by clear rules, and allow participants to simulate moral and immoral conduct. Some videogames are akin to extremely complex thought experiments, as they ask us to imagine entire worlds that are transformed by interrelated decisions. Games also incorporate countless dilemmas that call for moral reasoning skills, often doing so in ways that closely emulate the kinds of thought experiments employed by moral philosophers. The similarities between videogames and thought experiments are not incidental. They exist because they occupy the same distinctive ontological status of modeling the real world and potentially influencing it without being real themselves.

Throughout my responses to the critiques of videogames that simulate violence and sexual deviance, I have sought to show that many of the ostensibly dangerous features are illusory. At its core, the moral outrage directed at videogames is rooted in objections about the kind of content being simulated and the participatory dimensions of the medium. When the interface and realistic graphics are stripped away to leave issues related to content and participation, the similarities between videogames and thought experiments come into sharper relief. Both are preoccupied with moral deviance and encourage mental engagement with puzzles that involve immoral actions, yet the former spark moral outrage while the latter do not. Thought experiments are useful tools for moral analysis because they permit exploration of difficult issues with attention to both good and bad actions, without inflicting any real costs. The topics raised in philosophical counterfactuals may be uncomfortable, yet merely confronting them is not immoral and may even be an avenue for improving judgment. I argue that the same is true of videogames.

What Are Thought Experiments?

Imagine taking a walk along a trolley track and seeing a Y-shaped junction off in the distance. To your horror, you notice that five people are tied to one branch of the track and that a runaway trolley is racing down the hill toward them. You glance around for something that can stop the trolley but only find the switch controlling which branch the trolley takes. It is currently set to run over the five people, who are helpless to protect themselves. Diverting it will send the trolley toward an equally defenseless person who is standing on the other track, oblivious to the danger. What is the right thing to do? Allow the trolley to kill the five people, or intervene to save them and kill an innocent bystander?

This is the Trolley Problem, a classic thought experiment in moral philosophy. It has been around for decades, being most widely attributed to Philippa Foot but also described in various permutations by philosophers before and since.[2] The scenario has a degree of realism. Trolleys, trains, and subways do run out of control sometimes, and while those in the path might not be tied to the tracks as if by some mustache-twirling villain, it is entirely plausible that workers, stalled vehicles, and clumsy commuters could be stuck on the tracks, unable to move out of the way in time or ignorant of the danger. What is more important than the plausibility of the background details relating to who is in danger and why is that the scenario gets right to the heart of a pressing moral consideration that affects countless real-world decisions: how should we weigh people's lives against each other? This dilemma truly is routine, cropping up wherever competing interests in matters of life and death must be reconciled. It must be made when deciding who to prioritize for medical treatment, when to launch attacks during war, and where to focus disaster relief efforts. Wherever difficult moral choices are found, there are apt to be cases of prioritizing certain people over others. One day it may even be necessary for machines to make such decisions. For example, if autonomous cars must choose which way to swerve when multiple pedestrians are in the way. The ubiquity of this dilemma makes the thought experiment a useful hypothetical for reaching general conclusions about how to prioritize lives, and the rise of autonomous machines should give greater impetus for developing consistent guidelines that can be incorporated into their programming.

Thought experiments like the Trolley Problem are used across the natural and social sciences, in addition to philosophy, for analyzing an array of problems. They are typically purely imaginary experiments that take place, as the name suggests, only in a person's mind, with help from written or oral narrative instructions. These scenarios may also be developed in more detail with the help of simple diagrams. Essentially, a thought experiment is a model of a particular problem that is constructed by stripping away extraneous details to focus on a central question. As Julian Baggini puts it, "We can simply stipulate that all other things are equal, so the only question we need to settle is the core moral one."[3] This is evident from how the Trolley Problem gets right to the heart of the question of how to weigh people's lives against each other. The scenario forces a decision between two undesirable outcomes without leaving any avenues for weaseling out of the decision.

Weaseling out is precisely what many people attempt to do when hearing thought experiments. As someone who has taken and taught classes dealing with moral philosophy, I can attest that whenever these are introduced in a classroom setting, a clever student attempts to resolve the central dilemma by finding a way of circumventing it. Maybe the trolley can be stopped by driving a car in front of it. Maybe there is a way of derailing it before anyone is harmed. Maybe the lone person who is not tied down can be alerted just in time to jump out of the way. The undeniable appeal of dodging the horns of the dilemma as though the thought experiment itself was the runaway trolley highlights one of the challenges associated with narrative thought experiments. Because they are imaginary, they invite efforts to change the parameters of the problem in search of a better outcome. The result is a frustrated philosophy teacher explaining that the entire point of the experiment is to solve it within the confines of the variables that are left within the model. That is, these hypotheticals require much the same suspension of disbelief and acceptance of artificial rules as videogames. There may be no right or wrong answer to the Trolley Problem, but one way or another we must choose between one of the two undesirable alternatives. Sidestepping the problem is a kind of cheating, since doing this avoids resolving the dilemma directly, thereby failing to answer the core moral challenge.

Parallels between Videogames and Thought Experiments

The first clue that thought experiments have something in common with games should be the ease with which thought experiments can be reproduced as games and even improved in the process. Games can make hypothetical puzzles feel more real. They give the underlying rules a sense of immutability and confine the options available in a way that narratives by themselves cannot. That is, computer simulation forces participants to confront problems head on, leaving no opportunities for circumvention by attempting to alter the scenarios.

Pippin Barr presents the Trolley Problem using a graphical interface with a single game mechanic.[4] Players must decide who lives and dies in each of four iterations of the problem by pressing the space bar to pull the switch and divert the trolley or refraining from doing so. As videogames go, the mechanics could not be simpler. Barr even includes a tutorial in which players can choose whether to pull the switch when the tracks are empty, with no lives hanging in the balance. The simulation then confronts successively more challenging scenarios. In the first, there is a choice between allowing three people to die or diverting the trolley to kill one person. Next, the trolley is on a loop and will stop after it runs over the three people it is heading toward or after running over a very large person who will be struck if the switch is pulled. This is similar to the first scenario but helps to pave the way for a different type of challenge. In the third act, there is no junction, only a straight track with three people on it. Now the very large person is on a platform and can be pushed into the trolley's path. This is apparently just like the second case—a choice between one life and three—except now protecting three people requires physical interaction with the very large person, which may feel more like murder than when the choice is made by flicking a switch. The fourth scenario is the same as the first, except now the lone person is a relative. Players are asked to choose whether this should be a mother, father, brother, sister, wife, husband, boyfriend, girlfriend, daughter, or son, which essentially invites participants to make the puzzle as difficult as possible. This final iteration tests whether norms applied to strangers remain consistent when we know the people involved.

The rules of the simulation force players to make a choice. There are only two choices in each iteration of the problem as Barr presents it; there are no cars to drive onto the tracks or methods of alerting bystanders. The graphical representations are also helpful. Many of us are visual thinkers, for whom it is easier to imagine a problem when it is supplemented by diagrams. All decisions are final (at least until the game is reset). There is no way to flip the switch back to its starting position. This pushes participants toward making a decision rather than exploring all possible options. The game imposes time constraints that are absent in the narrative thought experiment by only allowing a few seconds of reflection before the trolley passes the junction and cannot be diverted. It is an admirable attempt to simulate moral decision-making under pressure, which may end up leading to different outcomes than in protracted philosophical discussions.

I will leave aside some of the more esoteric debates over what qualifies as a thought experiment in the strictest sense and argue that the medium probably is not among the necessary conditions.[5] There is no good reason to think that thought experiments must be presented in narratives when other media may function just as well or better. The use of narratives is mainly a practical consideration. It is usually cost prohibitive to construct counterfactuals using other media when the goal is only to make a specific theoretical point. Moreover, philosophical theories have traditionally been expressed using the written word, so this has been, and continues to be, the most natural medium when building counterfactuals. Textual descriptions also have the advantage of having existed long before computer simulations were able to convey philosophical puzzles.

The Trolley Problem is a thought experiment regardless of whether it is set out in the pages of a philosophy book or in a flash animation because it is a counterfactual scenario that invites participants to make imagined moral decisions. It may be tempting to deny that such a lowly medium as Flash Player can stimulate serious reflection, just as others have denied that videogames in general can convey deep content that would make them qualify as works of art.[6] However, in each case, this tendency to devalue videogames is deeply misguided.

Further support for my contention that videogames can be treated as presenting thought experiments comes from the fact that other media are frequently described as thought experiment analogues. Eva Dadlez says that "it is not out of the question to suggest that fiction can be and often is just such a thought experiment—one that can challenge or substantiate the judgments to which an individual adheres or which that individual contemplates."[7] Similarly, Thomas Wartenberg argues that some films function as thought experiments by creating imaginative scenarios that test our intuitions. He reads *The Matrix* as being a protracted thought experiment that touches on ideas from Descartes, Berkley, and Locke, among others—a conclusion that is supported by the number of high-profile philosophers who published commentaries on the film.[8] There are now entire book series analyzing literature, movies, comic books, and virtually everything else through a philosophical lens, often by focusing on similarities to classic thought experiments. All this underscores the folly of excluding videogames from philosophical evaluation.

Counterfactuals in books, films, and television shows offer useful parallels that can contribute to our understanding of videogames, yet this comparison is limited by the possibility of appreciating those media without having to directly confront the decisions presented. That is, we can read about a character making a decision or watch one on-screen without imagining what we would do under the same conditions. We can passively contemplate the dilemmas evoked. Thought experiments, on the other hand, have a closer affinity to games because they put us in the role of moral actors. We must make the imagined decision ourselves. Capturing this sense of interactivity in analogies that are used to understand videogames is essential because this is one of the key issues arising in claims that videogames are unique, and perhaps even uniquely immoral.

Comparing the content of media to thought experiments raises the possibility that entertainment could be a site of serious philosophical work. It suggests that books and films, among other media, can present hypothetical scenarios that, when formulated carefully, allow the media to perform the same function as more traditional narrative thought experiments designed by philosophers. Such media do not merely reflect or embody moral thinking; they are sites of moral analysis in their own right. Far from diminishing their importance, the popularity of these texts and their entertainment value actually adds to it. A relatively small number of people will contemplate the narrative version of the Trolley Problem as they read through a philosophical tome. Many more will experience an updated version of it in *Prey* when they are presented with it as a test during the game's tutorial.

The similarities between videogames and thought experiments are theoretically important. Comparing them can help us gain a deeper appreciation for how games explore moral questions and clarify the meaning of simulated immorality within game worlds. Like thought experiments, videogames create fictional worlds in which various courses of action can be explored. Both depend on constructing artificial challenges to create self-imposed tests, yet these challenges are never final. They can be replayed in endless permutations to explore possible outcomes. In videogames, these are set out by the developers and embedded in the game mechanics, though they can be broken by enterprising players who exploit a glitch or a loophole that the developers were not aware of. Those who design thought experiments likewise establish firm rules that are supposed to guide potential answers. These rules only set boundaries of imagination and are therefore less strongly felt, but they are nevertheless real and place certain solutions (such as stopping the trolley by pushing a car in front of it) out of bounds.

Games can function as thought experiments, but is the reverse also true? Barr's simulation is clearly a thought experiment, but is it also a game? Based on the criteria I discussed in chapter 1, it is difficult to see how the answer could be anything aside from "yes." There is a pedagogical component to the simulation, so perhaps it might be called a "serious game," but it clearly builds on the ludological elements that typically feature in things that we call games and incorporates narratological elements that give the gameplay meaning. Moreover, it would be fair to call it a videogame. After all, it must be played using a computer and is purely digital. The graphics and gameplay mechanics are simple, but the same can be said for many other games for early console systems, Flash Player, and mobile phones. One could object that Barr's simulation falls a bit short of qualifying as a game because there is no way to lose, but if a game must have winners and losers, then an array of games without these outcomes (for example, *Stanley Parable* or *Firewatch*) would not qualify as games either. It may therefore be best to say that Barr's simulation fits best in the genre of exploration games in which the point is more to tell a story than to judge the player's skill. This further compounds the conceptual slippage between the moral dilemmas we experience in videogames and those presented by narratives or other media.

If you are unconvinced that videogames can function as thought experiments or that thought experiments can be played like games, then look no further than *Life Is Strange*. Players take control of Maxine Caulfield, an eighteen-year-old student who discovers that she has the ability to travel a few seconds back in time. The game is essentially a series of paths that branch depending on player choices.

Moral decision-making is the key gameplay mechanic, while time travel just facilitates it by giving players a chance to test different approaches. As in the Trolley Problem, there is no winning or losing. Choices lead to different outcomes, which range from fairly mundane social interactions to matters of life and death. Some outcomes are better and some worse, though even what is better or worse depends heavily on personal tastes. Whether it is better to report Nathan Prescott for having a gun in school or to conceal this fact is up for debate, as are the dozens of other decisions players must make, which is why the decisions have given rise to long discussions on Reddit and other online message boards.

The series ends with an infamous decision that is essentially just another iteration of the Trolley Problem. Players must choose whether to save the protagonist's best friend, Chloe, or the town of Arcadia Bay. It is a decision about whether to prioritize the lives of many or the life of one, in this case made weightier because Chloe becomes a close friend over the course of the game and because Arcadia Bay is a town of thousands, not three or five. In this case, the Trolley Problem is not the entire game, but it is a key part. The game as a whole could be described as a series of similar puzzles held together and imbued with emotional weight by an overarching narrative. *Life Is Strange* is a prime example of how a fairly sophisticated and successful game can incorporate thought experiments as a gameplay mechanic. In this case, they are so central that there would be no game at all without them. In their absence, the game would present virtually no opportunities for player engagement and would be difficult to classify as a game at all. A thought experiment may therefore not only be a game but may also be integral to making certain digital models qualify as games.

The Utility of Thought Experiments

Thought experiments are employed in virtually every field of research because they make it possible to develop plausible inferences when empirical testing is impossible. For example, in another classic counterfactual, Hilary Putnam imagines two Earths that are identical except for one key detail: what people on Twin Earth call "water" is not H_2O but instead XYZ.[9] The two substances are alike in every way other than their chemical composition. Putnam builds an entire hypothetical planet just to consider whether people on Twin Earth would mean the same thing as we do when they talk about water. Such an experiment would be physically impossible, of course, but it is still useful for illustrating a specific problem about how names function. The experiment yields results by making it easier to zero in on circumstances in which a disagreement about the meaning of a name could crop up even though the same word is being used and in precisely the same social context. This kind of experimentation is not an alternative to empirical research but rather a way of filling in gaps that lie beyond the boundaries of our experience.

Despite their emphasis on rigorous empirical testing, natural scientists are some of the most avid users of thought experiments. Einstein came up with some of his most famous insights with their assistance. When contemplating the speed of light, he imagined what it might be like to ride a beam of light.[10] Developments in string theory, quantum mechanics, and multiverse theory have depended heavily on thought experiments and are often explicated with their help.[11] Who could forget the infamous Schrodinger's Cat case used to explore quantum uncertainty? In these and countless other cases, good imagination is instrumental in facilitating scientific advancement. Thought experiments can also precede empirical testing. It is useful to imagine different ways an actual experiment could be structured and what the various outcomes might be prior to performing the experiment to ensure that it is run properly and that the best results are obtained. This means that thought experiments are not necessarily alternatives to empirical research. They may be deployed in advance to ensure preparedness, increasing the odds that physical experiments will be successful.

Karl Popper's typology of thought experiments offers still more evidence of the various ways in which they can assist thinking when they are deployed in relation to specific theories. He groups scenarios into heuristic, apologetic, and critical forms according to whether they explain a theory, support it, or challenge it.[12] A particular scenario may play two or more of these roles depending on how it is presented. The classification schema is useful for appreciating why thought experiments are so pervasive across various disciplines and how they contribute to research on morality in particular.

First, thought experiments can be instructional tools that clarify a theory and its implications. Because these hypothetical scenarios are made as simple as possible by extracting irrelevant details, they make it easier to focus on the most essential elements. Moreover, theories are much easier to grasp when abstract ideas are made concrete. It may be difficult to understand the implications of the utilitarian exhortation to "maximize the greatest good for the greatest number" but easier to understand that it is better to divert the trolley to kill one person rather than five. Examples are also helpful if they raise issues that might not be immediately evident, such as how a normative theory would actually affect the world or what the world would be like if certain descriptive claims about it were true. Here the explanatory usefulness goes beyond conveying the basic outline to filling in the more specific details and considering broader implications. Pippin Barr's presentation of the Trolley Problem exemplifies this because it gradually ratchets up the challenges with new information that tests the utilitarian inclination to prioritize the lives of the many over the lives of the few under slightly different circumstances.

Second, thought experiments can support a theory, which is often done in the process of explicating it. Counterfactuals can present the theory in the best possible light by evoking situations in which it seems as though the theory offers better guidance than alternatives. The Trolley Problem is again instructive. We could attempt to solve it using aretaic theories based around individual virtue, yet these do not seem helpful. No level of excellence will allow the person facing the dilemma to stop the trolley, and without knowing anything about the potential victims, their individual characteristics cannot be introduced as supporting considerations when deciding whose life is worth more. Including the fat man in some iterations of the problem may even present a tacit critique of aretaic reasoning; fat people are often portrayed as lazy and therefore as less virtuous than thin people. Yet most respondents would probably be inclined to say that people are equally valuable regardless of their weight or presumed laziness.

The critical function of thought experiments is often where they get the most attention. Exposing flaws in a dominant theory is a sure way of provoking a general search for alternatives. This is why Thomas Kuhn says that thought experiments are "one of the essential analytical tools which are deployed during crises and which then help to promote basic conceptual reform."[13] R. M. Sainsbury argues that thought experiments are "associated with crises in thought and with revolutionary advances. To grapple with them is not merely to engage in an intellectual game, but is to come to grips with key issues."[14]

Popper's typology is not exhaustive. He focuses on what thought experiments can do with reference to theories themselves, but they may also be used as tools to facilitate moral development. Thinking about a single moral thought experiment can clarify how a person should act in a given situation, even one that has not yet been encountered. As David Edmonds says, "Thought experiments are designed to test our moral intuitions, to help us develop moral principles and thus to be of some practical use in a world in which real choices have to be made, and real people get hurt."[15] A scenario may prompt personal reflection into what existing values would dictate. In this case, thought experiments would not impart some new moral knowledge but rather test a person to formulate their values more explicitly and to imagine what those would look like when enacted. This is probably the most natural inclination when encountering an unexpected moral challenge, since people tend to confront novel decisions while keeping their existing cognitive framework intact.

Scenarios can also prompt reconsideration of values or decision procedures in cases where they are clearly inadequate, though of course this depends on the extent to which a person is open to revising deeply held beliefs. Shocking scenarios involving terrible costs may be the most effective in doing this. As I will discuss later, those deploying thought experiments to persuade large audiences tend to establish extreme costs and benefits that can push audiences toward a particular conclusion. Pedagogical thought experiments for learning new behaviors or rehearsing the implementation of values are common in socialization programs. Upon joining a new organization of virtually any type, whether for work or for fun, members are apt to learn about proper and improper behaviors with help from hypothetical scenarios. For example, military ethics training courses make heavy use of counterfactuals in which soldiers are asked to think about the right course of action in terms of institutional values.[16] Among the most recent innovations for training soldiers and police officers in use of force decisions are immersive shooting simulations that bear a striking resemblance to live-action shooting games such as *Crime Patrol* and *Mad Dog McCree*.[17]

Perhaps the most important advantage of counterfactual scenarios when it comes to moral reasoning is that they bring us to the boundaries of morality—and sometimes far beyond—without ever committing a genuine transgression. In particular, they allow us to explore dilemmas without causing harm. This benefit is most acute when it comes to dilemmas that involve disconcerting premises, such as those dealing with murder, genocide, rape, and torture. Many thought experiments are deliberately macabre to test our reasoning in those extreme cases when it is most apt to break down or fall into inconsistency. The scenarios do not reflect some kind of deviance on the part of their creators but rather an effort to clarify moral thinking by directly confronting the worst actions imaginable. The Trolley Problem shows the kind of violence that philosophers can inflict, but the scenarios get far more extreme than this.

Bernard Williams describes one scenario in which a character named Jim finds himself held captive by a repressive government in South America.[18] Government forces have also captured twenty rebellious Indians, who are lined up and prepared for execution. The captain of the militia discovers that Jim has no part in the conflict and decides to release him, but first he offers a choice: Jim can personally kill one captive selected at random to send a message to the population or he can refuse and watch all twenty die. In other words, Jim would either have to become a murderer to save nineteen people or kill everyone by omission. This choice is deliberately uncomfortable. It has the power to provoke self-examination precisely because it is uncomfortable. Some who hear this scenario might think that it is shocking and violent, and they would be right. However, moral guidance is supposed to serve us in difficult moments like this and will count for little if it is never tested against hard cases. The same goes for those of us who seriously reflect on the decision. There is no right or wrong answer, but simply thinking about the problem pushes us to exercise moral reasoning skills and to decide what really matters when making a choice between terrible alternatives.

Finally, thought experiments can expose problems in a theory by raising situations in which a theory cannot be applied or that elucidate contradictions within a theory. Thought experiments are especially useful for developing difficult cases that a particular theory is unable to solve, thereby showing that the theory in question cannot provide a general moral guide. Williams's case of Jim and the Indians is a prime example of this critical intent. He deploys this hypothetical as an argument against utilitarianism. According to utilitarianism, the explorer is obliged to shoot one of the rebels in order to save the others. A cost-benefit calculation shows that it is worth saving nineteen people rather than allowing all twenty to die. Utilitarians would go even further than this to say that the explorer is morally obligated to execute one rebel and that failing to do so makes him guilty of killing them by omission. Williams's point was that the utilitarian reasoning is flawed; Jim would become a murderer by pulling the trigger even once, and he would have to endure severe psychological trauma.

It would be misleading to say that videogames and thought experiments are the same thing, and I certainly do not mean to suggest that they are identical by drawing parallels between them. Videogames rarely purport to explain, support, or critique a particular theory, nor do those marketed for entertainment purport to be tools of moral pedagogy. Game developers may not even be aware of the theoretical significance of some of the problems that they raise, though I will consider persuasive games at length in chapter 6 to discuss those that do indicate such intent. Additionally, videogames do not have to incorporate deep theoretical challenges. They may be based around building mechanics that do not have a moral component, and many games that lack complex narratives do not provide enough information for theoretical puzzles to emerge. This means that there are many games that do not address morality. My point is therefore not to collapse the categories of videogame and counterfactual but rather to show that there is considerable overlap between the two that opens up a useful line of analysis when focusing on the moral significance of videogames.

Although videogames and thought experiments differ in some important ways, especially when it comes to whether they explicitly relate to theories, it is nevertheless appropriate to say that they are highly similar with respect to how they simulate ethical problems, such that theoretically significant challenges in videogames can function heuristically as thought experiments. This is the similarity that matters when it comes to assessing the moral significance of videogames, as it is the engagement with moral controversies that makes gaming controversial. Drawing a parallel between narrative models that explore moral issues for scholarly purposes and digital models that explore moral issues for entertainment is a useful way of understanding the moral implications of actions taken in videogames by way of analogy. In particular, the analogy brings greater clarity to the ontological status of models that permit simulated deviance, the moral implications of being bad within a simulation, the potential benefits of testing intuitions via counterfactuals, and the implications of constructing models with persuasive intent.

Improving Counterfactuals

So far, I have considered some of the general advantages of using thought experiments to approach philosophical questions and pointed out the similarities between narrative thought experiments employed by philosophers and those included in games. Despite appearing in different media, being used for divergent scholarly and entertainment purposes, and functioning differently in terms of their role in theory development, the two are alike in terms of how they model moral challenges and transform them into interactive experiences. In fact, this is not so much a similarity as a point of partial overlap where the affinity is so strong that the categories of thought experiment and videogame blend together when the former are represented digitally. In cases like Barr's Trolley Problem, it can even be difficult to say whether the simulation is more of a thought experiment or more of a game. In other instances, as in *Life Is Strange*, a videogame's ludological elements depend on their incorporation of thought experiments to such an extent that there would be no game at all without them.

I will spend the rest of the chapter considering some of the unique benefits of videogames when it comes to representing moral challenges and, in particular, how their simulated challenges improve on narrative thought experiments by taking advantage of unique characteristics of the videogame medium. In chapter 4, I turn back to debates over the morality of videogames and consider how this analogy can help us understand the implications of simulating good and bad conduct. Broadly speaking, thought experiments have two limitations. First, there is a concern with how thought experiments may distort moral reasoning because of how they are presented. Second, there is a concern with the realism of thought experiments. These overlap to some extent, with the lack of realism being one factor that could distort moral decision-making, but for clarity it is helpful to separate them into distinct problems.

Counterfactuals may distort moral reasoning by encouraging overreliance on intuition at the expense of new information. Daniel Dennett calls thought experiments "intuition pumps" because they promote intuitive judgments about the problems presented, thereby reinforcing intuitions and giving a sense that they are correct. The consequence is that "even great intuition pumps can mislead as well as they instruct."[19] Dennett goes on to criticize the tendency to use counterfactuals in place of arguments rather than as a way of illustrating an argument that can stand on its own merits. Similarly, Gilbert Harman argues that moral thought experiments are fundamentally flawed because they invite audiences to think about how they would intuitively solve problems.[20] He considers this a conservative way of thinking about morality that leads to the application of common sense and directs attention away from alternative perspectives. As Harman sees it, a more profitable approach would be to challenge moral intuitions. J. N. Mohanty denies that you can actually discover truths using this method and says that counterfactuals tend to be circular practices that result in the clarification of meaning without new information. This suggests that they may be able to illustrate how we think about morality without teaching anything new. When taken together, these objections identify a tendency for thought experiments to be structured in ways that make a particular conclusion seem natural. The result is confirmation bias—experiments that appear to be testing moral intuitions but actually show how some favored intuition will lead to the most desirable outcome under the narrowly defined parameters of the narrative.

The degree of realism is another potential concern. Georg Lind argues that thought experiments are not likely to help much in everyday life because they are so far removed from the moral decisions that we actually make.[21] This does not threaten the usefulness of counterfactuals when it comes to developing theories but does provide grounds for thinking that they cannot have much value in moral education. Don MacNiven goes even further, arguing that "real moral dilemmas cannot be properly captured by lifeless abstractions, no matter how ingenious. If moral dilemmas are to be fruitful in practical ethics they must at least reflect reality. The element of realism must always be there whether we are trying to verify a substantive moral claim, validate an ethical theory or clarify moral experience."[22] Here the concern is that counterfactuals veering too far away from the real world may lose their connection with it altogether, which would make the resulting theories useless at best and misleading at worst.

There is considerable disagreement over whether a lack of realism is problematic. Jonathan Glover contends that this can be advantageous because "it is often best deliberately to confront the most extreme possibility."[23] As he sees it, "thinking about the desirability of different futures cannot be separated from thinking about present values. And our values often become clearer when we consider imaginary cases where conflicts can be made sharp."[24] Julian Baggini echoes this point, saying that "if an impossible scenario helps us to do that, then its impossibility need not concern us. The experiment is merely a tool to aid our thinking; it does not pretend to describe actual life."[25] These advocates of liberal experimentation get at an important point about how unrealistic scenarios push us to think about familiar problems from a different angle. They may even upset ethical prejudices that we have not stopped to consider. This is crucial for developing a stronger theoretical understanding of moral issues and could help to circumvent confirmation bias.

Concerns over reinforcing intuitions and realism come together to create a potential disconnect between how problems are resolved in a narrative counterfactual versus the real world. Lawrence Kohlberg finds that moral thought experiments encourage people to find abstract principles to justify their actions, which can discourage people from adapting their values to fit the context and force them to endorse extreme values that lack the kind of nuance that is essential when resolving real moral problems.[26] Bernard Williams raises similar concerns that moral philosophers are mistaken when they think about thought experiments in purely abstract terms, because they impose unrealistic standards on their hypothetical actors.[27] In the real world, we face many constraints that do not arise in thought experiments. Limits on time and the available information prevent us from stepping back to consider scenarios in detail and force us to be decisive. Moreover, real people have to live with the consequences of their decisions, which in the Trolley Problem could mean the guilt of intervening to kill an innocent person. A good response to a real-world moral challenge may not stand up to tests of philosophical rigor but instead be based on making the best use of the resources available. This exposes a limitation in what is ostensibly a great strength of thought experiments. When these arise in narrative form, they strip away extraneous details to focus on a specific question and offer all the morally relevant information. Yet this extreme focus is precisely what makes it tempting to rely on abstract principles rather than thinking about what it would actually be like to make a moral decision under real-world conditions.

Some philosophers have correctly predicted that computers may provide a way around some of the limitations associated with narrative thought experiments by increasing the complexity and sophistication of the models. For example, Dennett notes that computer simulations could get around the confirmation bias that he identifies by providing a more reliable model than a person's imagination.[28] Roy Sorensen likewise notes that "since computer graphics specialists and producers of documentaries have already converted many thought experiments to new media, there is a chance that some future thought experiments will acquire a significant moral dimension."[29] These hopes of taking advantage of new technologies offer further evidence of the affinities between thought experiments and moral challenges in games. They are especially prescient in acknowledging that the former may be improved by moving away from a purely narrative format. My argument extends this prediction by showing that thought experiments not only crop up in purpose-built computer models but also are integral to videogames that simulate moral and immoral conduct for entertainment purposes.

The problems of intuition pumping and drifting too far from reality emerge from a common source. As Sorensen points out, real experiments have an "execution element."[30] They are enacted and have effects. Because thought experiments are imaginary, they are never truly executed. Their effects are hypothetical, which is to say they are unreal and depend on our imaginations. This is advantageous when it comes to analyzing problems without inflicting harm. After all, "executed experiments involve action and so can greatly help or harm people and animals."[31] Nevertheless, because thought experiments are not executed, the world never pushes back against them to introduce elements of chance or the unexpected occurrences that lead real-world experiments to produce counterintuitive results.

Like narrative thought experiments, videogames do not take place in the real world and therefore do not impose real costs. However, unlike narrative thought experiments, videogames are set in their own closed worlds that can be built to model not only a particular problem but also how that problem and its solutions impact the world. Rather than offering the kinds of abstract, decontextualized problems that are common in narratives, videogames present problems embedded in a particular world. This sense of context that is missing in thought experiments is a large part of what makes them feel different from real moral decisions. By providing a much richer sense of context, games may bring us closer to the considerations that actually influence moral decisions and their outcomes. The differences between videogames and narrative thought experiments—the former's greater complexity and the fact that the developers rarely set out to make a specific theoretical point—therefore turn out to be significant advantages.

The value of context is especially clear when it comes to simulating time constraints and uncertainty. Narrative thought experiments are designed for careful deliberation over a potentially endless time period, with the good ones leading to decades-long debates. The moral dilemmas that arise in games likewise facilitate lengthy discussions that play out in online forums and informal discussions, yet in the first instance these usually have to be made quickly and without all the relevant information. *The Walking Dead* offers a good example of this. Early in the game, players must decide whether to cut the arm off a companion who has been bitten by a zombie. In that moment, there is no way of knowing which decision is right and what the long-term effects may be. Players must simply decide then live with the consequences. This brings the decision into much closer alignment with how we typically experience moral dilemmas than in thought experiments, in which we have all the relevant details. Player discussions over the right choice show that many appreciate the weight of this dilemma and its appeal as a theoretical puzzle.[32]

Building on this point, videogames can simulate multiple theoretically significant issues that are operative at different levels. Narrative counterfactuals create the misleading impression that decisions are discrete events, made in one moment and then gone forever. But life certainly is not a series of discrete choices. Serious moral quandaries are generally composed of multiple overlapping problems. For example, the ongoing debate over the ethics of preventing climate change is not simply an issue of whether we should strive to pollute less. There are a host of other ethical challenges related to research ethics for those scientists who produce fraudulent results, determining how much influence oil companies should have in the debate over global warming, intergenerational justice, animal rights, and general issues about our ethical attitudes toward the world we inhabit. This list could go on, as could the list of the many facets of other real problems. Decisions are complex and feed into each other, especially over a long time span. One advantage of videogames is that they create nested moral challenges. An entire game can be seen as a thought experiment inviting players to imagine what it is like to control time (*Life Is Strange*), to live in a postapocalyptic world (*Fallout*), to create a utopia (*BioShock*), or to live with dementia (*Ether One*)—the list could go on, with dozens of examples. Within each of these games are dozens of other challenges that are shaped by the overall premise and that often affect each other. The result is a richer moral environment that more accurately captures interdependence.

We can question whether videogames accurately model the world, and in many cases they do not. Some games also reflect an effort to make a particular political or moral point rather than accurately re-creating the world. I devote chapter 5 to discussing different strategies of representing moral challenges, and the remaining chapters to addressing the implications of bias in the models that game developers create. For now, I will say that greater complexity in the moral decisions that arise in videogames is generally advantageous and that, as in narrative thought experiments, unrealistic or biased hypotheticals can be instructive in their own ways.

The execution element is also central to building a sense of player investment in the hypothetical decisions. Players must simulate the performance of any potential solution, which means going beyond just imagining what choices are available to also consider how those choices would have to be enacted. In other words, videogames not only model the effects that decisions could have on a fictional world but also promote reflection on whether the actions themselves are reasonable and plausible. Digital scenarios are just as unreal as narratives and therefore never as accurate as real experiments, yet they can achieve better approximations of what a real context of action might be like than narratives alone. Over successive generations, games have developed to the point that they can more effectively model the decisions they incorporate.

Conclusion

Comparing the moral challenges that arise in videogames to the narrative moral thought experiments that have been a fixture of philosophical investigation is a useful heuristic for reconsidering the ethical significance of digital actions by way of analogy. The close links between these two types of simulations are so strong that the boundaries between them cannot be clearly located. The possibility of realizing identical dilemmas in narrative form, simple digital models, and videogames is evidence of deep family resemblances in terms of how they confront ethical issues. This does not mean that videogames and thought experiments are the same. This is clearly not the case, since neither is reducible to the other. Rather, my point is that they embody comparable approaches to modeling moral decision-making.

The similarities between videogames and thought experiments help to establish the value that videogames *can* have when it comes to moral exploration. I say *can* because there is no requirement for games to explore moral issues or for players to engage with them. However, as I will show in the following chapters, videogames regularly exercise this capacity with varying degrees of sophistication. The videogame–thought experiment analogy also marks an important step toward answering the question of why simulations of immoral behavior can be morally significant without themselves having moral quality. In chapter 4, I draw on this analogy to argue that simulations of moral decision-making are valuable because they are tools that allow us to test different possibilities of action without inflicting real consequences, enacting real destructive habits, or having ill will toward others.

4

Digital Morality

Chapter 3 established the similarities between the ethical challenges presented in videogames and those that appear in traditional thought experiments, as well as in films, literature, television shows, and other media. My point in doing this was not to reduce videogames to another medium. *Videogames are unique.* This is underscored by my claim that games include an execution element that distinguishes them from other types of ethical models. Moreover, this comparison is only meant as a heuristic that can help us think comparatively about the significance of the simulated acts of moral and immoral behavior that appear in videogames. In this chapter, I build on that analogy and show what theoretical insights can be derived from it, focusing on two central points. First, understanding games as models in which players can explore moral questions without taking real actions explains why games can be morally significant without being sources of corruption, as critics fear. Second, this analogy can help to identify the difference between videogame content that is offensive and content that is immoral. Many of the arguments that identify certain games or actions within games as being immoral make the mistake of conflating these categories.

The experience of resolving a moral challenge in a videogame is much the same as when confronting a thought experiment. These puzzles demand an effort to identify the moral problem at hand, to weigh the various options available, and to decide on a course of action. This gives participants a chance to exercise their reasoning skills and clarify their values by applying them as a guide for hypothetical choices. A well-designed scenario could even present a problem from a new angle that encourages reconsideration of existing biases. This is true regardless of whether the model appears in narrative or digital format or whether it is packaged as pedagogy or entertainment. When these problems arise in video-games, some players may choose to be evil or neutral, yet their actions are not truly evil or neutral. These players show the same reasoning skills as players who choose good courses of action, as they must likewise exercise judgment to deter-mine the moral valences of the available options. Players who make good, neu-tral, and evil decisions in the game are therefore equally morally faultless and have the same potential to benefit from entertainment that exposes them to weighty questions.

I am not arguing that videogames are morally beneficial or that all players will experience moral epiphanies. Only games that have fairly complex narra-tives can evoke moral challenges, which means that games such as *Grand Theft Auto*, *Fallout*, and *Portal* can be morally significant, while games such as *Tetris* or *Snake* have little if any moral import. Whether a game has moral weight depends heavily on the developers' choices and, in particular, what kind of nar-rative they construct. Moreover, I am not arguing that videogames will make players more moral. It is doubtful that any thought experiment presented on any platform can create better people. The merits of moral education are diffi-cult to establish and beyond the scope of my analysis, and mere contact with moral ideas cannot guarantee that a person will agree with those ideas or have the desire to enact them in practice.[1] I want to make the more modest point that videogames present opportunities for moral exploration and that if these have any effect on players at all, it is likely to be a positive one. Unlike the shoot-ing skills I discussed in chapter 2, moral decision-making is largely mental and can therefore be meaningfully simulated by current-generation game systems.

Some critics argue that imaginary misconduct can be genuinely wrong even if it does not reflect ill will or inflict visible harm. Many critiques of videogames hinge on claims that it is inherently immoral to enjoy certain simulated actions. This would present a problem for my claim that moral exploration is not mor-ally blameworthy, so I conclude the chapter by discussing it in detail. Many phi-losophers who approach videogames from a virtue ethics standpoint think that simulating immoral behaviors habituates players to performing them, which corrupts players even if games never cause real immoral actions. I argue that the Aristotelian strategy of critique builds on a faulty understanding of Aristotle's philosophy, mischaracterizing his account of virtue, ignoring the distinction he draws between real and simulated actions, and failing to appreciate his advice that we need to experience moderate pleasure to live well. The concerns with cer-tain types of game content do raise the real possibility that people with objection-able beliefs or the intent to commit terrible atrocities in real life could express them in videogames. However, these concerns pertain not to the videogames themselves but rather to the attitudes players have in advance of playing them. Even more importantly, these objections tend to wrongly assume that offensive content is inherently immoral.

Choosing Good and Evil

It is rare for players to have the ability to be so overtly good or evil as in the Power of the Atom quest from *Fallout 3*. The central dilemma is whether to detonate a nuclear bomb sitting in the center of the town of Megaton. The bomb is active and therefore a constant threat to the town and its citizens, but it cannot be triggered or defused without the player's assistance. Mister Burke, a mysterious outsider, offers to pay the player to detonate the bomb because his employer thinks that destroying the town will improve views from a nearby residence for wealthy ghouls. The town sheriff requests the player's help in disarming the bomb, which will end the threat that it could kill the town's inhabitants. Destroying the town leads players to suffer a massive drop in karma—the game's metric for a player's moral status—and to win a sizable financial reward, while saving it results in a smaller karmic gain and a smaller reward.

Many commentators have cited this quest as evidence that moral choice engines in videogames are flawed because they create simplistic challenges that are unlike anything we encounter in the real world.[2] The tendency to dismiss this quest is unfair. For one thing, it comes early in the game and is followed by far more demanding decisions, making it more like a tutorial than a reflection of the game's puzzles. More importantly, even extreme decisions can raise interesting questions. Just as in thought experiments, realistic dilemmas are apt to be more applicable to everyday life, while outlandish ones may help to clarify what general moral principles we employ—a particularly useful exercise early in a game that features moral decision-making as a key element of gameplay and that pushes players to define their character's moral identity. Power of the Atom is based around a sharp binary with unrealistically high stakes, yet this is precisely what makes it an interesting moral challenge. It is an invitation to be cartoonishly evil and to think about what such a decision tells us about players who take that approach.

For my purposes, Power of the Atom is useful as a thought experiment about what it means to be good or evil in a game. Choosing to save Megaton is clearly good, while destroying an entire town just to improve the landscape is clearly evil. Such a simple and easily agreed on binary is actually immensely helpful because it allows us to say unequivocally that there are good and evil paths through this particular dilemma. There is little room for legitimate disagreement over the ethical implications of the choice, which means that any player who chooses to destroy the town is probably *trying to be evil* rather than simply making a mistake of judgment. What does it mean for a player to deliberately choose to be bad in this context? Is such a player blameworthy?

It is important to recognize that players' motives are complex and must involve at least two different components that lead to two different conceptions of how players may be good or bad. In one sense, being good is a moral judgment, which is the sense of being good that I am focusing on. Players can also be good in the instrumental sense of being skilled at the game. These two senses of goodness are not always aligned, as players may gain an advantage for being bad that would entice good (skilled) players to simulate bad (morally) actions.[3] The decision to be bad may simply be a gameplay strategy for achieving the higher rewards of the evil path. Whether this is a sound strategic choice depends on the game and a player's broader goals. Power of the Atom offers evil players a material reward at the expense of sanctions from other characters in the game. *BioShock* does much the same thing by allowing players who take the evil path quicker progression when developing fighting skills, while punishing them later by denying them assistance from an important nonplayer character. There may therefore be a strategic rationale for acting immorally.

Some games may not offer a choice; they may simply demand immoral conduct to be successful. As Ken McAllister explains, "To win a computer game requires the player to perfect his or her role in the game: adventurer, sniper, quarterback, starship captain, railroad tycoon. Failure to accept and actualize this rhetoric is not merely to lack understanding, as it would be among filmgoers. Rather, it is to lose, to be inferior, to be a detriment to one's group."[4] If the role that players take on is that of a villain, then they are compelled to adopt a particular moral stance within the game world for the purposes of progressing. The *Grand Theft Auto* and *Saints Row* series are examples of this; it is difficult to imagine beating the single-player stories without simulated evil. In these cases, malicious choices tell us little about whether players agree with the actions they perform. With this in mind, we cannot take moral decisions as solely embodying moral goals. We likewise cannot take the decision to act immorally in a game as a reliable indication of players' real moral character.

However, what if players have a choice to be good and instead deliberately take the evil path? Or what if they want to play games that put them in the role of a villain because they enjoy it? What if they destroy Megaton just because they think it is fun and not for any strategic benefits? I argue that players who choose to be evil and do so for enjoyment are not doing anything that is genuinely immoral. From a consequentialist perspective, destroying a real town is wrong because it inflicts massive harm on real people and the environment. Destroying a virtual town does not inflict any real harm and has no adverse consequences beyond the game world. Moreover, simulating mass destruction can be enjoyable for the millions who played *Fallout 3*. The evil choice is even fun for those who do not destroy the town. After all, the decision to save the town depends on having the choice in the first place and opting against it. The net effect on the real world is therefore a positive one—zero real damage and considerable pleasure—that leaves players better off without adversely affecting anyone. Pretending to be evil can therefore be good from a consequentialist perspective. It is cost-free and enjoyable.

Being evil is equally blameless from a deontological perspective. Players who intend to blow up Megaton do not intend to kill thousands of innocent people. Rather, they intend to destroy a digital representation of a town and to kill while knowing that it is all pretend. Without any real moral agents on the receiving end of the actions, there is no sense in which players can intend to inflict real harm. Even if players choose to be evil, enjoy being evil, and revel in the game's condemnations, they are only intending to be evil *in the game* and achieving this identity by *simulating* harmful acts. There is no reason to suspect that a desire to pretend to be evil and enjoyment of this simulated identity reflects any general moral ill will. On the contrary, the most reasonable explanation is that players who simulate evil acts do this simply because it is fun.

It is possible to imagine some players simulating evil because they intend to commit evil acts in real life. Maybe a person wanting to destroy an actual town but lacking access to the requisite bomb plays through the simulation as a fantasy of violence. Such a person would certainly be deeply disturbed, yet the moral character of the simulated action would not change. From a deontological perspective, it would only be immoral for players to willfully destroy the town while thinking that its inhabitants are real, as this would display genuine malicious intent. Only such a mistake of simulation for reality could allow a player to intend physical damage within the virtual space. A person making this mistake would certainly be an aberration, as we can expect all players except the very young or those with severe cognitive impairments to recognize that the game is unreal.

The thought experiment analogy I developed in chapter 3 is useful for understanding why simulated evil is not immoral. One of the primary reasons for discussing ethical puzzles in terms of thought experiments is to explore immoral, illegal, or harmful actions without actually performing them. Neither option in the Trolley Problem causes genuine harm that would make the choice truly objectionable. Philosophers have developed dozens of even more perverse counterfactuals that involve more death and destruction, yet the stakes are always purely imaginary, just as they are in videogames. Merely creating a model that can permit immoral actions or imagining oneself as the wrongdoer causes no harm. Moreover, the intent to use a simulation to imagine ourselves murdering or committing other objectionable acts is not the same as an intention to actually do these things. Philosophers explore terrible atrocities to develop theories; gamers do so to have fun. One could argue that the former motive is nobler, but neither intention is immoral.

There is something to gain from projecting ourselves into evil acts, as doing this requires an imaginative exploration of the moral choices available and awareness of what considerations would make a choice good or bad. Ethnographic research with players reveals that those who take the evil course of action often do so deliberately because they enjoy playing an evil character.[5] Amanda Lange confesses to being intentionally evil in the games she plays and describes enjoying it precisely because this permits her to do things that would normally be unthinkable. As she explains, "I know I am not my avatar in the game, so I like to experiment. Sometimes it's entertaining to me to see the results of a choice I would never make in reality. Sometimes it's just plain fun to be the bad guy."[6] Quotations like this mirror those of students in philosophy classes who enjoy being contrarians by attempting to defend counterintuitive solutions to thought experiments, perhaps while advocating choices that most of us would intuitively say are wrong. If they do this for the sake of being provocative, then it causes no real harm. In fact, this is beneficial because it forces others to work harder to defend their own choices. Research has borne out that dissent is inherently valuable as a means of reducing polarization in groups.[7] There is immense value in having a devil's advocate, or in this case an imaginary devil. Simply exploring the wrong course of action does not commit such a person to acting that way in practice, nor does it necessarily reflect a desire to do anything wrong.

It is important to note that whether these decisions come up in entertainment or educational contexts does not really matter. It could be that contrarian students exploring a thought experiment in an ethics class want to imagine being bad for no other reason than because it is fun, yet this would not change the fact that it causes no genuine harm and that it is potentially pedagogically beneficial to approach moral decisions by thinking about what not to do. Videogames may cause greater discomfort because the imagined acts are represented visually rather than narratively, yet the actions have the same ontological status: they are fictions created for the sake of exploring a counterfactual.

Moral Exploration, Not Pedagogy

Someone who enjoys pretending to be evil because they think it is fun or to spark controversy is not actually guilty of performing the imagined actions. Deliberately choosing to be bad in a simulation still requires moral judgment. Simulated good and bad choices depend on the same ability to distinguish good from bad. A good player must identify the evil course of action and decide not to take it, while the player pretending to be evil must be able to identify the good path. Intending to be good or evil in Power of the Atom or any other simulated moral puzzle that includes clear right and wrong paths presupposes the ability to assess the moral implications of that scenario. Players must intuitively map out the moral terrain prior to acting if they intend to ground their actions in a particular moral identity. This is the skill that we should value, regardless of which pretend choice the player enjoys more within the context of a simulation. One reason why videogames are morally significant is that they often give players opportunities for exercising this type of reasoning—opportunities for deciding whether they want to simulate good or evil—in which they must think about what actions would qualify as morally significant within the counterfactual.

Regardless of the choice players make, they are navigating the moral thought experiment and exercising judgment skills.

This point becomes clearer when we look more carefully at how players approach moral decisions in videogames. It appears that in practice most players prefer to be good when they are presented with moral choices. In a nonrepresentative survey of 1,067 players recruited online, Lange finds that 59 percent tried to be good, 39 percent did not attempt to have a consistent morality, and only 5 percent were deliberately bad. Those who played a game more than once were more inclined to experiment with distinct moral playing styles, with 63 percent attempting to be good and 9 percent evil the first time through.[8] On the second playthrough, 49 percent were deliberately evil and 16 percent good. In a study of *Fallout 3*, A. J. Weaver and N. Lewis concluded that "not only did most players avoid anti-social behaviour, but they cited moral considerations for their behavior."[9] Mia Consalvo, Thorsten Busch, and Carolyn Jong reached similar conclusions based on interviews with players. Most chose to be good and enjoyed acting like heroes. "Players who consider themselves essentially 'good people' are rewarded via game logics for playing the hero, for making choices that (re)affirm their desires to enact justice but also to attain glory, wealth, and power by doing so."[10] Some who chose to be evil said that they felt uncomfortable doing so, while others enjoyed this path because it allowed them to act differently than they would in real life. These players felt that being evil was fun precisely because it provided opportunities to temporarily set their values aside.

The research on players' moral choices is encouraging for three reasons. First, it indicates that when a game incorporates moral choices, most players make decisions with moral considerations in mind. They see their avatar as good, evil, or neutral and are later able to describe simulated events in moral terms. Players exercise moral judgment skills by evaluating the puzzles they confront and categorizing actions. This indicates that players have comparable experiences thinking in moral terms, regardless of the choices they actually make. Second, it appears that most players are more comfortable pretending to be good than they are pretending to be evil. This should not lead us to conclude that these players are somehow better than those who choose the evil path or that they have more sophisticated moral judgment, especially when those who start out good are apt to become evil if they play the game a second time. The preference for being good suggests something about comfort. Even though actions taken during a game do not inflict harm, they can make us profoundly uncomfortable because of the kinds of scenarios they simulate. Virtual murder is not real murder, yet it evokes thoughts of murder and invites us to think about what it might mean to kill someone. Shooting avatars in a Russian airport does not make players murderers, but it is, as many players have reported, a disconcerting experience because it gives us some sense of what it might be like to carry out such an attack. Just because an action is morally blameless does not mean it is comfortable.

Sorensen notes that some people are repulsed by the kinds of scenarios narrative thought experiments present but rightly says that this feeling is not triggered by genuine wrongdoing: "Squeamish visualizers are sickened by the blood-and-guts scenarios favored by contemporary ethicists. But this is no more momentous than the revulsion experienced by readers of gory novels."[11] The scenarios imagined may be troubling because of the character of the actions being imagined and not because there is anything wrong with imagining them. It is vital to distinguish between what is uncomfortable and what is immoral. It is uncomfortable to imagine facing a choice between killing one person and allowing five to die, yet conjuring such an image in our minds does not make us guilty of a misdeed. The same goes for videogames. These feel more real and are therefore more apt than mere narratives to cause discomfort. Far from being immoral, the feelings of discomfort push us away from unreflective play and encourage us to consider *why* we feel upset. Uncomfortable moments in videogames are often the most effective in conveying moral questions and provoking further discussion of them among players.

Third, players tend to change their moral alignment during a second playthrough of a game. From this, we can ascertain that players are not attempting to perform their real moral identities. Rather, they are engaging in moral exploration. They are working through the same puzzles from different perspectives and deriving at least some of their enjoyment of the game from considering those puzzles from alternative perspectives. This is further evidence that videogames incorporating moral choices function less as training simulations that inculcate a particular attitude, such as a desire to murder, than as thought experiments in which players can explore different courses of action without incurring any real costs. As Consalvo, Busch, and Jong explain, "Playing evil or good in games is not a monolithic or even consistent activity. Some players initially decide on their character's ethos but then change their mind during play. Others play a game multiple times, and so playing good or evil is one choice among many, while others play some games in altruistic ways and other games as selfish or in repugnant ways."[12]

When making moral decisions in the real world, we face three central challenges. The first is recognizing that there is a moral challenge. This can be harder than it sounds, as information shortages, misperceptions, and cognitive biases can interfere with gaining perspective on the problem at hand. The second is determining the right course of action, which requires an ability to identify what principles or values should be used to resolve a particular problem and to use those general guidelines to choose the right course of action. This skill is especially difficult to exercise when it comes to moral dilemmas, in which there is a choice between competing imperatives that cannot be satisfied simultaneously. The Trolley Problem is a prime example of such a dilemma. There is room for reasonable disagreement about which course of action is best and therefore considerable value in reflecting on the problem. Finally, there is the challenge of actually enacting the moral decision. Doing the right thing may be unpopular, financially expensive, or even dangerous, so it requires tremendous willpower.

I argue that videogames that incorporate moral choices should be judged positively, as spaces of exploration that give players the same chance to experiment with different possibilities for action as narrative counterfactuals, but with the help of computer simulations that make the choices far more compelling. Videogames force players to exercise the first and second elements of moral decision-making: evaluating the challenges and the courses of action available. Even those games that are charged with promoting violence or corrupting players' empathy, or those that do not give players the freedom to opt out of immoral acts, are praiseworthy for bringing into entertainment moral issues that players might not otherwise think about.

It might seem like I am trying to have the argument both ways—that I am suggesting that games can make players better people but that they cannot make them worse. It may also seem like I am making the dubious suggestion that playing games is a form of moral education. To be clear, I am not arguing that simulated engagement with moral challenges actually makes players morally better. Videogames are morally advantageous in the same way as thought experiments— they encourage the exercise of judgment faculties associated with identifying and mapping out moral challenges. They cannot in themselves cause moral improvement, so we will continue to see gamers acting immorally just as we continue to see some ethics professors acting immorally. There are three reasons for this.

First, moral issues are extraordinarily complex and often lack clear answers. Power of the Atom is not a true dilemma because the right path is abundantly clear. There is little room for reasonable disagreement about what it is. On the other hand, many narrative counterfactuals in videogames lack clear good and evil paths. In these instances, games' moral valuation systems break down and the right decision is open to debate. *Fallout 3* includes several dilemmas that require considerably more acuity than deciding whether to destroy a town. One expansion DLC (downloadable content) leads players to a postapocalyptic Pittsburgh that is badly contaminated with radiation. Ismael Ashur uses his raider gang to enslave workers and claims that this is necessary for establishing order amid anarchy. Players go on to discover that Ashur's baby daughter Marie is immune to radiation and that she is being studied to create a cure for radiation poisoning. Such a cure has the potential to save countless lives in a postapocalyptic world where radiation is a constant threat. Players must choose between supporting the slaves in an uprising against Ashur or protecting his rule and his daughter. To side with Ashur, players must kill the rebel leader. To help the slaves, players must kill Ashur and many of his raiders. Favoring the slaves puts a new leader in power—someone who is eager to create a more egalitarian regime but who also expresses concern about being able to maintain control and continue rebuilding the city. Helping Ashur protects the innocent

Marie and allows research on her to continue, yet this comes at the expense of a tenuous order founded on tyrannical control.

This quest offers material rewards for each course of action, yet it does not impose any karmic rewards or punishments. That is, the game presents a clear moral dilemma and suggests that there are costs and benefits associated with each choice, but it concedes that there is no easy answer about which decision is right. The scenario asks deep questions about the nature of legitimate political authority, the proper trade-off between coercive rule and anarchic autonomy, and the status of individual rights during desperate times, without pretending to have the answers. It is a counterfactual that forces players to make up their own minds. Although thought experiments are often introduced to answer ongoing theoretical disputes, good ones tend to raise more questions than they answer, and they are always open to different interpretations. This quest in The Pitt, like many others in *Fallout 3*, such as The Oasis and Election Day, do exactly this.

Moral dilemmas are dilemmas for a reason. They force us to choose between undesirable alternatives that produce suboptimal outcomes. The lack of conclusive answers makes thought experiments a useful framework for analyzing moral intuitions, values, and the consistency of decision procedures. There is value in using these thought experiments to focus on key moral considerations and in developing multiple scenarios that can get at them from different perspectives to see how the background details influence the outcome. Nevertheless, the complexity of the issues at hand means that we should not expect that practice thinking about them would yield any straightforward improvements in a person's moral character that we can say are unequivocally good. Thus, players may gain greater insight into the moral dilemmas being simulated, but they do not become morally better in any straightforward sense because of the complexity inherent in the choices and the absence of a definitive good path.

Second, as The Pitt example demonstrates, game developers are usually reluctant to take a firm stance on controversial issues. The dilemma tests players, but it does not take a pedagogical tone, because there is no clear right answer. The moral dilemmas that lack clear good and evil outcomes are opportunities to think about difficult issues in new ways and to consider what impact various choices would have on the world, but developers leave players to draw their own conclusions about what course of action is right. Moral choice engines tend to assign values only when the right course of action is relatively clear, as in the case of Power of the Atom. In those instances, games provide a chance to exercise moral reasoning skills but do not attempt to teach anything new. The fact that blowing up a town is evil should surprise no one. This quest does not show us what it means to be moral but rather invites us to consider the implications of acting well or badly in this particular scenario. That is, the quest is all about enacting our existing moral feelings. With genuine dilemmas avoiding a clear correct answer and easy problems having obvious answers, games fail to provide a simple moral pedagogy. They are more proving ground than instruction manual.

Finally, sometimes the most difficult part of doing the right thing in practice is acting. We may recognize a moral issue and know what we *should* do but still fail to do it because of a weakness of will. Perhaps we are too afraid to act or are lured in by the promise of an illicit gain. Counterfactuals cannot be of much help when it comes to learning to be better at enacting moral decisions, because they do not simulate the real costs we endure. Doing what is right in a game is apt to be much easier than doing what is right in real life. Even heavy in-game losses are fictional and relatively easy to bear. No matter how serious, they can be erased by the reset button. Moreover, as I established earlier, actions in a game look and feel very different from those taken in the real world. Pressing a button to make a character apologize for a moral infraction bears little resemblance to delivering an apology to a real person and having to navigate the dialogue without being guided by prompts. The ability to act on moral intuitions requires skills that games and narrative thought experiments are poorly suited to teach. Once again, games provide an arena for thinking about morality without necessarily improving behavior.

Ways of Playing

Sorensen argues that those who take the wrong course of action in thought experiments may be guilty of "at most, *minor* moral praise or blame" if their reasoning shows poor judgment.[13] This is an important insight, as it indicates that counterfactuals can display flawed reasoning even though they are not themselves the sources of corruption that critics are concerned about. The same point holds up when it comes to videogames, since players may receive minor moral praise and blame for poor judgment if they lack the awareness to recognize and work through moral dilemmas. Returning to Power of the Atom, we would have to question a person's moral judgment if they are unable to see that destroying Megaton would be wrong if the action were real. Unlike players who choose to be immoral, those who take a path, good or evil, without recognizing that the choice involves a moral decision would reveal a serious lapse in judgment. This would not indicate any moral problem with the game, since it reveals, but does not cause, this failing. It would only indicate that there is possibly something wrong with the particular players who do not have the moral judgment needed to evaluate such a clear instance of right versus wrong. Thus, the source of moral concern when it comes to how people imagine acting when they think about models of moral decision-making should not be those who enjoy being bad but rather those who are unable to identify moral questions when they appear.

Those lacking in moral judgment must be distinguished from those who just have other priorities or are indifferent. It is unlikely that most players who do not choose the good or evil paths in games that offer these choices are revealing a paucity of ethical judgment. The most reasonable explanation is that these players are either not interested in the moral component of the game—that they are more concerned with making strategic calculations that will ensure that they continue progressing—or that they want to remain neutral. Being neutral in a game that incorporates a moral calculus like *Fallout*'s karma system can be a challenge in its own right, forcing players to exercise the same judgments they would if they wanted to be good or evil. Any effort to deliberately cultivate a particular moral or amoral character depends on having or learning the ability to read counterfactuals for moral implications before making a choice. It requires the same imaginary leap into simulated dilemmas as narrative thought experiments.

There probably is a large population of unreflective players who simply avoid confronting moral implications, but they are not guilty of any misconduct, regardless of whether the choices are explicitly graded by a moral choice engine. Some players may recognize that Power of the Atom has a moral component and just not care about this element of the game. *Fallout 3* forces players to work through dialogue options that convey the decisions at hand and their significance, but many games reserve their most complex moral questions for cutscenes that players can easily skip. The *Call of Duty: Modern Warfare* series is a good example of this. The games are often interpreted as celebrating American empire and contributing to the narrative of a global war on terror. Conversely, they may be read as critiques of a corrupt U.S. military (one of the central villains is an American general) and of the quest to win wars without obeying moral constraints, which becomes evident when players participate in terrorist attacks and detonate a nuclear weapon to halt a Soviet invasion of the United States. The juxtaposition of pro-war and critical messages within the narrative raises interesting questions, but players could avoid them by simply skipping the cutscenes and playing through the missions as decontextualized battles. The same is true for many other first-person shooter games, in which play is possible without having a sense of the narrative context. Multiplayer combat is even more decontextualized, as it is typically just a contest between two competing teams attempting to capture flags or kill all the enemies.

Are unreflective players immoral? Like those of players who make intentional moral choices, unreflective players' actions are purely imaginary and have no impact beyond the game world. They are simply missing out on one dimension of play. There is an important difference between lacking the ability to understand the moral component of decisions that games present and just not caring about them. It is ignorance versus indifference. I would argue that in many cases unreflective players are missing out on two of the most gratifying aspects of videogames. They forgo the chance to consider the deeper questions that games evoke and they fail to appreciate part of the gameplay experience. Nevertheless, there is nothing morally repugnant about treating the games purely as entertainment and neglecting philosophical issues when there are no harmful consequences or expressions of bad will toward others. Morality is a key component of most narratively complex games. It helps to imbue players' simulated actions with meaning and greater weight. Decisions can be far more fun when they feel significant and controversial. This may be why many games highlight the moral significance of the issues they raise.

Spec Ops: The Line is a third-person shooter with close thematic and visual similarities not only to other third-person shooters but also to first-person shooters like the *Modern Warfare* series. It is the type of game that is usually easy to play unreflectively, with minimal concern for why the violence is being enacted. Early in the game, players are lulled into a false sense of security with familiar battles against generic masked enemies, but things quickly become complicated. Soon players find themselves in the unusual position of fighting against fellow American soldiers in an attempt to protect civilians. Then players launch a white phosphorus mortar barrage that accidentally kills dozens of innocent people as well as additional soldiers, who claim they were trying to protect the civilians. The game forces players to watch a cutscene that vividly imagines the carnage of charred bodies, including those of young children. The scene urges players to confront the moral costs of such an attack as the protagonists struggle to come to terms with their actions. It is also noteworthy that players do not really have a choice in this counterfactual, and there is no moral choice engine evaluating them. They do not decide whether to be good or evil. Instead, they become accidental participants in terrible war crimes in a way that suggests a certain inevitability to misconduct during war.

Spec Ops further attempts to foreclose the possibility of playing unreflectively by continually reminding players about the moral implications of their decisions. The loading screens are particularly interesting because they break the fourth wall and encourage players to not only think about the meaning of the actions they are simulating but to also consider the moral implications of the simulation itself. Early in the game, loading screens offer gameplay tips and pieces of background information, which is standard for the genre. The tone changes as players begin to realize that they are descending into darkness. The messages say things like, "To kill for yourself is murder. To kill for your government is heroic. To kill for entertainment is harmless" and "The US military does not condone the killing of unarmed combatants. But this isn't real, so why should you care?" Such messages urge players to think critically about the game even as they enjoy its simulations of violence. They do not instruct players to take a particular attitude toward their real or simulated action but rather pose challenges that encourage greater self-awareness and reflexivity. Above all, the game makes it difficult to ignore the fact that some actions simulated for entertainment purposes are horrific. Players never truly act immorally, and the game is certainly not corrupting, but it would still be fair to say that players who lack adequate sensibilities to recognize the moral dimensions of the game are in some sense misguided—deserving of minor blame, as Sorensen rightly puts it. This blame is not for the game but for the players themselves. It does not indicate a problem with the game but instead a pre-existing issue with a prior cause.

The Contagion Effect

In chapter 2, I discussed what I called the "contagion theory of simulated actions," according to which mere exposure to simulations of violence, sexual deviance, and other morally questionable actions is treated as being akin to an infection that players involuntarily receive and are largely powerless to resist. Now that I have analyzed the similarities between moral decisions in games and narrative moral thought experiments, as well as the implications of being evil or unreflective when playing, it is easier to see why the contagion theory is implausible. Players are not mere recipients of harmful stimuli in ways that are akin to contracting a disease, nor are they like drug users who are overcome by addiction. They are active agents who interpret and interact with games, as evidenced by their ability to describe their play in moral terms and reflect on the meaning of simulated choices. The ethnographic research showing players deliberately choosing good, evil, or neutral paths reveals a broad array of different gameplay strategies and an ability to evaluate in-game actions for moral significance.

Within the context of the scenarios I have discussed thus far, moral issues turn out to be more complex than proponents of the contagion theory imagine. Critics treat violence in videogames as being uniformly bad, yet in many cases it is morally justifiable within the game narrative. In Power of the Atom, killing may be necessary to prevent a nuclear explosion, while in Oasis—a *Fallout 3* quest that addresses euthanasia—it may be an act of mercy. The changing moral character of violence in videogames requires a nuanced assessment of what violence means within a particular context, rather than a simplistic causal narrative. When violence is unjustified, as in *Spec Ops*, games may question it and question players themselves. In that game, the simulation of unjustified violence is precisely what makes the game so meaningful as an indictment of war. Simulated immorality is therefore a conduit to promote peace in the real world in this instance. This underscores the polysemy of videogames and the importance of looking at actions within both their narrative contexts (where violence may be justified) and within a broader social context (where imaginary violence may be essential for commentary on real-world issues).

Grand Theft Auto is one of the most controversial franchises in videogame history and is regularly at the center of controversies about whether videogames are morally problematic. *Grand Theft Auto V* continues this tradition by forcing players to torture one of the nonplayer characters to progress through the game. It is a horrific scene in which players can beat the victim with a wrench, extract his teeth, waterboard him, and subject him to electrical shocks. Critics are inclined to interpret the mere representation of torture as immoral and as advocacy for torture, disregarding the attitude the game narrative takes about it.[14] They are also inclined to think that participating in simulated torture could teach players to torture or could desensitize them to the practice. Arguments against this simulation of torture tend to focus on a supposed moral problem linked to the contagion of violence, and a problem associated with the desensitizing effects of realistic violence. I argue that this badly misreads the game and underestimates players, and that the extremely graphic scene is yet another counterpoint to critics spreading moral panic.

YouTube and Reddit comments reveal that dozens of players feel uncomfortable when playing this part of the game or merely watching it.[15] Some even claim that it gave them nightmares. Moreover, the game strongly suggests that players should feel uncomfortable by linking the scene to the U.S. government's use of torture during the second Bush administration. Players are ordered to torture by agents of the Federal Investigation Bureau (FIB), with the protagonist characters expressing objections throughout. Players who torture using waterboarding alone earn the achievement "It's Legal!" in reference to the efforts made to defend the legality of using this practice against terrorists. This builds a number of backhanded critiques of U.S. government security agencies. Renaming the FBI as FIB transforms the acronym into a colloquial term for a lie. One of the game's protagonists, Michael De Santa, is hiding from a former life as bank robber Michael Townley, who helped the FIB kill his criminal associates. The name Michael Townley is a reference to a CIA agent of the same name who was implicated in the assassination of high-profile Latin American politicians at the behest of their conservative opponents. The game thus builds a critical framework in which the actions being represented are challenged far more than they are endorsed.

The torture mission is justifiably controversial because it is extremely uncomfortable. And yet, it is the feeling of discomfort that establishes this as a simulation of something morally problematic and that gives it a critical force when we see it in the context of the real policies it is commenting on. This moment in the game provides a compelling simulation of what torture might look like when it is enacted that goes far beyond the narrative descriptions of waterboarding that are offered in defense of torture. The attempt to realistically model the experience, blood and all, makes it look profoundly unattractive. The vivid re-creation of torture in pursuit of realism therefore serves to create a more effective critique. Thus, the game is extremely violent and realistic, yet neither of these attributes changes its underlying moral worth or lends credence to the criticisms directed against violent videogames. This is not to say that violence in games is always justified or that unjustified violence always serves a higher purpose. There are, of course, countless examples of gratuitous violence in videogames. Unreflective players may likewise miss these contextual considerations. Videogames are not always meaningful, and players are not always thoughtful. However, the room for interpretation, importance of context in constructing meaning, and role of player agency are evidence that we need a careful analysis of games that avoids reducing them to a contagion or reducing players to drug users.

A critic could argue that it is unfair for me to draw assistance from the comparison between videogames and narrative thought experiments because of the former's realism. After all, one of the main lines of critique I discussed in chapter 2 was that videogames produce a morally problematic realism. To this, I would say that being visually realistic does not equate to being real or having real moral weight. Representations of humans do not become human simply by virtue of being more accurately constructed. An empty caricature in a thought experiment may feel less real than a well-developed and modeled videogame character, but both fall far short of being real people to whom we would owe moral obligations. It would be strange to say that we have moral obligations to fictional characters. The torture victim in *Grand Theft Auto* is no more real than a character in a thought experiment and therefore no more deserving of moral consideration.

Player participation is another potential concern. One could argue that there is a difference between imagining immoral actions and participating in them, even though the participation itself is imaginary. Such a response holds some appeal because it draws on the ludological character of games that distinguishes them from other media that represent immoral actions without demanding active engagement with them. A critic of my argument could go one step further by claiming that the videogame simulation is far more participatory, and potentially more corrupting, than moral counterfactuals that take other forms. To consider the possibility that simulated action could make a moral difference, it is useful to go beyond the deontological and consequentialist perspectives that I have focused on thus far to consider how games should be judged from the standpoint of virtue ethics.

Matt McCormick argues that virtue ethics exposes a problem with simulations of immoral activities. Virtue ethics is not as directly concerned with whether particular actions are good or bad as deontological and consequentialist theories are. It instead focuses on the moral qualities of the actor involved. Aristotle argues that we become good people by habitually doing the right thing and training ourselves to do this instinctively. We become bad in much the same way, through activities that cultivate bad character and habituate us to making bad choices. As McCormick sees it, "By participating in simulations of excessive, indulgent, and wrongful acts, we are cultivating the wrong sort of character. The Aristotelian would respond that the holo-pedophile or the holo-murderer is re-enforcing virtueless habits and dispositions in themselves."[16] McCormick goes on to argue that players can suffer character damage even if games do not actually cause them to commit immoral acts. That is, simulated immorality may be inherently wrong on Aristotelian grounds regardless of whether it involves malicious intent or produces the kind of measurable bad effects that consequentialists privilege.

Christopher Bartel takes a similar approach. He does not think that the simulated immoral acts players take in games are inherently wrong, yet he does think that players can act wrongly if they have the wrong attitude toward these actions. Reflecting on the torture scene in *Grand Theft Auto*, he says that "the unwilling player does nothing more than witness his monstrosity. By contrast, the willing player does not merely witness Trevor's monstrous acts; he also cheers them on."[17] Bartel wants to excuse those players who merely witness immoral actions as well as those who practice immoral actions but dislike doing so. As he sees it, only players who enjoy pretending to be evil deserve condemnation. This is similar to McCormick's argument, except this version leaves open the possibility that players could practice being immoral and still remain guilt-free if they do not enjoy it. Stephanie Patridge makes a similar point, saying that "even when we determine that a game with morally worrisome content is worthy of being played, a virtuous gamer will refuse to enjoy the offending content because such content will bring to mind real-world, moral conditions."[18]

Corrupting influences may seem like a personal concern, but Adam Briggle contends that entire societies have a character that arises out of the aggregate decisions made by their members and that they are susceptible to habituation. "Computer games, like other aspects of new media culture, contribute to the character of the culture, the 'soil' in which we find ourselves, thereby influencing what we do and how we think, or in short, who we are. These influences, then, can be evaluated in terms of their goodness and badness."[19] Once again, the pattern of the personal becoming political emerges when it comes to videogames. Societies can be described as having a character that is shaped on the macrolevel in much the same way as the Aristotelian explanations of individual character formation. For those who accept this argument, it may provide a rationale for imagining that videogames have serious societal costs even if these cannot be seen or measured.

There are a few problems with these arguments grounded in virtue ethics, and because they are so closely bound up with Aristotle's philosophy, it is worth a digression to see just how far they drift from Aristotle's own thinking. First, it is misleading to suggest that Aristotle is solely concerned with character development in the abstract and not with actions in the real world. One gets the impression from critics that videogames corrupt players but that this corruption may always remain invisible. This is a convenient way of raising moral objections that are immune from contrary evidence, yet it does not align with Aristotle's theory. Aristotle does emphasize the importance of having appropriate feelings and argues that we should want to cultivate good character. However, he says that these things are desirable because they lead to *eudaemonia*, which is usually translated as "flourishing" or "living well." He describes this condition as being a result of virtuous conduct and as something that can be disrupted by misconduct. This means that if games were immoral in an Aristotelian sense, we would see the effects of game-induced character flaws showing up in other expressions of character and hindering a person's overall pursuit of *eudaemonia*, making the effects of gaming observable in the real world. Throughout his writings on ethics, Aristotle likewise gives examples of bad character being revealed through action, so we should expect to see bad consequences such as increased violence when character faults take root.

Second, Aristotle's theory of tragedy shows that he is attuned to the differences between real and simulated actions and that he thinks these differences have distinct moral implications. Aristotle celebrates the cathartic power of tragedy, saying that confronting uncomfortable thoughts and feelings through fiction has a purgative effect. This raises the possibility that counterfactuals act like a kind of moral holiday in which we act badly to release tension within a safe space while maintaining high ethical standards in everyday life. As Jon Cogburn and Mark Silcox rightly observe, "Aristotle suggested that, if placed in the right context, certain displays of violence in art can actually have a morally edifying effect on their audience."[20] Whether or not this kind of release works in practice, it is part of Aristotle's philosophy and should give us grounds for thinking that simulated immorality may be advantageous.

Aristotle's *Poetics* also introduces the concept of *mimēsis* (imitation), which is probably the closest he comes to dealing with the kinds of representations we find in videogames.[21] According to Aristotle, imitation is a natural human capacity that involves representing reality while also changing it in artistic ways. He argues that there is a clear separation between reality and its mimetic reproduction, and that the imitation gains much of its value from being a space for exploring possibilities beyond our normal experiences. As Gunter Gebauer and Christoph Wulf explain, "For Aristotle, the critical point is that mimesis produces *fiction* (emphasis in the original); whatever reference to reality remains is shed entirely of immediacy."[22] That is, mimesis makes reference to the real world while still being artificial and bound by different rules. It seems doubtful that someone so firmly articulating his own version of Johan Huizinga's magic circle argument would think that fictions divorced from reality would be morally compromising.[23]

Third, when Aristotle talks about being virtuous, he is not only talking about morality but also excellence in terms of skill. He relativizes good conduct to a degree by arguing that what counts as good or bad partially depends on the context and the actor involved. It may be good to kill during war, for example, but wrong to do so in everyday life. Likewise, a soldier's act of killing an enemy is virtuous because it is a display of excellence that is sanctioned by the context. When it comes to videogames, an Aristotelian conception of virtue must encompass both senses of being good that I discussed previously: moral goodness and skill. Being skillful in a game frequently requires simulated immorality and is therefore in a sense virtuous. It is perfectly consistent with Aristotle's philosophy to argue that videogames are morally distinct from everyday life, with values and expectations that are appropriate to that specific context and to the identities players assume.

Fourth, Aristotle says that we experience *eudaemonia*—that type of flourishing that is the ultimate purpose of life—when an activity is an end in itself rather than merely being a means to something else. *Eudaemonia* is an inherently desirable condition. Based on this characterization and Aristotle's frequent comparisons between virtue and mastery of a technical skill, it would be reasonable to infer that the flow state gamers experience when they are totally immersed in gameplay that they appreciate as an end in itself is at least a glimpse of *eudaemonia*.[24] It would be dangerous to foreclose such a meaningful experience. Aristotle is also clear in arguing that the happy life must include pleasures and that it is not based on depriving ourselves of fun, which adds further credence to thinking that moderate indulgence in simulated immorality may be healthy. The variants of the Aristotelian critique from Bartel and Patridge reveal a strangely puritanical attitude toward games that is not only at odds with Aristotle's advocacy for moderately indulging in pleasant activities but also strange in its own right. Their advice is essentially that it may be permissible to play violent and sexually explicit videogames but that it is not permissible to enjoy them. If we cannot take pleasure in the games, then what is the point of playing them at all? Our leisure would be seriously impoverished if we had to pretend not to enjoy it, and there is certainly nothing in Aristotle's philosophy to indicate that he would support such a self-flagellating approach to leisure.

Finally, there is the more serious issue of how easily the Aristotelian critiques of videogames slip between real and simulated actions as though they were the same thing. In this respect, the Aristotelian critiques suffer from the same problem of drawing firm distinctions between ontological categories as deontological and utilitarian critiques. Elsewhere I have argued that videogames can be a useful tool for developing *phronesis*, which is Aristotle's name for the practical wisdom needed to identify and evaluate moral decisions. Videogames are an exercise in *phronesis* because they give us opportunities to use moral reasoning skills. I made the same point in chapters 2 and 3, though without framing it in Aristotelian language. As I have shown, this skill of *phronesis* is just as likely to be improved by simulating evil or neutral actions as with good ones, so long as players are aware of what they are doing and why. However, improving *phronesis* is different from habituation. Whereas *phronesis* is a skill of judgment that is largely cognitive, habituation requires real action. Players who kill in a videogame are not practicing murder. They are playing a game in which they practice simulating murder. They can, and certainly do, get better at *simulating* murder. To the extent that games are realistic, players also learn about how a person might go about committing a murder. Nevertheless, the experience of controlling an avatar in a digital simulation is so far removed from the actual experience of killing someone that it cannot be a useful analogue.

Amoralism: Is It Just a Game?

So far, I have argued that simulating immoral actions in videogames is not genuinely wrong and that it can even be enlightening. However, this leaves another question: why do so many people have an intuitive sense that some actions performed in games are wrong if there is no wrongdoing involved? One of the central debates here revolves around an apparent contradiction that Morgan Luck calls the "gamer's dilemma." He argues that many gamers have permissive attitudes about virtual violence but that they will likely condemn virtual pedophilia. He says of gamers that "either they acknowledge that acts of virtual murder and virtual paedophilia are morally prohibited, or they acknowledge that both are morally permissible."[25] As he sees it, either conclusion leads to problems. Prohibiting virtual murder would make videogame content more restrictive than other media, such as films, while permitting virtual pedophilia would leave us sanctioning unpalatable simulated acts.

Luck's reasoning is reminiscent of an earlier point from Peter Singer, who comments on user-generated simulations of pedophilia in *Second Life*. As Singer explains, it is possible for adults to control child characters and then use them to have sex with other player-controlled characters.[26] There is no real sexual exploitation of minors because those involved are consenting adults who only use the child avatars as costumes for their fantasies. His argument then takes the opposite direction as Luck's, suggesting that violence is actually more problematic than pedophilia. As a committed utilitarian, Singer thinks that simulated acts must inflict some harm to be immoral. He draws on the studies linking videogames to violence that I discussed in chapter 2 to reach the conclusion that although there is often no harm in simulating pedophilia, there is harm in simulating violence. The underlying point is similar to Luck's: that we must be more consistent when evaluating simulated behaviors.

Various attempts have been made to solve the gamer's dilemma or to at least clarify its implications and foreclose possible answers. Young considers whether the difference between simulations of child murder and pedophilia could be attributable to divergent motives between players who enjoy one activity or the other, and concludes that the motives are indistinguishable.[27] He contends that there is no empirical evidence to suggest that players who enjoy pedophilia are more likely to engage in it than that murderous players are likely to kill, so the simulated actions cannot be distinguished in terms of players' intentions to enact their desires in real life. Young likewise argues that if finding enjoyment in virtual pedophilia is reprehensible, then the same must be true of murder.

Christopher Bartel thinks that it is possible to distinguish virtual pedophilia from murder because the former qualifies as pornography.[28] He claims that pedophilia sexualizes inequality and in doing so harms women. The imagery itself constitutes a harm, while images of violence do not. This argument rests heavily on being able to classify simulations as pornography and on showing that pornography is harmful, which are both questionable propositions that have yet to be adequately demonstrated.[29] Additionally, as Luck and Ellerby point out, representations of pedophilia need not be pornographic.[30] The acts could simply be referenced without being depicted on-screen, which would leave the gamer's dilemma intact. One could also take the objection in a different direction by questioning why if pornography is harmful, simulations of violence are not.

Rami Ali attempts to evade the dilemma by appealing to the importance of context when judging any simulated actions. "The morality of virtual acts will turn on whether the gamer engages with these acts in a morally perverse manner or not, and not on the type of act performed (whether virtual murder or virtual pedophilia)."[31] By this reasoning, virtual murder and virtual pedophilia can be equally acceptable or condemnable depending on the context and how they are represented. It all depends on whether these are necessary. If the player must perform these actions for the story, then they are done for the sake of enacting the narrative, but if players choose to engage in these actions without being forced to by the game, the actions indicate enjoyment and become objectionable. Ali's line of argument therefore constitutes a partial return to thinking that players can simulate immoral actions just so long as they do not take pleasure in doing so. If this standard were applied to virtual murder, then we would have to conclude that the many thousands of players who choose to simulate killing because it is fun are acting wrongly. This would solve the gamer's dilemma but with some profoundly limiting conclusions when it comes to permissible game content.

Before getting into the details of this argument, it is important to point out that the gamer's dilemma is itself a thought experiment—one more reason why that concept is so helpful is that it is not only an apt comparison with simulated actions but also one of the primary tools through which games are interrogated. As thought experiments go, the gamer's dilemma is fairly unrealistic. This is not a decisive problem, as I have shown that unrealistic thought experiments can be valuable. I only mention this as a caveat that we should treat the problem as a valuable one without overstating its descriptive accuracy. There are only a handful of games that allow players to simulate rape, and fewer still that permit pedophilia. Most treatments of this dilemma deal with imaginary games involving hypothetical sexual crimes. Real instances of virtual pedophilia tend to occur more from player modifications than by design. This is important to bear in mind when considering the dilemma to avoid conflating a counterfactual that is useful for interrogating moral intuitions with a genuine problem facing videogames in practice. The most immediate risk from the gamer's dilemma is that it could push commentators toward thinking that the more common acts of simulated killing must also be considered immoral for the sake of consistency, which is the response from Singer and Ali. This is what makes it an important objection to refute. Fortunately, there is good reason to think that the dilemma is illusory.

We already have a fairly strong comparison that can help us understand why the gamer's dilemma is not a genuine dilemma: the novel *Lolita*.[32] This story about a middle-aged man developing a sexual relationship with a twelve-year-old girl is widely considered a classic of twentieth-century literature, despite the fact that it involves pedophilia. The first question we should ask when thinking about the gamer's dilemma is: why does this double standard exist? How can a book, which has been converted into films and therefore spans several media types, be treated as a literary masterpiece while a hypothetical game dealing with the same topic is assumed to be reprehensible? Luck and Ellerby claim that there is something morally problematic about even alluding to illicit sexual relationships without showing or describing them, which is to say references that fall short of being pornographic. *Lolita* does exactly this, alluding to and describing illicit contact between an adult and a minor. The gamer's dilemma is therefore built on a double standard in how different media are approached, revealing a tacit assumption that videogames could not possibly take the right attitude toward morally troublesome topics compared to ostensibly more serious forms of entertainment. This creates a dilemma for the gamer's dilemma: whether to treat all media representations of pedophilia as immoral or extend the permissive attitude many take toward *Lolita* and other works that deal with controversial topics to games.

One could counter this by saying that there is something different about enacting the pedophilia as a player versus reading about it or watching it. However, it is not clear why interactivity should matter. Participating in pedophilia for the strategic goal of progressing through a game does not constitute any stronger endorsement than reading about it to get through a novel. Conversely, if someone enjoys reading about illegal sexual activities and fantasizing about them, then why should it matter whether the fantasy unfolds in their own minds or comes with digital assistance? In other words, innocent appreciation of a text that involves pedophilia and a deviant desire to fantasize about the act are equally possible in more passive and interactive media.

I would argue that the immorality of real acts of pedophilia lies in the wrongness of sexually exploiting those who are not able to give consent and who are highly vulnerable to coercion. The wrongness of pornography involving children lies in the continued harm of circulating images produced under duress, that are a reminder of the crime, and that allow others to benefit vicariously from wrongdoing. Virtual pedophilia does not involve these harms. There is no initial victimization of a person and no subsequent harm done if images of the abuse are recorded. Regardless of whether pedophilia simulated in a game is referenced or depicted visually, neither of these harms arises. From all the objections to simulated violence I have discussed thus far, it should be clear that many people are uncomfortable with simulations of immoral actions even if there is nothing genuinely wrong with the simulations. The simulations are not harmful, but they evoke actions that are harmful and that are therefore highly charged and likely to cause offense. Virtual murder feels wrong to many people, even though there is no compelling evidence of harm. This indicates that we cannot take revulsion to certain types of simulations as evidence that there is genuine wrongdoing.

I suspect that virtual pedophilia may feel more wrong than virtual murder—perhaps to the point of being objectionable even to gamers who enjoy virtual murder—because the simulations are more similar to the real activity and therefore more evocative. When it comes to murder, the wrongness lies in killing a person. Without an immediate victim or an increased propensity to kill in the future, there is no immorality involved in the simulation. Moreover, because real killing is so far removed from simulated killing, involving the click of a mouse or press of a button versus shooting a weapon or wielding a knife, they can be easily distinguished. When it comes to illegal pornography, the wrongness lies in the image itself, and this is precisely what the game may be simulating. A digital image of a child avatar engaged in sex may be difficult to distinguish from real images of sexual exploitation, and even if the simulation is clearly fake, it still bears a more striking resemblance to a real image of abuse than a simulation of murder has to a real murder. When it comes to illegal pornography, simulating the crime and actually participating in it involve comparable actions. This means that although virtual pedophilia is not actually any more wrong than virtual murder, there is a heightened likelihood of feeling the same discomfort that would be triggered by genuine abuse.

Disgust probably also plays a role in making pedophilia feel more wrong than murder. Sexual activities have a high propensity to attract that feeling, perhaps even more so than acts of violence. We should be careful about conflating disgust with genuine moral concern based on the former category's bad record of being applied to behaviors that are not morally objectionable, and feelings of disgust are commonly associated with sexual activities that are seen as being deviant. Only a few decades ago, interracial relationships were considered immoral by many. The same was true of homosexual relationships. Now transgendered people are in a battle for their right to live openly. Restrictions have been based not on genuine moral concerns but rather on feelings of disgust, yet the feelings of disgust were so powerful that they motivated serious deprivations of rights and abuse.[33] The lesson we should draw from this is that disgust is insufficient to make something immoral; there must be additional grounds for objecting to someone's behavior for it to be considered wrong.

Pedophilia and rape are in no way comparable to interracial relationships or being transgendered; the former are reprehensible, while the latter are not. The difference lies in consent. Unlike justifiable sexual expression, pedophilia and rape involve sex without consent from the victim. They not only evoke feelings of disgust but also involve genuine wrongdoing. However, when it comes to simulating these acts, consent cannot be an issue because there is no victim. The same feelings of disgust persist, but without the problem of consent that one experiences in real life. In other words, the feelings of disgust are natural because pedophilia and rape are abhorrent, and we may justifiably be disgusted when these actions are simulated in videogames or other media, but we should refrain from treating disgusting media as being morally objectionable because sexual disgust is generally an unreliable guide for moral evaluations that cannot by itself be used to determine what is permissible.

Returning to the example of *Lolita*, I can recall my feelings of disgust when reading the book. It was difficult to finish, and to this day I have no idea how anyone can defend its literary merit. For me, it is a profoundly disgusting story that does not deserve to be read. Nevertheless, I do not think that people who enjoy the story are pedophiles or that they act immorally by reading the book. The book involves no genuine harm, nor is there good reason to think that reading it will damage a person's character or foster malicious intentions. My disgust, then, emerges less from genuine moral considerations than from my aesthetic sensibilities. Perhaps those who enjoy *Lolita* see the same value in contemplating moral deviance to better understand it that I find in videogames. As far as the gamer's dilemma goes, any simulated pedophilia may well be disgusting, but it is not immoral. Inconsistent attitudes about violence and sex do not tell us anything morally significant. Instead, they tell us something about what kinds of activities we find too revolting to imagine.

Conclusion

As I have argued, the de facto moral thought experiments that arise in videogames have two important benefits. The first is to encourage players to be aware of the moral challenges that may exist in various situations. Videogames give players practice recognizing the moral implications of a broad range of scenarios from binary decisions between good and evil to nuanced decisions that mirror some of the most important controversies we face in the real world. By locating moral challenges in myriad contexts, players are challenged to recognize them amid various background conditions and to consider the extent to which those background conditions influence the moral problem. Second, videogames give players practice in exercising their moral judgment by allowing players to explore different strategies for resolving them. Players get to experience being good and evil as well as occupying the gray areas in between. Being evil can be just as informative as being good, perhaps even more so because this is a perspective that players are apt to have less personal experience with in the real world. The exact choices players make are of secondary importance compared to the exploration of various possibilities, as none of the actions cause actual harm. Even when games limit players' opportunities to make moral decisions or force players along a particular trajectory, they offer opportunities to think about the world from a different perspective and encourage players to temporarily act according to a value system that may differ from their own.

Does this mean that any videogame content should be considered permissible regardless of what is shown? I have focused on defending videogames against criticisms because the general effort in research on games and morality is to find grounds for condemnation. However, I acknowledge that there are reasonable boundaries on expression in games and that some limits are necessary, just as I earlier pointed out the importance of maintaining intelligent age restrictions on certain games. In this case, my defense of games has two limits.

First, there is an enormous difference between simulating morally questionable activities such as murder, rape, and pedophilia and actually advocating them or attempting to incite them. Even the most extreme games that attract critical ire, such as *Grand Theft Auto*, *Manhunt*, and *RapeLay*, address topics without attempting to incite players to carry out attacks. A game would become morally indefensible if it went beyond simply representing an activity or even mildly glamorizing it to encouraging players to emulate the actions being modeled. This would be the difference between a book about murder and a death threat, or a film about rape and an instructional guide on how to give someone the right dose of Rohypnol. It is a distinction that is already captured in most laws regulating free speech, which impose restrictions on content that goes beyond representing morally questionable behaviors to inciting them.

Second, videogames become morally problematic if they are able to represent an activity so accurately that they could reasonably serve as a training simulation for it. I have argued that existing games generally fail to qualify as training devices because of the gulf between what they simulate and the real actions. Learning to shoot in a videogame is nothing like learning to shoot a real weapon. Moreover, there is nothing immoral about learning how to shoot or how to operate a military jet. On the other hand, I would say that there is something problematic about a videogame that provided players with a step-by-step guide for how to rape someone or with a game that teaches players how to build a bomb and use it to kill innocent people.

I will deal with these caveats in more detail in chapters 6 and 7 to show that existing restrictions on speech provide ample guidance for dealing with games that cross the line into incitement. For now, I will conclude by saying that the caveats are hardly necessary. Most outrage is directed at games that lack these potentially harmful messages—games designed purely for entertainment. Games with immoral content in either of the senses that I described are exceedingly rare and unlikely to exist. Even if developers wanted to produce such games, they would have a limited commercial market and be subject to extensive restrictions.

5

The Many Faces of
Moral Reflection

Games are widely criticized for supposed harms ranging from school shootings to terrorist attacks, from desensitizing individual players to dulling entire populations' aversion to war, from instilling aggression to legitimizing racial violence. But games are often controversial because they take on important issues that are themselves controversial. If games were safe media that consistently steered clear of difficult topics such as crime, war, racism, and sexual violence, then they would forfeit their capacity to provide a critical vantage point. It is because games take on difficult issues and spark controversy that they are able to promote deeper reflection on moral questions. And this is by no means a feature unique to highbrow games that deliberately set out to explore serious issues. Even games that are routinely accused of promoting senseless violence have much to teach if we approach them in the right way. From *Grand Theft Auto*'s satire of racism, to the *Modern Warfare* series' disastrous invasion of the Middle East and villainous American general, to *Super Columbine Massacre RPG!*'s exploration of the causes of school shootings, games that are charged with being mindless murder simulators or with lacking any deep artistic merit can pose important questions that reach beyond the game world.

I devote this chapter to exploring some of the dominant approaches videogames take to raising and exploring moral problems. These include explicit moral choice engines, setting boundaries on what actions players can perform, rewards and punishments to establish moral context, branching paths at key junctures, and the tangential presentation of moral quandaries as background conditions structuring game worlds. These approaches to moral reflection are common in games, with some games making use of several at once. Looking at the various types of challenges helps to demonstrate that games can, and often do, create meaningful moral simulations that make them worthy of being treated as thought experiments rather than as mindless entertainment or as sources of corruption. The moral challenges games produce are not necessarily all deliberate. Some game developers may not intend to take on moral issues, yet when a medium empowers players to make decisions within simulated social contexts, moral questions are unavoidable. I make no assumptions about developer intent and instead explore what these various types of challenges look like from a player's perspective.

Mapping out the various moral challenges included in games is essential for showing that games have moral significance through their ability to produce counterfactuals that invite moral reflection from players. In many cases, these challenges are ones that players must solve directly, much as one would solve a narrative thought experiment. These are akin to the Trolley Problem, displaced into a game setting, although such problems can be portrayed in many different ways, depending on how they are embodied in the game mechanics and with different effects on the game narrative. In other instances, the moral issues arise indirectly in the background of the game narrative or implicitly through interactions with nonplayer characters. Each of the approaches I discuss in this chapter has strengths and limitations when it comes to exploring moral questions, highlighting their significance, and linking them to real-world issues. When taken together, the different styles of representing moral challenges show that gameplay is highly flexible and that morality is integral to constructing meaningful narratives. The styles of moral simulation not only allow games to prompt and reward deeper reflection but also help to make games more enjoyable and distinctive.

The breadth of the analysis in this chapter forces me to overlook many excellent games that deserve more sustained attention. I encourage readers to use the framework I develop (and to expand it). I also focus more on games that I think do well in presenting moral challenges with the admission that moral issues are not always handled perfectly and that some simulations muddle the issues at stake more than clarifying them. There are better and worse ways of executing each style of moral simulation, and better and worse ways of integrating them into gameplay. Above all, the examples I discuss are a testament to the insight that videogames can provide—even when the game in question is widely criticized for having some kind of harmful effect on players. This capacity to explore important issues from different perspectives is additional grounds for being skeptical about the moral panic attitude toward games and for embracing their power to facilitate moral exploration.

Moral Boundaries

One way of thinking about morality is to look for boundaries demarcating acceptable actions from unacceptable ones. After all, moral injunctions are often seen as limits on what we can do, or at least what we can do without fear of sanction. All games impose some boundaries—limiting how high players can jump, what areas of the map they can visit, and how many items they can carry. Most boundaries arise from attempts to mirror real physics or are necessary because of limited processing power, but some are morally significant. No matter how open-ended they are, most games impose constraints on how players can interact with other characters, which establish that certain acts are simply impossible within the game space. Such actions are just as impossible as jumping higher than the physics engine will allow or venturing beyond the boundaries of the map. That is, they are impossible within the normal confines of the game and can only be achieved if players cheat in some way.

Violence against children is a prime example of a moral rule built into most videogames. The first and second games in the *Fallout* series drew criticism for permitting attacks on children and even assigning players the "child killer" status for doing so. Later installments of the series made it impossible for players to attack children, and it remains unusual for any role-playing game to permit this. Bullets and punches pass straight through the intended victims, leaving the children unharmed. Developers may also simply omit children to prevent violence against them. For all the blood and guts in No Russian, there is a conspicuous absence of children. No major airport in the world would be populated exclusively by adults, but despite its pretense of realistically simulating terrorism, the mission censors the attacks by removing under-aged victims.

Every narrative game must incorporate some tacit moral structure, even if it is unintentional, simply because games are finite and some decisions must fall outside the scope of what they are able to simulate. This means that moral boundaries may exist even if developers do not mean to create them. If they fail to establish the requisite gameplay mechanics for extreme actions for any reason, then these are de facto beyond the game's normative range. For example, despite concerns over videogames simulating rape and pedophilia, it is rare to find games in which these (especially the latter) are possible. Developers might not always intend to forbid these actions, but they are forbidden all the same if players are unable to simulate them. Games therefore establish a kind of moral architecture as boundaries are created, all without labeling actions or the need for explicit moralizing. Thus, at the most basic level, we can say that games impose absolute moral limits that are embedded in the game rules. These limits may not be explicit, but they offer clues into which behaviors are normal within the game space and which are in some sense unthinkable.

In a slight variation on this style, games may allow acts that are clearly wrong but make them obstacles, such that crossing a moral boundary results in a loss. One of the most familiar instances of this is the punishment for killing civilians in first-person shooters and shooting simulations. From classic shooting games, such as *Lethal Enforcers* and *Virtual Cop*, to games using real actors, such as *Mad Dog McCree* and *Crime Patrol*, to the current generation of military first-person shooters, such as the *Call of Duty* and *Battlefield* series, civilians have been incorporated as obstacles that players must avoid harming during gunfights. In most cases, civilians can be killed—players can murder or incidentally attack the wrong person during a gunfight—but this causes players to lose a life or fail a mission. This makes the games more complex by preventing players from instinctively shooting anything that moves and forcing them to instead evaluate each target. The rules construct a repetitive moral and strategic choice that acts as a barrier against advancement on par with the enemies themselves, thereby asserting the wrongness of certain decisions on the use of force by making it impossible to play the game well without playing the game morally. These two senses of being "good" in the game are collapsed into one. Playing the game well demands staying within the moral boundaries that are embedded in the rules. In this case, the moral boundary can be transgressed, but only to a small extent, before the transgressions bring gameplay to a halt.

Games may also establish moral boundaries that are enforced by characters within the game world. Virtually every role-playing game, including those in the *Fallout*, *Elder Scrolls*, and *Baldur's Gate* series, treats stealing as wrong. Players can steal without losing a life or having to restart, but if they are caught in the act by nonplayer characters (NPCs), they can expect overwhelming retaliation. Picking up someone else's property can lead an entire town to turn against players in *Skyrim* and establishes just as strong a sense of moral reproach as when the game simply punishes players by removing health. Here the boundary comes not from a direct punishment in the game itself but instead from a norm that is consistently enforced by NPCs acting collectively. In each of these ways, moral norms are tacitly introduced into the game as boundaries on acceptable action, often without the need for explicit judgments of whether the player's character or choices are good or evil.

Moral Alignments

Perhaps the simplest and most overt way of explicitly incorporating moral evaluations into a game is by assigning a moral alignment. In these instances, a game asks players to choose their alignment at the outset, then leaves little or no room for players to revise those values as the game progresses. Nonplayer characters may likewise have overt alignments that offer clues about what to expect from their behavior and how they should be treated. This type of moral system was popularized by role-playing games, especially those from Dungeons and

Dragons (D&D). The appeal is easy to understand. In paper and pencil games, morality is relevant, but it may be difficult to incorporate dynamic moral evaluations alongside other considerations, such as fighting skills and magical powers. With dungeon masters managing dozens of characters, it is helpful to have some sense of what their beliefs and values are without the responsibility of making them all fully developed people who can grow and change.

Baldur's Gate, like most other role-playing games using the D&D rules, includes nine alignments that not only express moral sensibilities but also the characters' attitudes toward social rules. The alignments are lawful good, neutral good, chaotic good, lawful neutral, true neutral, chaotic neutral, lawful evil, neutral evil, and chaotic evil. According to the D&D rules, the spectrum from good to evil is primarily meant to gauge qualities such as respect for life and altruism versus selfishness.[1] The spectrum from lawful to chaotic indicates whether characters pursue those goals in a way that is consistent with societal norms and official rules. The two axes therefore distinguish between fundamental moral values and the methods of enacting those values in a particular social context. This makes it possible to capture divergence between these moral identities, such as when a good character flouts the law through vigilantism.

Nonplayer characters also come with their own moral alignments, which dictate their actions and how they relate to other characters. The divergent sensibilities are most evident when dealing with NPC teammates. Nonplayer characters are more manageable when they agree with the player character's values, and teams are easier to keep together when all members share roughly the same orientation. This group dynamic is among the most interesting features of the moral alignment system. Even though these games suggest that people have strict and clear moral codes that can be labeled good and evil, they indicate that there is a social aspect of morality such that people who collectively hold good or evil values will get along. There may therefore be group norms that organize life even for those who viciously attack outsiders. Heterogeneous teams erupt into violent conflicts, which makes the combination of good and evil personalities more destructive than homogeneous teams of either type.

There is much to dislike about fixed moral alignments. They are unrealistically rigid and formulaic, neglect capacities for growth and change, and impose more order onto moral decisions than we experience in real life. What person is truly so predictable as to consistently follow a moral alignment across different types of decisions? Nevertheless, it is important to avoid undervaluing these games' capacities to provoke moral reflection. One of the foremost benefits of this style of simulating ethics is that it makes morality overt and unavoidable. Subtler methods of posing ethical quandaries may lead unreflective players to overlook the moral weight of their actions. When moral status is attached to each character, including the player's own character, and influences gameplay, it is an unavoidable issue that must weigh into key decisions and the management of groups. Player forums even reveal fairly sophisticated discussions of the significance of choosing one alignment over others, in which players reflect on their own personal values and how this relates to choices about which alignment to select.[2]

Another interesting implication of the alignment system is that there are multiple routes to being moral or immoral, depending on whether the route is chaotic, lawful, or neutral. It suggests that one need not follow a linear path through moral decisions or even employ the identical types of reasoning when attempting to be good or evil. Despite the static nature of this alignment system, this degree of moral complexity is more nuanced than the sliding good versus evil scales that I discuss in the next section.

Omniscient Evaluations

Some games assign explicit moral alignments but allow them to change. Players are not confined to a particular identity and can find themselves moving from one to another—even crossing between good and evil alignments. This more accurately reflects the dynamic character of moral decision-making and the realities of personal development while still making morality explicit and a core element of the narrative. However, in contrast to the fixed moral alignment system, moral choice engines usually locate players along a sliding scale between good and evil extremes without distinguishing between different ways of being good and evil.

Fallout 3 is a prime example of this style. Its karma system moves along a scale ranging from −1000 (extremely bad) to 1000 (extremely good) each time players make an important decision, whether it is killing an NPC, blowing up a town, or rescuing slaves. Choices are weighted, with more serious actions, such as murder, producing a larger shift in karma than minor infractions, such as theft. Following the actions, changes are displayed on the screen alongside the number of experience points obtained. This serves as a constant reminder that every action has moral implications, and provides immediate feedback about what those implications are. The reminders informing players that they have gained or lost karma are particularly important because they create the sense that evaluations are coming from the game itself, with NPCs only reacting to a change that is an objective feature of the world. This is reinforced by the term *karma*, which refers to a kind of cosmic evaluation of a person's actions that exists regardless of whether they are seen. This stands in sharp contrast to later installments in the *Fallout* series, such as *Fallout 4*, in which NPCs seem to be making moral evaluations based on their own judgments rather than responding to an objective moral status.

Players of *Fallout 3* can check their karma score at any time by looking at their stats, a further reminder of the role decisions have in building individual character alongside practical skills. The game even attaches names to players based on their karma and experience levels, giving them a sense of what people in the game world actually think about the character. The names become more extreme as players gain experience, which suggests that the moral status depends not only on how decisions are made but also on the overall importance of the decisions and how they establish patterns of behavior. For example, players can start with the status of Vault Guardian, Vault Dweller, or Vault Delinquent, depending on whether their low-experience character is good, neutral, or bad. By the time they reach level thirty, they are labeled Messiah, True Mortal, or Devil for the same orientations. It is revealing that the highest level of neutral alignment is equated with humanness, while pure moral categories are profoundly inhuman. The game makes no secret of its expectation that normal people walk a narrow line between good and evil. The game world changes as a player's karma score shifts up or down. Characters in the game react to players based on the karma score and become more friendly or hostile accordingly. Certain factions attack players who belong to a different moral alignment, although in practice this does not have a major impact on the game because the good and evil factions are roughly equivalent.

InFAMOUS includes a karma system with similar effects on the course of the game. As in *Fallout 3*, players are labeled with titles that reflect their orientations. The good scale ranges from Protector to True Hero. The evil scale ranges from Thug to Infamous. A karma meter provides visual clues about which path the player is on and signals the game's evaluations of each decision. The player avatars and their actions also change, becoming more aggressive or noble in their mannerisms and language. As players reach higher levels, their reputation spreads to provoke stronger positive or negative reactions from NPCs. *Fable II* likewise includes a sliding scale between good and evil that is affected by interactions with other characters. However, some of its evaluations are strange and of questionable moral significance. Eating carrots and celery increases one's moral status, while eating chicken or drinking alcohol has a corrupting influence.

Mass Effect deviates from the single binary scale by introducing two different scales: Paragon and Renegade. The latter is not so much an evil rating as it is an indicator of aggression and moral disengagement. Because these are independent qualities, players can advance on both simultaneously or prioritize one over the other. This produces arrangements that are akin to the lawful-chaotic character alignments in addition to shaping the character's moral identity. Developing higher scores on either scale opens more dialogue options and can change the gameplay. *Mass Effect 2* experiments with a percentage system in which the proportion of Paragon to Renegade points becomes more important than the overall number of points but with a similar effect of creating a moral system that has less to do with being good or evil than with how aggressively the protagonist acts when completing missions.

Star Wars: Jedi Knight: Dark Forces II is a particularly interesting example of the moral scale because of how evaluations attach to the character. Here, morality is contextualized in terms of how far players have drifted toward the dark side or light side. Nonplayer characters do not give strong responses to this transition, and it has little effect on the game narrative until the end, yet the game attempts to show that the decisions mark a deeply rooted character transformation. It is largely invisible to others, but it is real in the sense of corrupting the character at a fundamental level that players themselves are unable to reverse after a critical threshold. The morality score does not come from how players respond to moral decisions, as in most other games with explicit moral evaluations, but rather from the choice to invest in light- or dark-side powers. It is therefore the result of training more than actions. One gets the sense that the reputation cost associated with a specific action is of secondary importance and that what really matters is what the player decides to become through deliberate educational choices.

Games that present explicit moral dilemmas and that explicitly evaluate the character's moral status are often criticized for taking a simplistic approach to moral issues and failing to recognize the gray area between extreme good and evil choices. Above all, critics attack a perceived lack of realism in the choices and the resulting moral statuses. Miguel Sicart says that games such as *Fable* and *Knights of the Old Republic* are "fundamentally flawed" because the decisions they include are largely procedural matters about which path to take through the games and not genuine moral dilemmas.[3] That is, the decisions do not engage real thinking about morality because they are so deeply embedded within a particular game choice. Michael Heron and Pauline Belford say of explicit moral decisions like those in *Fallout 3* that "moral choices then become flattened down into mere narrative flavouring rather than a reflection of an individual's ethical makeup. Moral choices within games are thus shallow and lack the ability to truly offer us an opportunity to reflect on the actions we have taken."[4] Grant Tavinor criticizes these kinds of games for introducing unrealistic problems, saying that "the fictional worlds of videogames are usually populated by moral caricatures rather than realistic ethical beings, where characters do things for morally banal reasons, and where the impacts of their actions are hardly ever revisited or reflected on."[5] Rather than encountering NPCs who are like ordinary people, players confront Nazis, aliens, superhumans, and zombies.

These commentators are right in noting that games routinely produce unrealistic and extreme moral challenges, especially when moral choice engines are a key element of gameplay. However, this is often unavoidable given the kinds of problems games establish. Playable characters are not ordinary people; they are immensely powerful, world-changing figures for whom decisions have far-reaching, extreme effects. The Power of the Atom quest that I discussed previously is a prime example of this. The quest does seem somewhat ridiculous because of the suggestion that one person could ever choose whether to destroy an entire city. This is certainly something that most people could never approximate in their daily lives. Nevertheless, if one did encounter this scenario, it seems likely that it would be resolved in some way that would either be extremely good or extremely bad, with little possibility of a neutral outcome. Given the choice of whether to detonate a nuclear bomb and destroy a town, it is difficult to see how there might be a middle ground. And given the immense influence players have over game worlds, actions with extreme moral implications naturally follow.

Even more importantly, these criticisms overlook the value of extreme and unrealistic scenarios—they recapitulate the arguments that thought experiments lose their value when they take on unrealistic cases, which again highlights the utility of that comparison. Unrealistic scenarios can be valuable precisely because they are unrealistic. A lack of realism may make it more difficult to bridge the gap between fiction and reality, yet it can also be valuable to disregard realism when this helps to focus on a specific moral issue or transforms a familiar problem. Even extreme cases in which the right answer seems to be as clear as the decision of whether to destroy a town can provide useful practice that can help us clarify our moral values, thereby making tough cases less difficult. This is why some of the classic thought experiments from philosophy involve unusual scenarios such as surgically joining bodies to share organs or manipulating brains in vats to create perceptions.[6] Thought experiments routinely involve scenarios that we would not be surprised to see in games because they are deliberately constructed to present extreme choices that are able to focus attention on a specific puzzle. Thought experiments in philosophy and in games need not be realistic if they in some way problematize our assumptions or if they help to clarify our intuitions.

Rowan Tulloch correctly points out that games with moral choice engines tend to take a pedagogical attitude toward players, as though they are evaluating decisions from a position of moral certainty and critiquing decisions in a way that presupposes moral truths.[7] This feeling is especially strong when games issue abstract judgments that seem to come from the world itself rather than embodying them in the attitudes of specific characters. However, Tulloch overstates the pedagogical overtones by arguing that in-game rewards, such as health and skills, reinforce the moral lessons by encouraging players to conform to the game's sense of what is right. Most games reward good and bad decisions in roughly equal ways, which is essential for keeping a game balanced. Bad decisions usually result in more immediate rewards, especially financial rewards, which can help early on. Good decisions tend to be the safer long-term investment. This means that games with explicit moral evaluations do strike a pedagogical note, but they also shy away from making this too heavy-handed by introducing parallel rewards and punishments. This reveals some degree of discomfort with disrupting gameplay for the sake of moralizing.

Even more significant is that developers tend to abandon the pedagogical tone whenever decisions become ambiguous. The Oasis and Free Labor quests from *Fallout 3* illustrate this. In both cases, the divergent quest branches do not result in the usual karmic rewards or punishments, so the game avoids passing judgment on the status of euthanasia or the permissibility of revolutions that result in anarchy. This break in the game's evaluations underscores the complexity of the decisions by violating players' expectations that their actions will produce some kind of judgment. The game only asserts that there are better and worse ways of achieving these goals by imposing some karmic costs if players enact their decisions with excessive violence. These quests reveal a more sophisticated use of moral choice engines than Power of the Atom (which does classify choices as either good or evil), as well as borrowing from fixed moral alignments by indicating that there are more lawful or chaotic approaches to good or bad actions. The moral choice still exists even though the method of evaluation has changed somewhat. Players are encouraged to think about the decision within a broader context of the karma system and the implications each choice will have on their status. Nevertheless, at the moment of action, it is unclear what judgment the game will provide. It is at this point that quests like Power of the Atom show their true utility. Such quests signal the importance of moral reasoning and give a false sense that karmic rewards will always be clear. Then, when truly difficult decisions arise, players who want to anticipate the game's response to moral ambiguity must think carefully about how they wish to proceed and attempt to predict what consequences their decisions will have.

Multiple Voices

One way of incorporating moral choices without drawing criticism for unrealistically extreme scenarios or explicit moralizing with a pedagogical tone is to relocate the judgment mechanisms from an objective moral rank like the karma system to informal mechanisms arising from nonplayer characters. This gives a sense that moral evaluations are subjective opinions coming from other characters rather than objective features of the world players inhabit. This subjective style of judgment is often used in games with fixed alignments as well as in those with moral choice engines, since a diverse array of reactions to a particular type of content makes for more interesting interpersonal interactions. However, some role-playing games make this the dominant form of moral evaluation, such that moral judgments only come from other characters and never from seemingly objective game rules. With massive worlds full of nonplayer characters, it is possible to have them serve as the mouthpieces for judgments. The social aspect of this kind of judgment also makes it closer to how we receive feedback in the real world, as our own sense of moral identity comes largely from peers and not from some kind of invisible metric that tracks everything we do.

The *Fallout* series has shown an evolution toward heavier reliance on this style of framing moral identity. The moral valuations in *Fallout 4* come through most clearly when players receive praise or blame from NPC companions. Nonplayer characters speak out for or against the player's choices and present a range of different perspectives that more accurately capture the range of responses people might have to decisions rather than seeing them as simply good or evil. Nonplayer characters' attitudes are also expressed through text messages that appear in the corner of the screen after players do something morally significant. For example, if players assist in espionage while partnering with the antiauthoritarian Piper, the game will display a message saying "Piper didn't like that." Acting against an NPC's preferences too often can cause that character to leave, while satisfying them can build a stronger relationship and even lead to romance. Because players can only have one companion at a time, they cannot gain multiple perspectives on a particular decision. Thus, in a given playthrough, players will only discover NPCs' attitudes one at a time as they react to players' choices. This makes the moral dimension of gameplay more central even as the evaluations become less overt. Players must not only be attentive to the moral significance of their actions but also mindful of which companion will match their moral reasoning style and how their relationship with the companion will change as a result of the choices that are made.

Factional alignments are similar to the evaluations that come from NPCs and allies, though in the context of game narratives these reflect a sense of institutional norms held by a group of characters rather than personal beliefs. There may even be variations between characters within an organization, despite their common cause. *Fallout 4* takes this approach as well, with a main quest that gives players the choice of joining one of four factions struggling for control over the Commonwealth. Each faction has its own values, and each imposes unique demands on how players should act. *Fallout 4*'s Minutemen have a hopeful vision of rebuilding the Commonwealth with independent settlements. They embody a sense of beneficence, yet they are relatively weak and decentralized, which renders them unable to provide adequate security. The Underground Railroad works to preserve the freedom of Synth androids and embodies an abolitionist spirit but lacks a credible political and moral platform beyond this and resorts to questionable methods. The Institute is secretive and violent, but it is guided by scientific goals and has the greatest potential for rebuilding. Finally, the Brotherhood of Steel is militant and seeks an android genocide but clings to traditional moral values and has the power to enforce order in a chaotic location.

No group is purely good or bad. Their motives and methods are mixed to the point that there is something to like and hate about each—to say nothing at all of the variations between individual group members. This leaves room for reasonable disagreement about which faction truly offers the best future for the postapocalyptic world. Each has its advantages and disadvantages in terms of gameplay, as well as unique quests, items, and allies. This leaves the game's difficulty fairly balanced regardless of what choice players make but changes the story to such an extent that the decision still feels meaningful. Helping one faction succeed actually transforms the environment and leads to changes in the kinds of NPCs players encounter when venturing outside the main quest. Playing *Fallout 4* or games with similar factional alignment systems presents an extended moral dilemma in which players must weigh costs and benefits of membership that are ambiguous and continually changing. *Fallout: New Vegas* likewise provides a four-faction choice, with a similar challenge of balancing a complex assortment of costs and benefits.

Far Cry 4 introduces a simpler version of the factional alignment decision, albeit one that raises similar questions about the nature of legitimate political authority. The story is loosely based on Nepal's Maoist insurgency, set in the fictional country of Kyrat. Players take the role of an American of Kyrati descent who travels to the remote country and is caught up in the war between King Pagan Min and the Golden Path rebellion. Players find themselves torn between two different factions within the resistance group, which represent opposing traditionalist and progressive standpoints and differing policies on the country's drug trade. Players intercede to determine which side the organization favors, helping to structure its ideology. The winning faction ultimately takes over the government to enact terrible policies, such as enslaving or persecuting rival political dissidents. Players must then decide whether to kill the leader of the Golden Path in an effort to end a new type of tyrannical government. The game raises some uncomfortable questions about the future of war-ravaged countries and their prospects for restoring stability, without providing clear answers. As with *Fallout 4* and *Fallout: New Vegas*, the complexity of the group value systems has led to lengthy debates on gaming forums about which of the suboptimal endings available is truly best, which in turn generates conversations about which policies governments should pursue and how coercive security should be balanced against the protection of individual liberties.[8]

Branching Paths

Another way of creating moral decisions and promoting reflective gameplay without imposing clear standards on players is to create branching paths that are not explicitly judged as better or worse than alternatives. *Fallout 4*'s faction system is an instance of this, with different factions having their own story arcs, but games need not introduce factions to create this effect. *Life Is Strange* offers an elaborate branching structure in which decisions not only determine the ending, as is the case in many games that include moral choice engines, but also dictate the course of myriad events throughout the game. Some decisions even build on each other in ways that cause path dependency, such that players who make different initial choices end up facing different dilemmas later.

Life Is Strange tells the story of Max Caulfield, a teenage girl who has to navigate the usual challenges associated with growing up and interacting with friends, as well as the immense burden of discovering that she is able to travel a few seconds back in time to revise her actions. Gameplay revolves around dialogue choices that explicitly signal the possibility of a branching path in the narrative. *Life Is Strange* does not label the moral worth of decisions; there is no gauge moving up or down with each choice. And yet, the game does remind players of the immense moral weight of each action because the time travel mechanic encourages experimentation. Once players make a decision, they may rewind time and test the effects of choosing a different option. This provides opportunities to take different branches in the narrative a few seconds into the future to see their immediate outcomes.

The game is particularly effective in showing how choices lead Max to become a particular type of person—at least in the eyes of others—thereby incorporating the interpersonal style of moral evaluation I discussed previously with reference to *Fallout 4*. For example, at one point, players have to decide whether to stop a security guard who is bullying a student. Helping the student will have players branded as troublemakers by the guard and good friends by the student. Failing to intervene will avoid upsetting the guard but disrupt Max's friendship. Even with the ability to rewind and try both approaches, players cannot truly have it both ways. Only the immediate outcome is visible, so players must think carefully about which strand of the narrative they want to follow into the next encounter. To underscore the significance of decisions, the game reminds players that "this action will have consequences" whenever they reach an intersection. Thus, time travel and the abundance of moral choices that have a substantive effect on the game narrative come together to make players reflect deeply about their choices, creating what Luis de Miranda calls "an existential simulator."[9]

Max remembers what happened before she traveled through time; the NPCs do not. At several points, the game makes entirely new choices possible based on the knowledge gleaned from choices that were already made. For example, at one point, players have the choice between looking at a friend's discarded pregnancy test, which will have them chastised by the friend for being too nosy, or ignoring the test altogether and leaving their friend without emotional support. Looking at the test once and then traveling back in time makes it possible to avoid offending the friend while still having the knowledge needed to provide assistance. What is particularly interesting in these cases is that the time travel ability is not actually necessary for making the ideal decision. Players can choose to take the delicate option first by seeing books about maternity on the friend's shelf and using these to draw an inference without searching through the friend's trash. The lesson here is therefore one that transfers readily from the game world—to be aware that choices may be more complex than they initially appear, that careful observation is vital, and that anticipating another person's reactions helps to generate new interpersonal communication strategies. The game reiterates this later when players must attempt to talk a friend out of suicide without the ability to rewind, relying only on their past treatment of the friend and memory of interactions with her. It is a frustrating moment for many players but vital for teaching a lesson about overreliance on a fictional game mechanic when real judgment skills are more dependable.

Perhaps the greatest advantage of this rewind mechanic is that players can experiment with decisions and reflect on their outcomes without having to replay the game. Studies of how players navigate moral challenges show that players tend to be good the first time through but that they prefer experimentation with neutral and immoral perspectives upon subsequent attempts. The problem is that many games are too long for players to go through more than once.[10] Being able to experiment with different choices and the immediate reactions they provoke lowers the barrier against testing various moral strategies. Another interesting feature of *Life Is Strange* is that after completing each episode players can see how their own decisions compared to those of other players. They get a sense of what the dominant perspective is on the optimal course of action through the game dilemmas. There is no right or wrong answer to these problems, which is part of what makes them so interesting. Nevertheless, comparing one's own choices against the trends encourages players to revisit their decisions and to reflect on whether they would act differently with the benefit of hindsight. Thus, *Life Is Strange* continually underscores the importance of choice, and of moral choice in particular. It largely avoids the pedagogical tone of other games by entrusting evaluations to the game's NPCs and to the innovative peer-feedback mechanic.

Rewards and Punishments

Regardless of whether games introduce explicit moral decisions that are quantified according to a moral calculus or present decisions implicitly, they generally offer rewards and punishments. These introduce material considerations into moral decisions, such that doing something bad might be more tempting because of the potential profit. This can make decisions feel weightier by not only raising the personal stakes of a decision but also potentially altering subsequent gameplay. However, as Heron and Belford point out, the consequences tend to make slight changes to game narratives or the items available without significantly altering the overall difficulty. They rightly point out that balancing gameplay is essential and that games could be considerably less fun if the outcomes of good and evil choices were asymmetric. As they put it, "Ludic considerations of game balance and playability virtually mandate that the distribution of benefits and penalties applied by taking one moral path through the game should be roughly mirrored by the end of the game if you take the other."[11]

BioShock offers one of the most famous examples of how the effects of radically different choices are gradually smoothed out to the point that rewards and punishments for good and evil paths are roughly symmetrical. The game's central and recurring dilemma is whether to harvest young girls called Little Sisters for ADAM, a substance that allows players to gain genetic modifications that assist in combat. Players face an explicit moral dilemma of whether to rescue the girls for a small ADAM benefit or kill them for a larger payoff. Killing is the more rewarding short-term strategy, but players who refuse to do this are rewarded later in the game with additional ADAM as a gift. The choice therefore has limited influence on the course of the game or its overall difficulty. Being good only makes a modest addition to the initial difficulty curve.

One of the strangest quests in *Fallout 4* comes when players discover the USS Constitution stranded on land in the middle of the Commonwealth. The ship's crew of dysfunctional robots asks players for help repairing it and defending it against scavengers. As players recover spare parts needed to repair the ship, they confront the scavengers' leader, who asks players to defect and help the scavengers. A choice emerges through this dialogue: help the robots, even though they are not human and only need their provisions to fulfill a delusional fantasy of sailing the Constitution again, or help the scavengers, who need the provisions to survive, even though this would force players to join forces with people of questionable loyalty and renege on previous agreements to help the robots. The stark opposition between the two groups and the impossibility of favoring both are emphasized throughout conversations with the respective leaders. A player's companion NPC may also comment on their ultimate decision of which side to help, delivering a few lines of praise or condemnation along with a text notification explicitly stating the NPC's attitude. In many ways, this is a compelling dilemma that raises questions about whether players have obligations to autonomous machines, and the game refuses to give a clear answer. In the end, players receive rewards of weapons and experience points regardless of which decision they make. The rewards differ and may be more or less attractive depending on players' preferences, but they are commensurate and do not seriously alter the game.

Dishonored takes one of the most interesting approaches to reward-based moral evaluation, as it finds a way to significantly alter the game narrative and increase difficulty while also adding to the game atmosphere. *Dishonored* takes place in a fantasy city that is threatened by a virulent plague. Players take the role of Corvo Attano, a member of the Empress's bodyguard who is framed for her murder. The game follows Corvo's efforts to assist a resistance group attempting to retake the city from those who had the Empress killed. *Dishonored* is primarily a stealth action game. Players have a number of techniques for staying hidden from enemies, including special powers such as teleportation and the ability to slow time. Players may progress through the levels nonviolently, knocking guards unconscious or bypassing them entirely, or they may choose to kill guards with an array of guns, grenades, and traps. The game discourages violence to some extent, as loud weaponry draws unwanted attention from guards and can lead players to be quickly overwhelmed. However, it is often possible to kill silently, and in many instances lethal attacks make a mission easier by completely removing the threats rather than just temporarily disabling them. The choice between high- and low-lethality approaches is clearest when players sneak up behind opponents, as they are given the option of performing a stealth kill with their sword or knocking the victim unconscious.

The game uses player actions to determine the city's chaos level. Killing more people escalates the plague by giving the rats more bodies to eat, leaves more communities and families broken apart by the consequences of a death, causes more NPCs to turn hostile, and increases the number of guards present during each mission. This amounts to a substantive change of the game's difficulty but one that also works from a gameplay standpoint because it complements the strategy players have chosen. The added difficulty for more violent players comes in the form of more opportunities for fighting. Conversely, players who use limited violence and rely heavily on stealth can continue to do this because they face fewer guards.

It is important to note that *Dishonored* employs a different type of underlying moral reasoning from many other videogames. Whereas most of the games I have discussed rely on a virtue-based way of thinking about morality, according to which players are marked as being good or evil and bear those qualities as character traits, *Dishonored* employs a consequentialist standard that focuses on outcomes. Corvo is not good or evil. Instead, the results of his actions have good or bad effects on the game world. This allows players to escape any direct moral judgment of their decisions even as the game emphasizes that the consequences of their actions go on to have a morally significant effect on the world. Nevertheless, the chaos meter is clearly a moral choice engine. It is a metric of whether players affect the world in ways that disrupt it or that help it, which is to say that it is a metric of the morally significant consequences of players' actions. Feedback about moral choices comes at the end of each mission, and the game's final sequence reflects the overall chaos level. *Dishonored* is fairly dark throughout, yet the game reaches something like a happy resolution if players maintain a low chaos level.

Implicit Evaluations

So far, I have considered some of the many ways that videogames can introduce moral challenges as an element of gameplay. There is no perfect method. Each involves trade-offs in terms of balancing difficulty, making choices feel meaningful, and preserving sufficient freedom of action. They are often mixed to provide greater complexity and deployed in distinct ways. Part of what makes videogames so interesting from a theoretical standpoint is that the methods used to simulate moral challenges are constantly changing. Any comprehensive taxonomy of the different types of moral evaluations would become quickly outdated as new strategies appeared. Explicit moral choices are important for overtly placing players in the role of moral agents and forcing them to make judgments. Explicit moral choices are thought experiments posed by the game and that must be executed with the player's assistance. They encourage players to be engaged with decisions and to think carefully not only about how choices will affect the game but also about what they will mean for the player's character. This is especially true when the character has a moral identity or when players want to take a particular path through the game.

Although explicit decisions are one important means of exploring morality, they do not exhaust the range of morally significant themes in videogames. Like films, books, and television shows, videogames also raise issues by exploring them indirectly, without making them into interactive puzzles that must be solved to progress. Here the moral issues arise within the narrative and invite reflection without involving choices that affect the course of the narrative. Virtually all narrative-based videogames introduce some moral considerations in this way. In many cases, the game worlds are caricatures that embody controversial background issues in addition to the dilemmas that players must actively resolve. The moral challenges are not entirely reducible to narrative, since they affect the overall look and feel of the game as well as how players' interactions with the game are framed. Nevertheless, the background issues tend to be heavily driven by narrative elements and are often created using exposition.

Each of the games that I have discussed in terms of explicit moral choices is situated in more complex game narratives that provide overarching commentary about how the game world came into existence to begin with. *BioShock* is based in the city of Rapture, a utopia for elites that echoes many of the central themes of Ayn Rand's novel *Atlas Shrugged*. Players arrive to find that the ideology of individualism has resulted in the total collapse of order. As players navigate the city, the game reminds them of Rand's Objectivism with news broadcasts, advertisements, and monuments celebrating that philosophy's ideals of rugged individualism. The game suggests that this philosophy leads to uncontrollable conflict, and as Joseph Packer points out, treats the Objectivists much like the evil Nazi enemies in games like *Wolfenstein*.[12] The game thus makes a tacit argument about how unrestrained individualism leads to a Hobbesian state of nature, giving players the chance to experience the war of all, against all, firsthand. The moral implications of this are embedded in the game, although players are never directly asked to take an attitude toward Objectivism.

In *Fallout*, it is the naive optimism of the 1950s and enthusiasm for nuclear weaponry that create the context for players' decisions. In *Spec Ops: The Line*, players make several choices about who to shoot and whether to surrender—choices that are more meaningful because they are situated within a broader context that is shaped by a disastrous U.S. military incursion that inflicts terrible harm on innocent civilians. These games encourage us to look for the interplay between the individual moral challenges that we face and the overall narrative that structures them. Decisions are not isolated but rather follow from a particular type of world that is being modeled along the lines of Objectivist philosophy, nuclear imprudence, militarism, or some other system of ideas that has uncomfortable implications.

Papers, Please offers a good example of how a game can intersperse direct and indirect moral challenges. On its surface, the game is relatively simple. The player character is an immigration officer working at a border crossing in the fictional country of Arstotzka. The goal of the game is to inspect the passports and supporting documents of people crossing the border and to give correct decisions about whether they can enter based on a list of rules that continually grows more complex. Players must accurately process a certain number of travelers a day, as they earn a small amount of money for each and can only progress by continually earning more. At the end of each day, players receive an overview of their finances and risk having a family member become sick or die if there are inadequate funds. Players themselves may die if they do not process enough travelers or if they make too many mistakes.

Despite the game's relatively simple mechanics, it continually raises weighty moral challenges. As players examine the passports of those attempting to cross the border, the travelers plead for admittance, talk about their families, or offer bribes. Some of the characters who are caught smuggling drugs claim that they were coerced and beg not to be reported to the guards. Some characters may be desperate for players to overlook an expired visa or to make an exception to the rules, as they are visiting dying family members or fleeing persecution. The bribes become more tempting as the game progresses, especially if a family member is sick. It is extremely difficult to consistently earn an adequate income as a passport control officer who obeys all the rules. However, deciding when to disregard the passport requirements raises myriad challenges. Permitting exceptions to the rules or taking bribes leads to citations, prevents players from earning money for correctly processing passports, and may ultimately end in the player character being arrested. Players also become embroiled in a terrorist plot as a shadowy group attempting to overthrow Arstotzka's government tries to enlist their help. Players are therefore forced into a series of explicit moral dilemmas that must be resolved to continue the game, while also experiencing a narrative context that raises moral questions about legitimate authority and individual responsibility.

Heron and Belford argue that *Papers, Please* externalizes ethical judgments because the decisions must be made without a karma system or other device for explicitly evaluating decisions. They see this as a major difference from games like *Fallout 3*, and an advancement over what they characterize as more simplistic approaches to morality. I would argue that *Papers, Please* is an excellent game with sophisticated moral choices, but the differences between it and other games are really a matter of degree. *Papers, Please* does not evaluate players themselves with a karma metric, yet it does create a framework in which decisions are evaluated morally via rewards and branching narrative paths. The real innovation, and what makes the game's dilemmas feel more compelling than many arising in other videogames, is that the moral lens is itself deeply flawed. The financial rewards of becoming corrupt are in some sense attached to the morally preferable options of undermining an authoritarian government. What is right in the government's eyes involves acting according to orders that appear to be unjust. Thus, the game relies on a familiar method of evaluating choices but asks us to reconsider what the costs and benefits of the different choices actually mean because of the narrative context in which following orders is morally questionable. The game therefore deploys a kind of unreliable moral schema akin to an unreliable narrator in a novel. This schema is an indirect moral challenge that players cannot question any more than the citizen of an authoritarian state can openly disagree with a nonsensical legal system. It is a background condition of life in the game world that is called into question each time an explicit moral dilemma arises.

The follow-up game *Beholder* presents a similar challenge, as players are tasked with monitoring tenants living in an apartment complex that is under the control of an authoritarian regime. According to the game's logic, being good entails making decisions that we would intuitively consider bad: intruding on privacy, assisting in the suppression of dissidents, and helping to imprison people guilty of trivial offenses. The implicit morality of the game's judgment system then comes into conflict with the explicit choices, encouraging reflection on both.

BioShock, *Fallout*, and *Papers, Please* are examples of games in which players must make moral decisions in worlds that are profoundly shaped by narratives that pose overarching moral questions and that make each specific decision more significant by adding context. It is also possible for games to raise big questions through world building and narrative exposition without allowing players to make moral decisions for themselves. At times, depriving players of choice may even be essential to constructing the background issues. This is especially true when games explore the concept of freedom. This is why we should not conflate freedom of choice in moral dilemmas with moral complexity.

The *Portal* series shows that games can raise morally significant issues while limiting player agency. The two games in the series follow Chell, a silent protagonist who is put through a series of puzzle-solving experiments in the Aperture Science's underground laboratories. In the first game, players navigate these experiments while being guided by the voice of GLaDOS, who players later discover is a robot. Over the course of the game, GLaDOS goes from a slightly eccentric overseer to a dangerous and dishonest enemy. Her comments become increasingly hostile, and eventually she attempts to kill Chell.

Portal 2 features commentary from the equally eccentric Cave Johnson, who is continually mentioning the harmful side effects of tests after they are performed. For example, "Just a heads-up: That coffee we gave you earlier had fluorescent calcium in it so we can track the neuronal activity in your brain. There's a slight chance the calcium could harden and vitrify your frontal lobe." The games emphasize Chell's lack of autonomy by making her a silent and, according to the game's other characters, unintelligent protagonist. She has no ability to speak in her defense and cannot attempt to persuade GLaDOS to release her from the testing. Chell must simply endure the tests until she can attempt to flee. Other characters' suspicions that Chell is stupid and mute are evidence that they do not value her life and that they have rationalized her instrumental treatment. *Portal* does not present players with any moral dilemmas, and it does not offer much freedom of choice, at least in terms of shaping the game narrative. Players are free to decide how they will navigate each of the game's many puzzle sections, but they must follow a linear course through the game narrative. This is fitting for a human lab rat whose life is carefully scripted by experimental manipulations. To become Chell, players must lose their autonomy.

Although the *Portal* series does not directly pose explicit moral challenges to overcome, the games raise many moral issues as background conditions in the game world, not least of which is that Chell is being subjected to dangerous tests against her will. The game narrative calls attention to the plight of humans and animals who suffer in the name of scientific progress—those who are deprived of their autonomy for a real or illusory greater good. Becoming a test subject who is exposed to constant danger without an escape route underscores the wrongness of denying individual autonomy.[13]

Moral Choice in Multiplayer Games

Single-player games often have more of a social character than is immediately visible. Fans form communities, discuss games in online forums, watch YouTube gameplay footage, and generate new content through modding. Even when play is solitary, the practices surrounding it present opportunities for interacting with others. The group character of gaming is essential to understanding games' moral importance, as interpersonal contact provides venues in which players can comment on the moral themes in games and reflect on their simulated decisions. As I have pointed out and will cover in more detail later, some of the best evidence of players' moral engagement comes from discussions among fans. However, it is also important to recognize the limitations of the group life surrounding single-player games. When interactions and a sense of community are largely extrinsic to a single-player game, players may experience moral decision-making in games as being solitary by avoiding fan communities. The same is not true of multiplayer games, in which decisions can implicate other players directly.

Just as in single-player games, moral problems arising in multiplayer games take place against the backdrop of a game narrative and are facilitated by the game rules. The difference is that in the former case challenges are largely produced by the developers and embedded in the game narrative, while in the latter they may be caused by contact with other players. These exchanges are shaped by the formal rules of the game but nevertheless arise because of decisions made by other players. Actions become more real in the sense that players do not simply interact with the simulation but also act with other people through the simulation. Intentions and consequences can then reach beyond the game world. The types of moral challenges also tend to differ in form. Whereas most of the decisions in single-player games are simulated high-stakes matters of life and death, the interactions in multiplayer games are more likely to involve interpersonal contact that includes verbal abuse and symbolic displays of disrespect. In more extreme cases, the interactions might lead to the theft of virtual property or the destruction of avatars.

Multiplayer game worlds provide structures in which moral challenges arise, helping to determine what challenges are possible and how they may be resolved. For example, virtual theft can only exist when players have property and when they have an ability to steal. Multiplayer games may be built to preclude theft by not permitting players to accumulate property, restricting the transference of goods, or punishing players who are caught stealing. There is a vast difference between what significance these actions have based not only on the rules of the game but also on the tacit rules that develop between players. Stealing may be technically permitted while still being shunned by players. Camping in multiplayer shooters (hiding in one place to ambush more daring competitors) is a prime example of a practice that games allow but that is widely reviled and considered to be a breach of etiquette because it slows the pace of combat and feels unfair. Multiplayer games therefore have an agenda-setting role that is exercised by preventing specific types of relationships and allowing others, but players can develop their own rules that further structure the moral considerations at work. Thus, formal rules encoded into the game exist alongside social rules generated by players; the former act like physical laws that cannot be altered, while the latter are akin to the group norms that regulate behavior in ordinary life.

The norms that develop between players but that are not inscribed in the game itself depend on a collective understanding of what the rules are. They are produced and sustained by the players and contribute to the construction of the world by giving it a social context in addition to the formal context established by the rules that work through the game itself. Much of the misconduct in multiplayer games consists in players obeying formal rules but abusing the social rules by going beyond what others have consented to. They may exploit the possibilities of the space to take unexpected predatory actions against other players. In this way, they may act unethically toward other players, taking advantage of trust and degrading the collective norms. This is not a serious moral breach, especially when it does not inflict physical harm, but it is nevertheless real. After all, the stakes of multiplayer games can be high, with people investing considerable time and money that may be lost when some players act wrongly.[14]

The rules of the game world help to structure the moral interactions between players and are the enabling conditions that determine what types of moral issues may arise through interactions. Games that permit players to kill each other raise the possibility of virtual murder. Those that allow players to have property and to transfer that property to others create the possibility of virtual theft. At the same time, games that prevent players from fighting, that do not allow players to have property, or restrict the transference of goods may ensure that these kinds of misconduct are not reproduced in the game world. Every multiplayer game must rely on interpersonal communication, which brings with it a host of challenges related to verbal abuse and intimidation that may or may not be policed by content filters. Moreover, the greater the scope of freedom in a formal sense, the more opportunities exist for players to mistreat each other by refusing to abide by social conventions.

At first glance, it might seem reasonable to think that aggressive actions taken against human-controlled avatars are more morally significant than those taken against computer-controlled avatars. It might seem like there is a difference between the virtual killing of an avatar controlled by a human player and one controlled by a computer. The former is a proxy for an autonomous person who is a moral agent capable of taking on rights and responsibilities; the latter exists only as lines of code. Throughout the book, I have argued that the lack of agency behind computer-controlled avatars is what exempts them from moral consideration—avatars are not real and therefore not worthy of being granted the same respect owed to persons. When it comes to multiplayer games, the people behind the avatars are moral agents and deserve respect as such.

Mediation complicates interactions with other people somewhat by transforming the structure of interpersonal communication. This is true of all types of mediation, such as telephones and email, and is not unique to games. Interactions in multiplayer games are usually facilitated by digital avatars. This change in form is significant, as some of the rights and responsibilities that are attached to our bodies become transformed or fail to apply when we extend ourselves through a nonphysical medium. One of the most basic human rights is the right to life, which is the right to not be harmed by other people.[15] This right creates an obligation for all other moral actors to respect our physical integrity and not act in ways that harm or endanger us. Many other rights derive from this. For example, when a person's life is threatened, we generally recognize that person to have a right to self-defense against the aggressor. The right to life and the ability to act in self-defense are among the most basic and important components of rights theory, which underlies many of our moral norms as well as domestic and international laws. However, we often attempt to escape from this right when we play videogames. Players willfully take part in games that expose their avatars to the risk of being injured or killed. Players simulate actions that would be outside the scope of ordinary morality and, in multiplayer games, do so as part of a collective activity in which they attack and are attacked by other people with the same rights and responsibilities as themselves.

Players join multiplayer battles or log into virtual worlds with the goal of participating in a collective simulation. They consent to enter worlds where certain kinds of simulated immoral actions are possible and could adversely affect them. In *World of Warcraft*, players must accept that others can attack and kill their avatars during quests. In multiplayer shooter games, players join in the collective activity for the sole purpose of being involved in a simulation of reciprocal killing with other players. This element of consent means that even in the most heated matches—even those instances where players lose virtual property and virtual lives—the game is more akin to a boxing match than it is to a street fight. It remains a consensual and strictly rule-governed activity. This gives multiplayer games distinctive ethical codes and helps to build a community ethos. Indeed, player communities are built out of the simulation of hostile interactions. Regulated competition can provide the foundations for a sense of group loyalty, and this in turn can foster trust relationships and a sense of ownership over the social rules that players follow. Simulated acts of violence and abuse between players are therefore morally permissible so long as there is consent.

Verbal abuse and disrespect in multiplayer games is troubling because it can slip beyond the boundaries of what players reasonably consent to when they buy a game. Such attacks are directed not at the avatars but instead at the players who control them. They are personal attacks that extend beyond the game. They may be an accepted hazard that players recognize when participating in games but in most cases are not consented to in the same sense as activities that are formally permitted by gameplay rules. We play games like *CounterStrike* and *Overwatch* to kill other players' characters and to be killed in turn. This is the entire point of the games. Insults and abuse from other players may be common but in most cases are not the reason for playing. Thus, when it comes to multiplayer games, the most important moral consideration is whether the simulated immoral conduct is consented to by the players and consistent with formal rules and social norms. Issues of violence, which are my focus, are rarely problematic, because players consent to this as a foreseeable component of gameplay.

Conclusion

An entire book could be written about the various ways of structuring moral challenges in games and the associated costs and benefits of each approach. This chapter's overview of the subject is only meant to illustrate the range of strategies that games have taken and how these address different dimensions of moral decision-making. As models of moral decisions, videogames can never perfectly approximate the real world; they must simplify morality and balance it against gameplay imperatives. This leaves endless opportunities for variation in how models are built and what role morality has. Moreover, I have argued that game worlds provide their own overarching moral themes, which are embedded in game narratives, often with help from well-crafted ludic elements that advance those narratives. When evaluating any particular game, it is essential to address both the decisions that players are directly involved in and the broader moral issues posed. Because of the comparatively limited narrative depth of multiplayer games, they generally lack the explicit moral choices of single-player games. Nevertheless, they provide a valuable platform in which players interact with each other and form group associations based on shared norms that are formally and informally enacted. These various types of moral challenges demonstrate a clear and consistent tendency for games with narrative elements to take on important issues. I would encourage anyone who remains in doubt of the impact these scenarios and others like them have on players to take a look at online message boards where players analyze these decisions in far more detail than I have been able to here. Even maligned quests such as Power of the Atom are the subject of lengthy and thoughtful discussions that reveal efforts to apply moral judgment.[16]

The moral challenges that arise in games underscore the functional similarity with thought experiments, or rather show that thought experiments continually arise within games. It is worth emphasizing that the decision to be good or evil is irrelevant for the purposes of learning, because the decisions have no immediate real moral value. What matters is the opportunity to work through the problem and reflect on the underlying issue. Videogames present counterfactuals in which players can engage in cost-free experimentation with different courses of action. This allows them to explore moral questions without ever acting immorally. Far from being murder simulators or sources of moral corruption, as critics would have it, videogames perform admirably in this work of moral simulation. Some games execute moral elements poorly, and some may disregard them entirely. Games certainly have no obligation to be morally sophisticated and should not be judged primarily on their merits as pedagogical tools, yet the trend over the past three decades has been for games to become increasingly effective in this respect. From *BioShock* to *Papers, Please*, *Life Is Strange* to *Red Dead Redemption*, it is evident that morally sophisticated games are often commercially and/or critically successful. There is a demand for games that encourage players to think.

6

Persuasive Games and
Ideological Manipulation

Critiques of videogames have expanded beyond the concerns over their cognitive impact on players that I discussed in chapter 2 to how they connect to broader political and social concerns. Here the focus is more on harmful ideologies and the unhealthy policy attitudes that games may cultivate than on the impact games may have on criminal misconduct or empathy. Nevertheless, these broader critiques share much in common with the psychological concerns I covered previously. The political and sociological critiques often encompass the psychological critiques and assume that those are generally accurate. Many of the same worries raised about videogames' influence on players become the basis for arguments about how gaming influences entire populations. The scope of the problem shifts from being about how videogames promote aggression among individuals to how they make entire populations more comfortable with war or from how they train individuals to carry out school shootings to how they prepare entire populations for violence. The underlying mechanisms for thinking that games are problematic therefore remain largely the same but appear at a different level of analysis, as collective rather than individual problems.

The affinities between psychological and political objections to videogames reveal the importance of gaining greater clarity about games' moral implications. They show that gaming is not just a matter of personal choice and that moral decisions cannot be confined to the home. Individuals' entertainment choices may have far-reaching effects that could prompt a collective responsibility over what content is considered permissible. Nowhere is this clearer than in the debate over military videogames, and *America's Army* in particular. Military first-person shooters have attracted widespread condemnation for promoting war and increasing popular support for militaristic policies. *America's Army* stands out as being especially controversial because it was developed by the U.S. Army and triggered fears about a new, more potent form of propaganda. Just as psychological critiques view gaming as being uniquely harmful because of its interactivity, political critiques have charged videogames with transforming gamers into willing participants in American empire.

I spend the first part of this chapter exploring some of the problematic assumptions that have arisen in writings on military videogames, using these as a case study for moral concerns related to persuasive games more generally. Critics are right to be skeptical about the messages games present, but they tend to make two errors. First, they often treat persuasive games as being deliberately deceptive when in fact most reflect an effort to convince players of a perspective that the developers appear to genuinely believe. There is an important difference of intent between an effort to deceive and an effort to convince. This does not mean that the game messages are correct, but it does mean that disagreements over game content have more to do with differences of opinion and divergent values than with an immoral attempt to dissimulate. Second, critics often suggest that it is possible to unmask the ideologies embedded in games by adopting a neutral perspective or with the help of games that present opposing viewpoints. I argue that videogames are inherently biased because decisions about how to model the world necessarily simplify real events and processes in ways that reflect assumptions about what information is important and what underlying logic governs those real events and processes. We should think of military videogames and other persuasive games not as mere propaganda but as arguments posed through counterfactuals. These arguments express different ideological orientations and conceptions of events that can broaden our understanding by allowing us to see the world from different vantage points.

My goal in looking at persuasive games, and military games in particular, is to show that there is room for reasonable critique of the content of games without giving in to moral panic that either overstates the extent to which game developers are attempting to manipulate players or assumes that players are passive dupes. It is even possible to enjoy playing these games while disagreeing with the arguments they make. I hope to chart a middle path for analyzing these games— one that can show why they have some value when it comes to exposing us to different perspectives and that being open to these perspectives does not sacrifice opportunities to critique games or their ideological underpinnings. According to my analysis, attempts to persuade by using videogames are not morally problematic, so long as they are not *deliberately* misleading. That is, persuasive games that embody a good-faith effort to make reasonable and factually supported claims are justifiable. However, the models are still open to critique by looking at how extensively the narratives and rules of the simulations diverge from those they attempt to model and by examining contradictions within the assumptions embedded in games. Arguments that are empirically and logically flawed can be challenged on those grounds without dismissing persuasive games out of hand. The right response to these games is to adopt a critical standpoint when playing (something that games often encourage players to do) and to develop pluralistic tastes that encompass games taking different perspectives.

The Military Entertainment Complex

Military videogames are a particularly challenging subset of violent games when it comes to theorizing moral and political implications. They not only allow players to participate in the simulated violence that is widely condemned but may also teach tactical skills and encourage players to identify with real armed forces. These include the familiar characteristics of violent videogames—the blood and gore, the virtual weaponry, the permissive attitude about killing—while also situating them in a context where the killing is justified in the interests of national security and subordinated to reasons of state. This elevates violence beyond the purposeless killing of games such as *Postal* and *Saints Row*, as well as the criminal violence of games such as *Grand Theft Auto* and *Mafia*, celebrating it as heroic and necessary violence that helps to preserve international security. Moreover, when military videogames come from armed forces themselves, as in the case of *America's Army*, then there is arguably an organization working to impart violent attitudes and skills to players. This might be expected to increase games' capacities for moral corruption.

There are also concerns related to the production processes that give rise to military videogames. First, some games from civilian developers are produced with extensive help from military advisers. This assistance may be contingent on presenting the military in a positive light, or it could encourage self-censorship on the part of developers. For example, the creators of *Medal of Honor* enlisted help from special operations veterans, which may partly account for the game's overt celebration of American martial valor.[1] Second, there is concern over armed forces becoming directly involved in the production of videogames, either as customers remaking commercial videogames for internal use or as producers of videogames that are designed as strategic communications tools directed at nonmilitary audiences. The U.S. armed forces have a long history of appropriating games such as *Doom* to create military variants,[2] contracting their own version of *Full Spectrum Warrior* for training purposes, and even developing their own recruitment and training simulations.

Military videogames have inspired a subset of videogame critique that is specifically devoted to showing how games function as a new, more potent form of propaganda. In a comment that captures the general tone of this research, Aaron Delwiche says that "video-games have the potential to shape attitudes and behavior in ways that Goebbels could never have dreamed."[3] Marcus Power likewise asserts that "digital war games put a friendly, hospitable face on the military, manufacturing consent and complicity among consumers for military programmes, missions and weapons."[4] The claims made in this research parallel the four arguments I discussed in chapter 2, as they accuse games of training players for war, promoting militarism (the aggression argument projected onto the national level), desensitizing audiences to the costs of war, and making violence feel less real.

Concerns over the morality of videogames and their political importance become especially serious when games closely mirror real attacks and do so along geopolitical fault lines. Here, the controversy surrounding No Russian is revealing. On January 24, 2011, Moscow's Domodedovo International Airport was struck by a suicide bomb. The attackers were part of the Caucasus Emirate, an Islamist organization attempting to create an autonomous region in the Caucasus. The bomb killed 37 people and injured 173 in the baggage claim area. *Russia Today*, a state-run news station program, linked the attack to *Modern Warfare 2*. Reporters juxtaposed real videos of the attack with scenes from the videogame to evoke a sense that these are merely two different versions of the same event and that they must therefore be understood in conjunction. One report emphasized that it is a "popular American videogame sold worldwide" and thereafter continually pointed out that the game could be traced back to the United States. The message in this framing is that U.S. media companies were responsible for inciting violence against Russia by scripting the attack. The report substantiates this characterization with comments from Walid Phares, who is introduced as a "global terrorism expert," about how terrorists can use videogames as training simulators. Other experts affirm this argument, though no alternative viewpoint is shown.[5]

Of course, this evaluation of *Modern Warfare 2* misses the broader political context of the attack—that terrorists from the Caucasus had been bombing targets in Russia for over a decade, that Russia's harsh treatment of the people in that region has done far more to incite violence than any videogame ever could, and that dozens of previous attacks had been launched without any resemblance to videogames. There was certainly nothing new about terrorists attacking airports. Just as with school shootings, videogames offered a convenient explanation for the attack that shifted the burden of guilt away from political and military elites. It was especially egregious to conflate the game with a more general American effort to undermine Russian security—an intimation more dangerous than any videogame.

Although military videogames, and especially military first-person shooters, are generally controversial, *America's Army* stands out as being the dominant target. It was first released in 2002 and has been continually updated since then to become an entire franchise that now includes four computer games, dozens of expansion packs, games for other platforms, virtual-reality experiences, and comic books. As of 2015, around 14 million people had played *America's Army*.[6]

Each installment in the series follows a similar pattern of leading players through simulated U.S. Army training programs, then sending them into multiplayer battles as American soldiers. The games are designed so players on both sides of a match see themselves in American uniforms, while adversaries consistently appear as insurgents. Robertson Allen argues that the franchise asserts that the Army is always a force for good, as it is impossible for players to envisage themselves as anything other than American soldiers.[7]

Power echoes Grossman, Funk, and others who profess videogames' ability to desensitize players when he says that the games "may suppress an aversion to killing."[8] Peter Mantello extrapolates concerns about videogames promoting aggression onto the state level by arguing that *America's Army* is an attempt "to advance an aggressive, neo-orientalist frontier logic that sees the horizons of globalization, the fringes of Western power, as a gamer-type utopia."[9] He also says that "*America's Army* is the most spectacular example of the militarisation of videogames and of this reprogramming of the citizen as a participant in Netwar." Mark Salter contends that "war games represent a militaristic, masculinist, Western geopolitical frame of violence." Dozens of other studies have reached conclusions similar to these.[10]

The U.S. military is not alone in using videogames for strategic communication. The infamous private military contractor Blackwater licensed an eponymous videogame in which players could pretend to be members of the organization participating in a humanitarian intervention. Hezbollah produced the games *Special Force* and *Special Force 2*, which re-create the fighting in Lebanon in 2000 and 2006, respectively. Sustained interest in gaming by the U.S. Army, combined with the forays into gaming by contractors and violent nonstate actors, indicates that violent organizations see the medium as being a promising way of cultivating a sympathetic audience and propagating their own narratives of recent conflicts.

Modifications of existing games and subversive play styles are another approach that violent nonstate actors can take to promote themselves. According to reporters from the U.S. Army, members of the Taliban are suspected of playing *America's Army* as a way of gaining information about U.S. tactics.[11] The Islamic State has likewise explored videogame messaging, using *Grand Theft Auto* to create a montage of simulated attacks against American cities.[12] Here they take advantage of the game not only to produce violent imagery but also to cue sympathetic players to interpret the game as a terrorism simulator, just as so many of the game's critics have seen it.

Anxiety about Influence

Armed forces have a long history of using popular culture for strategic communication across all available media.[13] This was evident long before videogames, in films and television shows produced with military assistance, and armed forces continue to search for new communication outlets on social media platforms. Videogames are not special when it comes to their potential use by armed forces and may actually be in a stronger position to resist this influence. Civilian film and television producers routinely seek military assistance because they need expensive military equipment that must be borrowed. The usual exchange is to sacrifice some editorial control to obtain use of military hardware, which ends up with media that are overtly pro-military or that at least refrain from casting their sponsoring armed forces in a negative light.[14] Filmmakers who refuse to yield editorial control must either pay for expensive equipment themselves or do without it.[15]

Civilian developers in the military gaming market have an advantage over companies producing other types of media. They are under no similar demands for borrowing military hardware, as they can simply model it digitally. The medium makes it easier to engage with military themes and show the appropriate equipment without the demands of seeking assistance that may give military institutions leverage over civilian producers. The prospect of modding existing games or developing relatively simple games for mobile platforms also lowers the entry cost of using games to present persuasive messages that circumvent elite control. This could explain why the *Modern Warfare* series has cast American officers and military contractors as villains—and in a few instances made it possible to fight against them—while most Hollywood films that rely heavily on U.S. military assistance lack American villains.

Media producers also seek advice on military affairs to create a sense of realism. They need to rigorously model the language, tactics, and dress to create a sense of authenticity. This is a demand that applies to videogames just as much as other media. Videogames have made extensive use of military technical assistance, but it is not always as clearly in the service of military interests as it may appear to be. Soldiers working on *Medal of Honor* actually did so without permission from the military and were reprimanded.[16] They were cooperating with an entertainment company as soldiers but not doing so with a military strategic communication mission in mind. Other advisers may be retired and not acting as agents of a military organization. Thus, even in instances when civil-military collaboration exists, it does not always reflect official policy decisions. It is essential to take a nuanced view of civil-military collaboration and to note that the many different motives at work create a more complex picture than one of armed forces controlling content in the kind of consistent and straightforward way described by critics who decry videogames for serving as propaganda.

None of this contextualizing should exempt military videogames from critique. My point is only that videogames from civilian developers may be more immune to pernicious influences than other entertainment media. Of course, this is irrelevant when games are created by armed forces themselves or are in fact heavily influenced by them, which can more plausibly have harmful effects because of the creators' clear interest in promoting military service. When it comes to these games, Sparrow et al. argue that there is a contradiction between the gaming industry and many players arguing that videogames do not have any adverse effects while the military attempts to use videogames for training purposes with help from civilian game developers. These authors are especially critical of what they see as a contradictory tendency on the part of developers to defend themselves against charges of promoting violence while actively cultivating links with the military. They contend that "either military organizations are wrong to think that digital games have the training power they assert they do, or some digital games do, in fact, have the power to influence the real-world behavior and dispositions of players in morally significant ways."[17] Despite claiming to be agnostic about which of these claims is accurate, the authors take a fairly clear stance in this debate by saying that "it is likely that in training skills digital games are also shaping moral dispositions."[18] Furthermore, they attempt to dispel three prominent arguments that purport to show why violent videogames are not harmful.

It is worth considering the article by Sparrow et al. in detail, as they show one of the most plausible recent efforts to rehabilitate the arguments about the adverse psychological consequences of gaming as well as an attempt to link this material explicitly to concerns about military videogames. The authors start by evaluating the defense that military videogames may influence soldiers while not influencing other players because these two audiences have different intentions when playing games. Soldiers play with the goal of learning military skills, while recreational players simply seek enjoyment. Sparrow et al. consider this the least convincing defense of military games. They reason that recreational players may fantasize about becoming real soldiers and attempt to acquire the requisite skills. Moreover, they say that "an explicit desire to learn real-world skills or dispositions need not prevent such learning from taking place."[19] Fighting skills and value changes may therefore come inadvertently, regardless of the player's intentions.

Another defense Sparrow et al. reject is that there is a meaningful difference between military and civilian gaming technologies. The difference between the two may be in the kinds of experiences military and civilian games provide or in the divergent levels of realism. The authors acknowledge that military simulations create more embodied experiences by accurately re-creating vehicle controls, yet they say that civilian games are able to do the same thing with motion controls like the Wii Remote and Microsoft Kinect or virtual-reality technologies like Oculus Rift. They also point out that some military control systems, such as those for tactical drones, are modeled on videogame console controls. Additionally, they say that it is not the skills themselves that matter but rather the "goals and motivations" that players learn by practicing these skills.

This leads Sparrow et al. to consider the defense that games do not alter players' beliefs and values. Here they point out that other media, such as books and films, can alter people's beliefs. They argue that the Bible and Koran have clearly influenced audiences, and that it would be strange to think that videogames lack a similar power to affect players. The argument that games are influential rests heavily on readers intuitively accepting the influence of these other media. The authors' effort to link adverse psychological effects of gaming to the military's use of games brings out some of the comparisons between training for war and desensitization that I discussed in chapter 2 while also linking them more clearly to claims about military videogames promoting militarism and causing disengagement from war. However, the effort to join these two bodies of research leaves their respective limitations intact.

To start, the argument about gaming technology reiterates the familiar fear that videogames make it possible to enact violence in such a way that killing skills may be learned. Sparrow et al. are right in thinking that motion controls and virtual reality can help to make games look more like the simulations used for training soldiers. However, as I discussed in chapter 2, the comparison between military simulations involving real weaponry and commercial videogames involving Wii or Kinect motion controls vastly overestimates the similarity between them. Sparrow et al. are right in saying that videogame controls sometimes resemble the controls used for military equipment, but the same resemblance between military and civilian technologies exists in the case of computers, tablets, and smartphones. Missile systems are guided using computer interfaces, tablets can help to coordinate attacks, and small reconnaissance drones can be operated with smartphones. The critique is therefore both too broad, in the sense that it mistakenly associates Kinect motion controls with real weapons training, and too narrow, in the sense that it focuses solely on a limited range of technologies among the vast array of devices that have military and civilian variants.

Equally important is that there is nothing inherently wrong with learning the skills in question. Anything players learn about controlling tanks and fighter jets would be relatively useless to them outside the military. Even a perfectly realistic tank simulator cannot assist in readying a player for an attack if no real tank is available for use. Sparrow et al. say that simulations also teach things like how to drive trucks and how to shoot rifles; the former is a desirable skill that would be wonderful for players to improve. Claims about improved shooting are dubious for the reasons that I discussed in chapter 2. Moreover, teaching players to shoot is also not itself immoral. In most countries, the lack of access to guns means that these skills cannot be used in everyday life, and in countries where guns are permitted, they doubtless provide far more opportunities for realistic training than videogames. The same strange reasoning that I pointed out in chapter 2 crops up again here—the fear of simulated gun practice when real guns are infinitely more problematic.

The weight of the argument made by Sparrow et al. is on the supposition that simulating military skills in a videogame will alter players' beliefs and values. The authors think that the realistic rifle training and tank simulations will make players think differently about wars, even if they are never personally involved in one. The risk here is a societal shift in attitudes about war that could have dangerous consequences. For the most part, Sparrow et al. direct this point against a straw man. They conflate arguments that games do not train players to kill or promote aggression with claims that videogames have no effect on players whatsoever. They claim that it is patently false to say that videogames have no effect on players (which is true) but then move from this premise to the conclusion that games must have the power to cause serious changes in the propensity to use violence (which is dubious and does not follow from the first point). Chris Ferguson comes off particularly badly. Sparrow et al. mischaracterize his work dispelling myths about videogames spreading aggression as an attempt to show that the content of games has no influence of any kind, which is a claim that Ferguson has not advanced.

I readily concede that videogames can influence players' perceptions and values, just as other media are able to, but this is not analogous to the claims that critics of videogames make. Critics say that games cause antisocial behavior, including school shootings, which goes far beyond simply suggesting that they have some influence on players' perceptions and beliefs. Critics accuse games of causing violence in the same way that Goethe's *The Sorrows of Young Werther* was accused of promoting suicide[20] or Salinger's *The Catcher in the Rye* was accused of inspiring serial killers.[21] Those books were doubtless extremely influential, but the danger they present is so low that we do not think twice about making them required reading in schools. It is entirely possible for media of any kind to influence audiences in modest ways, but it does not follow from this that media can transform people into murderers. Just as links between those classic works of literature and real acts of violence have been debunked without downplaying the works' power to move audiences in more subtle ways, we can (and should) reject strong claims about the adverse effects of gaming while still accepting that subtle influence is possible.

Above all, what I (and, I suspect, most others who are skeptical about videogames' corrupting influence) take issue with is the idea that videogames' influence operates through the contamination model that is assumed by so many commentators attempting to show that videogames promote immoral behavior. Contrary to Sparrow et al., it is perfectly reasonable to accept that videogames can persuade and influence in subtle ways without thinking that mere contact with them is enough to radically transform players. In fact, this position fits much better with existing psychological research. Models of cognition show that people are influenced by new information and experiences but that they organize it in terms of existing beliefs and values. The result is path dependency, with new information usually being molded by existing biases. Research has likewise shown that it is extremely difficult to convince someone to change their values even if there is some evidence that they should.[22] Ideas do not spread upon contact but rather come into conflict with each other and must filter through perspectival biases.[23] This should be intuitively clear, as it explains why a single text can give rise to radically different interpretations. To put it simply, we play games through the lens of existing biases and are more inclined to read games in terms of those biases than we are to reorient our entire worldview.

Critics of *America's Army* routinely cite statistics showing that many new recruits have played the game, but this proves little because anyone who is contemplating a career in the Army will likely be drawn to the game. Those who experience a rush of militant fervor when playing *America's Army* and other military videogames likely already have a strong inclination toward this outlook. In other words, we should expect that people who are attracted to military service and who may one day join will enjoy fantasizing about combat before entering the ranks. The game may help to convince these people to join or to develop stronger pro-military feelings, but more through confirming their existing beliefs about the benefits of military service than by substantively changing attitudes.

The real test of the game's impact would be evidence that players with strong antimilitary sentiments rethink these after playing, and so far the voluminous literature on *America's Army* has failed to uncover anything of the sort. There is good reason to think that critics of U.S. military operations can play the game with their values intact. Joseph DeLappe famously protested the Iraq War by posting the names of dead American soldiers in the *America's Army* team chat. Playing did not change DeLappe's convictions as the pro-Army content he experienced came up against his entrenched antiwar values. We do not know how *America's Army* influenced members of the Taliban who played it, but I doubt that it filled them with a newfound love of the U.S. military. The Taliban fighters were probably slightly influenced by the game. They may have learned more about American weapons and tactics as well as the Army's strategic communications message. However, learning new information does not automatically translate into the kind of sweeping transformation that critics of videogames imagine taking place. Information does not instantly contaminate.

Crediting games with having some kind of hegemonic influence overstates their power while also underestimating the extent of polysemy. As Felix Ciută points out, the same videogames attract complaints from those on all sides of the political spectrum. Some of those that are most often charged with promoting militarism and American empire "have come under attack from the political establishment for being insufficiently regimented to the nationalist/ideological mainstream."[24] *Medal of Honor*, which incorporates strong pro-American and pro-military messages, incited controversy for allowing players to take the role of Taliban fighters. *Call of Duty: Modern Warfare* includes strong pro-American and pro-military messages, but it also allows players to participate in a terrorist attack, features an American general as the villain, and includes several missions fighting against the U.S. military. These and other military shooters do not straightforwardly or consistently support a particular ideology. They are complex texts open to an array of meanings, which means that they will lack a clear and consistent influence on players and that interpretations of what the games mean will depend heavily on players' existing beliefs.

Just as the data about violent crime has shown a sharp drop as the popularity of videogames has gone up, enthusiasm for war appears to be dropping in the era of military videogames. Virtually all major studies of American public opinion toward the use of force show the population becoming more averse to war except in cases of self-defense.[25] There is likewise evidence of the American public becoming more sensitive to foreign civilian casualties,[26] which suggests a heightening of moral appraisals rather than the diminution critics predict. Public opinion about war is a complex issue that is beyond the scope of this book, yet just as with the crime statistics, it provides prima facie grounds for thinking that the moral panic about videogames is misguided.

In most cases, it takes quite radical and disruptive experiences to make us reconsider existing biases. The more deeply held the beliefs, the more of a shock is needed. Terrorist attacks and major natural disasters are the kinds of experiences that social scientists have linked to major attitudinal changes.[27] There is no evidence that videogames have this kind of jarring impact, especially on adults, whose cognitive biases are firmly entrenched. There certainly are experiences that could transform a person into a killer—the loss of family members, the outbreak of war, childhood abuse—but it is doubtful that videogames could have this dramatic effect. The influence of playing videogames is likely to be comparable to the influence of other forms of media consumption, which is to say that they will have subtle effects that are mediated by existing beliefs and values.

Ideology Is Inevitable

Critiques of military videogames do have some merit. They raise reasonable concerns about how videogames present information and how they engage in political advocacy. In particular, while there is little evidence that videogames have an appreciable effect on attitudes toward war or on aptitude for fighting, it is nevertheless clear that some developers wish to celebrate military service and attempt to attract recruits. The developers of *America's Army* have a clear intent to advance the interests of the U.S. Army, which they never shy away from stating. Nevertheless, critique needs to be reframed to avoid drawing on the dubious conclusions of research about the cognitive impact of violent videogames or perpetuating a moral panic. It is more useful to focus on the institutional goals and on the content of the games to determine whether these are morally problematic. To chart this more productive line of inquiry when it comes to military videogames, as well as other games with persuasive intent, it helps to return to the example of thought experiments. Counterfactuals are not neutral. They are created with theoretical goals in mind. Whether intentional or not, those goals are reflected in how the imagined scenarios are structured and the kinds of solutions they favor. As Philip Tetlock and Aaron Belkin point out, "From a broadly psychological perspective, it is difficult to imagine avoiding serious bias in thought experiments. Bias can creep into every stage of this inherently subjective process."[28] This is unavoidable in any model of the real world, as choices about what information to include and what to omit, how to frame the stories, and what costs and benefits to describe inevitably shift moral calculations.

The effect of bias is clear from the many iterations of the Trolley Problem that have been developed. The Trolley Problem is often used as an argument for utilitarianism, as though it were clear evidence in favor of privileging the interests of the majority. However, opponents of utilitarianism have altered the parameters of the scenario to promote different conclusions. Judith Jarvis Thomson exposes a serious contradiction between utilitarian reasoning and our moral intuitions by imagining a hospital in which five patients are awaiting organ transplants. Each needs a different organ and will die if a replacement is not found immediately. A relatively healthy person then arrives in the hospital for a routine checkup. The question is whether the surgeon should kill the healthy person to save the five who need organ transplants. Here the inclination to sacrifice one life for the sake of five seems less compelling, to the extent that this scenario or variations of it are often used as evidence against utilitarianism. Nevertheless, the fundamental question remains largely unaltered. It is a choice between one life and five, just as in the Trolley Problem, but reconfiguring the thought experiment introduces new considerations that make the utilitarian perspective seem less compelling.

Just as different ways of formulating moral hypotheticals reflect different moral orientations and attempts to promote a particular perspective over others, persuasive videogames reflect attempts to build models that promote a particular way of seeing the world. Persuasive games even perform the functions of philosophical thought experiments I identified in chapter 3. They attempt to explain, support, critique, and offer guidance. *America's Army* does each of these quite clearly. It explains the U.S. Army's institutions and values. It supports the Army's mission by conveying that information. Its critical intent is evident from the game's insurgent enemies, who signal that the Army sees its primary enemies as violent nonstate actors. Finally, it tries to guide players toward military service or at least toward a more favorable view of the U.S. Army.

Philosophers tend to work with fairly abstract and arcane theoretical details that can make their counterfactuals feel far removed from the real world, yet the narrative models they construct are significant. For one thing, the issues at stake are typically central to urgent political disagreements, covering topics such as euthanasia, abortion, or killing in self-defense. Attempting to substantiate or reject moral arguments relating to these issues is therefore not a theoretical exercise divorced from reality but a political intervention that may have a real impact on public discourse. Compelling thought experiments can have a profound influence over the course of political debates, perhaps even steering the attitudes of policymakers and the general public. The use of the ticking bomb scenario to advocate for torturing suspected terrorists is a prime example of this. The typical scenario is that a terrorist who planted a nuclear weapon inside a crowded city is caught and refuses to reveal the location of the bomb. With only an hour left until the bomb explodes, interrogators must decide whether to torture the terrorist to reveal the bomb's location or forgo torture and allow the bomb to detonate. The welfare of a terrorist and prohibition against torture must be weighed against the safety of thousands or even millions of innocent people. This thought experiment derives much of its value as a persuasive tool in favor of using torture from the level of violence imagined. With no physical constraints on the counterfactual space, the number of victims can rise into the millions to find a point at which not torturing becomes reckless and disproportionate.[29] How convincing the scenario is as an argument for torture depends heavily on how the counterfactual is constructed and how high the costs become. Torture is doubtless more convincing when ten million potential victims are at risk and there is certainty about who placed the bomb than when there is a single potential victim and multiple plausible suspects. This has led to extensive debate over whether this counterfactual is fair to use in support for torture when the enormous costs of not torturing and the certainty about having the right suspect are unrealistic.

Thought experiments like the Trolley Problem or the ticking bomb are not simply right or wrong in a moral sense. They are fictions that do not actually cause the harms they consider. They function as tacit arguments and often have a great deal of value in political advocacy. The ticking bomb thought experiment has been a fixture of the debate over torture, appearing in entertainment media, political speeches, news commentary, and academic research.[30] The debate over whether torture is justified is to a large extent played out over this scenario. Disagreement over the moral issue of torture therefore slips into disagreement over how we should imagine torture working when we consider its costs abstractly. The same possibility arises in persuasive games—the possibility of imaginative models being unfair in some sense because of the distortions introduced.

In critiques of military videogames, there is a tendency to suggest that they are propaganda in the simplistic sense of being deliberate distortions that are intended to mislead. This follows in the Marxist tradition of ideological critique, in which ideologies are understood as false images that obscure reality and that must be unmasked to reveal an underlying truth. The Marxist approach makes two critical errors that have been imported into the research on persuasive games. The first is the assumption that ideologies are mere distortions and that those who produce persuasive media are therefore guilty of attempting to mislead audiences. This is a dubious premise. For one thing, efforts to persuade are often overt. *America's Army* is explicit about its persuasive intent. One game manual states that "it is part of the Army's communications strategy designed to leverage the power of the Internet as a portal through which young adults can get a firsthand look at what it is like to be a Soldier."[31] The pervasive pro-Army rhetoric and imagery leave little doubt about this stance. From the second they turn on the game, players are immersed in a simulation that is overtly linked to the U.S. military's efforts to attract recruits and provide civilians with a positive impression of military service. For those who have made a career out of military service, this probably seems like an honest and worthwhile goal—not an attempt to mislead. It would be fair to argue that this goal is misguided, poorly executed, or wrong to convey through a videogame. It is probably also true that those who attempt to persuade knowingly engage in small distortions along the way. However, it is a mistake to treat political expressions as being simply dishonest without evidence of an intent to mislead. Critique of persuasive games must be able to accept that ideologically charged messages express genuine beliefs. It should then engage these beliefs based on their own merits rather than simply suggesting that they are dissimulations.

The second error is more serious. This is the assumption that it is possible to reach a nonideological perspective in which all distortions are stripped away. Commentaries on games that present perspectives opposed to *America's Army* and other popular military videogames are often described as though they cut through illusions to get at the underlying facts. *Spec Ops: The Line* is praised for creating a more authentic vision of war, as is *This War of Mine*, which shows the impact of fighting on civilians.[32] However, these games are not necessarily more accurate by virtue of presenting a contrary viewpoint, and we should not assume that any videogame model would be able to express the true nature of war. Games make different arguments about what war is like and what the costs are, encouraging us to take a different perspective than the one we tend to experience in mainstream war games. These perspectives may be more convincing, for reasons that I will address in the next section, but they are still ideologically charged in the sense that they do not reflect a purely neutral perspective on conflict. They embody choices about what information to include and what to omit—choices about how to build the game world and what assumptions to embed in its algorithms. Lacking any purely neutral model of the world, we should accept that every videogame will carry ideological baggage and avoid arguing that games are problematic simply because they are biased.

Michael Freeden provides a helpful conception of ideologies as "imaginative maps drawing together facts that themselves may be disputed."[33] Ideologies are complex assemblages of beliefs that inform our perceptions and help to orient us. They are essential for making sense of political reality. Major political disputes often come down to irreconcilable differences between competing maps—disputes that cannot be resolved by simply unmasking one side or the other and in which there is no perfectly neutral vantage point. It is useful to see disagreements as perspectival disputes. As James N. Druckman points out, "Much of politics involves battles over how a campaign, a problem, or an issue should be understood."[34] Those on opposing sides of a political controversy must have some ability to present their viewpoints and advocate for them—an opportunity to present their perspective and its conception of how issues are rightly understood. Videogames are an ideal tool in this sense because they enact a perspective shift. They go beyond narrative thought experiments by making inhabitable worlds in which players can explore another viewpoint in detail. They make the figurative ideological maps into literal maps that structure persuasive games. Assumptions about how the world works and what values are correct dictate the ludic and narrative structure of games. The resulting simulations are never neutral; they present different arguments and attempt to make them attractive in much the same way as in other types of political disagreement. The arguments can be evaluated for empirical accuracy (via what I will later call external critique) and logical consistency (via internal critique) but should not be prejudged simply because we dislike the source of the arguments or differ on matters of opinion.

The Value of Persuasive Communication

Although they are particularly controversial, military videogames are only one genre among many persuasive games that convey information about current events and that may help to shape players' knowledge of and opinions about controversial issues. Ian Bogost, Simon Ferrari, and Bobby Schweizer show how videogames can be used as tools for reporting or commenting on current events. They distinguish between three types of news games.[35] Editorial games make arguments about current events. Tabloid games contain soft news stories about celebrities and sports. Reportage games attempt to stand in for regular news reporting by presenting purely factual accounts of events. In each case, videogames provide information about current events, often with persuasive intent. Many of the games in each of these categories fall into the "casual games" category in the sense of incorporating gameplay mechanics that are easy to grasp. Keeping the games fairly simple makes it possible to produce them contemporaneously with the events being re-created, thereby making the information more relevant when it comes to shaping audience perceptions. Simple gameplay mechanics likewise help to reach the broadest possible audience rather than just hardcore gamers. As in thought experiments, simplicity is often helpful for focusing on a central problem and making it memorable. Although the games often purport to give a neutral perspective, they are always inherently biased, because they selectively present information when building models and give players a specific view. These games embody arguments about how the world works and what meaning we should attach to events.

One of Bogost, Ferrari, and Schweizer's examples of an editorial game is *September 12th*, an online flash game that gives players an overhead perspective of a stereotypical Middle Eastern city complete with sandy streets and stucco buildings. Cartoons dressed as civilians and terrorists wander the streets below, moving in haphazard patterns that make them difficult to predict. Players interact with the game using a single gameplay mechanic: they may launch missiles into

154 • Simulating Good and Evil

the city. The ludological structure of the game says a great deal. The dominant narrative following the 9/11 attacks was that a violent response was the only viable option, so the game gives players no choices aside from war. Players quickly find that each missile strike to kill terrorists invariably kills civilians as well. Each time a missile comes down, more of the avatars transform into terrorists, suggesting that they are radicalized by the deaths of friends and neighbors. The game is broadly accessible, simple, and presents a strong argument. It is a perfect digital counterfactual.

Dozens of other editorial games about current events have been produced. It is now common for activists with opposing perspectives on armed conflicts like those in Gaza, Ukraine, and Syria to create simple games that argue for their perspective by enlisting players' assistance on one side or the other. Other games simulate nonviolent political and social issues. For instance, *PeaceMaker* tasks players with resolving the Israel-Palestine dispute, which must be accomplished by developing a two-state solution. Political activists likewise make games to glorify their party or candidate—or to demonize opponents. Other games teach players about humanitarian disasters, piracy, the illegal drug trade, surveillance, and countless other topics.

Although games are uniquely suited for immersing players in events as active participants, the persuasive strategy of convincing audiences through a shift of perspective borrows from a long-standing trend of using media to introduce alternative viewpoints. Writers such as Charles Dickens and Upton Sinclair led readers to see the world from different angles as a method of social critique. Films and television shows have promoted tolerance for marginalized groups by offering a sympathetic glimpse into their lives. There is nothing inherently illegitimate about the use of media to convey persuasive messages in this way. On the contrary, it expands the scope of political engagement by transforming entertainment into a forum for learning more about alternative viewpoints. As with videogames functioning as moral thought experiments, the games that take on political issues create opportunities for exploring divergent perspectives and value systems within a safe space.

Bogost, Ferrari, and Schweizer offer valuable insight into how games are used to present news, and it is a credit to their research that the insights can be extended further. They focus on games that are designed to stand in for various styles of journalistic reporting, but games also proffer information and make arguments about the past and future, as well as making more general claims about how social practices work (for example, in political games set in fictional contexts). Many games attempt to mirror historical events and time periods, and are therefore in just as much a position to shape beliefs about them as news games covering recent events. The intermingling of fact and fiction raises major challenges when it comes to accuracy. Games sacrifice some details to create more engaging stories and for the simple reason that no model can perfectly re-create its source material. Changes made in the interest of fun lead games such as *Battlefield I* to replace ponderous World War I era weaponry such as bolt-action rifles with machine guns and rocket launchers. Such changes are an affront to historical accuracy but tend to be more innocuous than the framing of contentious events. Aaron Hess shows that *Medal of Honor: Rising Sun,* which is set in World War II, emphasizes the wrongness of Japan's attack on Pearl Harbor, then fails to consider American misconduct or the decision to drop atomic bombs. He argues that "the use of narrative memorializing in interactive space creates an experience of public memory, giving video game players an active but private (in the home) role in memory-making."[36] The costs of games that cause misperception about World War I era weaponry are low; the costs of misperception about nuclear warfare are much higher.

Games about the future do not have to contend with issues of factual accuracy, yet they tend to be based on hypothetical futures that we could imagine reaching based on current circumstances. The *Fallout* series is set in a postapocalyptic United States that is generally reasonable given what we know about the dangers of nuclear warfare. *The Homefront, Modern Warfare,* and *Battlefront* series take liberties with political realities but are loosely grounded in real political enmities that could potentially lead to war in the future. In each case, the imagined future tells us something about the world we inhabit and what conflict scenarios seem plausible. As with the controversial military videogames, the key to understanding games that reflect on social and political issues past, present, and future is in terms of the arguments they make. The games are not neutral but instead instantiate models of issues in ways that favor a particular perspective. *September 12th* argues that attacking terrorists will incite terrorism. *PeaceMaker* argues that political disagreements can be resolved nonviolently. *Medal of Honor: Rising Sun* argues that America's war in the Pacific was a heroic and justified crusade. Postapocalyptic games argue that the end of the world is a foreseeable risk. Whether intentional or not, these arguments arise through ludological and narratological design decisions.

The contamination view of videogames suggests that we should shy away from videogames that make us feel uncomfortable or that show perspectives hostile to our own, lest we risk becoming victims of their influence. It assumes that there is some risk that playing a game about crime or terrorism could transform us into criminals and terrorists—that simply encountering one of these arguments entrenched in entertainment media entails acceptance of that argument. This is deeply misguided. Now that videogames are an important medium for presenting different perspectives, efforts to avoid contamination threaten to limit our contact with alternative viewpoints and different ways of experiencing the world. As Bogost, Ferrari, and Schweizer say, "Clearly a person cannot become an expert just by playing a game, but games can teach a mindset, a way of approaching problems through a set of rules, values, and practices."[37] Looking at these rules, values, and practices from an insider's perspective can be enlightening and does not presuppose that we agree with them. I can say from my own experience that

I have learned a great deal about the U.S. Army from playing *America's Army* and that I have learned about Hezbollah from playing *Special Force*, though I am highly critical of both institutions. The critics of military videogames mentioned previously have likewise managed to play these games with skepticism. I suspect that most gamers have similar abilities—they can shift perspectives and see through ideological messaging without blindly accepting it.

Even games that may at first glance seem like they lack any deeper meaning or that present dangerous messages may have something to teach us. The *Grand Theft Auto* series is heavily fictionalized, yet it does encourage us to give more thought to what it might be like for people growing up in poverty or immigrating to a new country. I would argue that it is completely reasonable to take pity on the series's protagonists who are pushed into crime by life circumstances. We do not know which games offer enlightening perspectives until we experience them, so we are in danger of impoverishing our experiential horizons by prejudging games as being too simplistic to be of any interest. A far more profitable approach is to play many games that pose an array of different arguments, all while maintaining a critical perspective on the arguments.

There is one important caveat to make in this endorsement of videogame pluralism. Persuasive games that are designed to incite players to commit immoral or illegal acts should not be afforded the respect of ideological expressions. It is reasonable to accept some limitations on games, just as with speech, in extreme instances when there is clear evidence of incitement. For example, it would count as incitement if the Islamic State were to produce a game exhorting players to carry out their own terrorist attacks and that offered guidance for building bombs or ramming vehicles into innocent people. Genuine examples of this kind of incitement are exceedingly rare, and there is no simple rule for deciding when a game meets this standard. Given critics' tendency to mistakenly blame games for serious moral transgressions, the burden of proof for demonstrating that a particular game is guilty of incitement should be high. I will return to this issue in chapter 7 to offer some thoughts on how extremely offensive games may be treated when they threaten to cross the boundary into incitement.

Two Critical Pathways

Rethinking the risks associated with persuasive games is essential not only for understanding their moral and political significance but also for reorienting critiques of these games along more productive lines. We can give up the assumption that ideological messages are mere distortions and the fantasy that objective, non-ideological perspectives are possible while still critiquing the arguments that games make. Accepting that arguments and alternative perspectives are legitimate is not the same as accepting that they are correct. Broadly speaking, two useful critical approaches remain: one focusing on the relationship between games and what they are attempting to model, the other focusing on contradictions in the ideological assumptions embedded in games. I call these external and internal critical strategies, respectively. These are not new strategies. Both appear routinely in analyses of games and other media. The problem is that they are not clearly disaggregated from the misguided criticisms that I have discussed throughout the book. In particular, their value is regularly undercut by excessively strong claims about games' harmful influence. More care should be taken to present them as distinct strategies and to divorce them from the unhelpful assumptions that I have contested. We can deploy external and internal ideological critiques while still recognizing that those responsible for the games may genuinely believe in the content and that we lack the ability to ever reach a truly nonideological perspective.

The external critique strategy looks for factual inaccuracies, omissions, and framing effects that call into question the argument being made. Videogames differ considerably in the extent to which they attempt to mirror the real world. Classic franchises such as *Super Mario Bros.*, *Sonic the Hedgehog*, *Spiro*, and *Mortal Kombat* have little resemblance to any real events or people, which suggests that the developers have limited interest in mimetic realism. However, the military videogames, historical simulations, persuasive games, and news games that make arguments about important issues generally strive for some degree of realism in the sense that they attempt to mirror real events or in the sense that they reimagine real issues in fictional worlds. These games construct models of events and issues that inevitably leave a difference between reality and simulation that Bogost calls the "simulation gap." Imperfect models cannot be dismissed as mere deceptions if they reflect genuine beliefs and are designed to convince rather than mislead, but they are open to critique in terms of what information is presented or omitted, how issues are framed, and how the overall model is designed. That is, games are open to critique based on how they respond to the simulation gap challenge and on the extent to which their treatment of it distorts the issues and events being re-created.

Games that purport to model specific events offer the easiest targets for fact checking. Like news reports, such games frame the issues through decisions about what information to present or omit, what to focus on, how information is arranged, and what judgments are made. Games are open to criticism in terms of how framing decisions are made and how they attempt to mitigate bias. Returning to Hess's example, the decision to focus on Pearl Harbor but not address American bombings of Japanese cities reveals a strong pro-American framing of World War II. True neutrality may be impossible, but a game that includes atrocities committed by both sides would have a stronger claim to fairness by including a greater variety of relevant factual information about the conflict. It would be unfair to say that the game is mere propaganda, especially when the developers do not demonstrate an intent to mislead players. At the same time, it is clear that design decisions obscure the historical record and avoid important moral issues. Perfectly re-creating the past is doubtless impossible, yet it is easy to imagine a game presenting a fairer representation of the war that references the questionable conduct by all participants.

Rather than re-creating specific events, some videogames create abstract models of real-world institutions and issues that are reconfigured within counterfactual narratives. *America's Army* is a prime example of this. Games in this series are set in hypothetical future conflicts and therefore cannot include factual inaccuracies to be uncovered by comparison against historical evidence. However, the games make claims about what the U.S. Army is like and how it operates; the Army is a real organization, so these claims are open to factual evaluation. The games' claims of being highly realistic are undermined by the omission of so many of the harsh realities that we know are associated with the Army's operations.[38] In particular, the games do not give much attention to civilian suffering and fail to show the physical costs of violence, such as blood and disfigurement. The games' model of war therefore leaves out vital elements of the experience of war. We do not need details of specific events to know that simulated combat in urban areas with virtually no blood and no civilian casualties creates a problematic vision of war. *America's Army* provides useful insight into how the Army envisions future conflicts and how it sees itself—insights that probably have more to do with genuine beliefs on the part of developers than an effort to dissimulate. In particular, the absence of physical violence illustrates the U.S. military's doctrine of carefully managing the effects of war.[39] Rather than critiquing the game as being merely deceptive propaganda, it should be seen as granting useful insight into a perspective that can help us understand the U.S. Army's doctrine. At the same time, the doctrine itself can be justifiably challenged as a naive idealization of war. In other words, the problem with the game is not that it is intentionally deceiving audiences but rather that the model embodies misconceptions about war that exist in the Army's own vision of itself.

Part of what makes videogames so interesting is that questions about framing and modeling are themselves moral and political questions. They are inconclusive and open to contestation. They present different arguments that may be more or less factually accurate, but no particular game is able to get at the reality of war or of other issues. No model is ever a complete re-creation, so every model is open to analysis based on framing decisions and can be judged in terms of how these decisions are made. *This War of Mine* compares favorably against *America's Army* when it comes to showing the impact of war on civilians, and *Spec Ops: The Line* certainly does better than *America's Army* in exploring the psychological costs of fighting. However, whether these games are truly better models is a political question that must be resolved by analyzing these various models and considering what information is truly most appropriate when it comes to representing war. I will not attempt to offer an answer to that question here but instead point to the overall importance of fostering pluralistic perspectives and considering the various arguments available. One benefit of avoiding the heavy-handed critique of games or attempting to restrict games' content is that we end up with an array of different models that can be compared against each other. This gives us a better range of viewpoints on gaming and on the issues being simulated.

Although no game can be neutral in the sense of building models that are free from bias, it is possible to frame issues in better or worse ways and to develop models that include more or fewer relevant considerations. Some games even go a step further by problematizing information. They not only call attention to the diversity of perspectives on any given issue but also encourage players to think carefully about the impact of the simulation gap on their virtual experiences. Bogost, Ferrari, and Schweizer offer two examples of this. *Beyond Good & Evil* includes two newspapers with opposing ideologies. The interplay between them shows the dispute over narratives and the effort to critique the presentation of information. *Fallout 3* does something similar with continual radio news announcements that comment on the player's decisions with varying degrees of accuracy. In both cases, the games signal that reporting cannot always be trusted, even if there is no attempt to lie outright. We could add other examples from the many games in which different factions present competing narratives of events, such as *Fallout: New Vegas*, *Skyrim*, *The Witcher*, and *Far Cry*. These games model the competition between ideological perspectives and encourage players to reflect on how this process shapes perceptions. Players must exercise judgment when interpreting information and attempting to orient themselves.

The strategy of internal critique seeks to uncover contradictions in a game's narrative or rules. Videogames create closed worlds built from mutually reinforcing ontological and epistemological assumptions. These worlds facilitate certain types of gameplay. The world of a first-person shooter is violent and replete with opportunities to fight. The world of a building simulator is an endless sea of raw materials and opportunities for creation. The worlds are radically different, yet they gain a sense of plausibility when we are immersed in them, because they are closed worlds, carefully governed by gameplay possibilities that naturalize these ways of being. One danger that arises is that closed worlds are designed to function consistently even when the models they offer are not really viable. They can operate as games because of how the rules fit together, regardless of whether the same logic could pertain in the real world. The world of *Grand Theft Auto* feels intuitively plausible because of its immersiveness and resemblance to real cities, but it is an impossible world. It is a place in which violence lacks serious repercussions. A real Liberty City would quickly descend into chaos; it would be a war zone, not a prosperous metropolis. Its extreme violence can only continue without consequences because the world and its population can be infinitely regenerated and repaired. The rules governing the virtual space are contradictory; they are unsustainable and cannot continue on their own momentum. They can only exist in fiction.

Identifying the internal contradictions within the logic of game worlds that would make them unsustainable without being continually reset opens the possibility for using what is often called "immanent critique," which first developed as a strategy for exposing contradictions between ideological assumptions. Ideologies are networks of interconnected beliefs that rarely fit together perfectly and that are vulnerable to attack from within. Ideologies can collapse under the weight of their own conflicting assumptions without introducing any factual inconsistencies. For example, there would be a contradiction in a political platform that calls for an end to immigration but does not explain how to maintain productivity without migrant labor. Proposals to restrict immigration and to increase productivity are often contradictory unless some other policy changes are made to smooth over the contrary implications. Contradictions within ideologies are common, especially when ideologies are assembled from different sources or are attempting to appeal to diverse constituencies whose values do not perfectly align. Real politics is messy because it requires efforts to patch up the adverse effects of contrary policies or because ideologies must be moderated to prevent serious contradictions. This opens further opportunities to challenge ideologies from within based on how they compromise on core beliefs. In contrast to the external approach of comparing claims to facts about the world, this strategy of critiquing from within is a matter of locating logical contradictions that exist apart from factual errors.

When it comes to persuasive videogames, there is ample room for critique based on identifying the rules of the models they construct and finding contradictions in these models. Such an effort can be undertaken without dismissing the ideas as mere deceptions or ignoring their value as communicative acts that grant us insight into political interests. *America's Army* is rife with contradictions even if we approach it in this way. Internal critique can proceed by looking at how the arguments set out in the game come into conflict with each other at the narratological or ludological levels. For example, the game embodies a contradiction within the Army's doctrine, which Colin Kahl calls the "annihilation restraint paradox."[40] Like soldiers, players learn about the immense destructive power of the weapons they control and are urged to mercilessly attack enemies; they are also told to avoid inflicting any civilian casualties and are punished for misusing force. The gameplay experience mirrors a real contradiction of competing imperatives, which is both grounds for critiquing the game and one of the great insights that players can reach. There is likewise a contradiction between the goals stated in the game and the U.S. Army's orientation. Missions involve simulated conventional battles with insurgents, which expose an ideological tension within an Army that is striving to retain its prowess in conventional wars even as it is continually drawn into asymmetric conflicts against insurgents. Building on that, the game reflects a naiveté of U.S. military operations treating battlefield success as the key to victory, which is at odds with the country's political aspirations of nation building and democratization.

Some previous studies of *America's Army* have called attention to these themes, as well as the importance of looking at game rules. Ken McAllister provides an excellent example of what I mean by external critique when he says that "computer game scholars will want to differentiate between, for example, a player who realizes that a particular battle in a war simulation can be won only by means of an air strike and the player who realizes that the entire simulation is constructed on the idea that air dominance is the key to victory in all modern warfare. The former case causes the player to change his or her strategy only vis-à-vis a particular scenario in the game, whereas the latter causes the player to reconsider both local game strategy and the history of real wars."[41]

Nevertheless, critics of military videogames have all too often used these themes to support a reading of *America's Army* and other games as mere propaganda. These critiques make important contributions to research, but they need to be rehabilitated to serve a different sensibility about persuasive games. We can enjoy these games and accept that they are not mere deceptions, while being attentive to the underlying assumptions and the problems they generate.

The strategy of immanent critique can also be extended beyond persuasive games that are designed to advance a particular message or goal to those that attempt to model ideologies enacted and taken to their logical extreme. *BioShock* provides an excellent example of this. I already discussed how the city of Rapture is a utopia turned dystopia because of the contradictions inherent in the founder's ideology of self-reliance and extreme competition. The goal of individual perfection inspired the creation of genetic modifications and propelled the community into civil war. As players discover this story, the events turn out to be eminently plausible because the game attempts to model the contradictions that are really present in Randian egoism and similar ideologies. *BioShock Infinite* does much the same thing by first modeling a world built out of an extreme racial, religious, and nationalistic conservatism and then modeling the world created by resistance fighters who impose an uncompromising vision of egalitarianism. In each case, the world creates a physical manifestation of political ideologies. And while the constructs are simpler than the philosophies they mirror, they raise important questions about whether the ideologies do incorporate these contradictions. The result is that the games entertain while also offering some compelling insights into political theory.

Conclusion

I have argued that military videogames and other kinds of persuasive games can and should be critiqued but that the strategies of critique need to be reconsidered. Arguments about extremely harmful psychological repercussions of gaming overstate videogames' power to transform players and perpetuate an unproductive moral panic. I contend that persuasive games are best seen as arguments for particular perspectives on issues and events. They make claims about what we should believe and what we should value. For the most part, developers seem to genuinely believe the messages their persuasive games propagate. They do not simply seek to mislead players but rather aim to convince them, though this effort may involve stretching the truth. Persuasive efforts may influence players in subtle ways, but this is not morally problematic. We are shaped by our experiences, including experiences of entertainment. Games, like other media, may offer us new information and alter our perspectives, but our interpretations of media are heavily dictated by our existing biases. We tend to see what we want to see when engaging with polysemic media. Above all, games' influence is apt to fall short of the kinds of major events that are usually responsible for having a substantive effect on people's core beliefs and values. Thus, it is possible to acknowledge that videogames have some influence on players without assuming that they have a contagion effect. Players are not blank slates to be remade by playing a game for a few minutes, so it is essential to abandon the contagion model of thinking about persuasive games and approach them with far more nuance.

I have defended controversial videogames against some of the criticisms they have received and highlighted some of the analytical mistakes that appear in those criticisms. My effort to challenge certain critical strategies is meant not to foreclose critique of games but rather to resituate critique with more promising strategies. We can recognize the persuasive games as arguments and acknowledge that the developers may genuinely believe in the messages presented, while still striving to expose the errors within those arguments. We should strive to evaluate these games in terms of what kinds of models they build, with attention to the external problems related to factual inaccuracies and omissions and the internal problems associated with inconsistent ideological assumptions or inconsistent rules governing the games.

7

Speaking through Games

From torture to mass murder, rape to pedophilia, suicide bombing to nuclear annihilation, videogames never cease to shock. Some commentators wonder whether the discomfort is worth it or whether the risks outweigh the rewards. Moreover, for each example of a thoughtful use of shock, there are many examples of games presenting gratuitous violence and sexual content without any apparent redeeming goal. Games such as *Custer's Revenge*, *RapeLay*, and *Ethnic Cleansing* not only upset sensibilities but do so in ways that arguably conflict with social mores and glorify aggression. Even hardcore gamers report being dismayed at gruesome acts of simulated violence or when games allow players to commit atrocities.[1] Disturbing moments are a magnet for controversy and condemnation. They also encourage us to reflect on our simulated experiences and on our attitudes about the real events re-created.

My goal in this chapter is to demonstrate the importance of distinguishing between offensiveness and genuine immorality when it comes to videogames. Offense is not in itself grounds for moral concern. Offensive content may be uncomfortable or even profoundly disgusting, yet in most cases it is not actually harmful. Moreover, offensiveness is often essential for taking on difficult issues. A game that addresses racial inequality, sexual deviance, or violence cannot help but present troubling situations and evoke real atrocities. I demonstrate the value of offensive games by looking at the messages conveyed by some of the most controversial games. *Super Columbine Massacre RPG!* is a troubling simulation of a real school shooting, but the game's offensiveness is vital to its investigation of the attack and the ostensible link between videogames and violence. *Grand Theft Auto* simulates extreme violence and presents racial stereotypes, but it does so satirically. *Grand Theft Auto V*'s simulated torture is an effective critique of this practice because it is brutal, just as *Spec Ops: The Line*'s white phosphorous attack is more effective at conveying the horrors of war because it re-creates civilian victimization. Games featuring highly sexualized female characters have been blamed for objectifying women, yet some of these characters have helped to move games beyond the ubiquitous white male hero. In each case, shock and even disgust are vehicles for making significant points.

It is essential to contextualize offensive content and to consider the range of interpretations it may support. Many games that have been charged with racism and sexism do not advocate discrimination. Rather, they represent real activities or events in which the logics of racism and sexism are already inscribed. To be offended by these games misses the point that games are not responsible for the existing inequities they call attention to. Games have the potential to subvert racism, sexism, and other pernicious beliefs, and they deserve praise when they do this. However, subversion is itself a controversial project that is subject to divergent interpretations according to the logic of polysemy. Efforts to make progressive simulations are apt to offend and to provoke disagreement about whether they are truly progressive or what it even means to be progressive. The pursuit of more politically engaged games requires a proliferation of viewpoints that will inevitably cause offense and discontent. The more serious the issues games take on and the more they attempt to challenge conventions, the greater the odds that others will disagree with the approach taken or the messages presented.

The lesson I want to emphasize in this chapter is that we should adopt a more permissive attitude toward offensive games in the sense of being less outraged by offensive content and more attentive to how content that initially appears to be immoral may take on a different meaning when seen within the game narrative and within the social context. We certainly should not accept every game as being meaningful or insightful, but we must be on guard against the tendency to search for moral fault wherever possible. The risks posed by videogames are infinitesimal compared to the risks of overzealous censorship. Moreover, we should be cautious about the treatment of offensive games that lack any moral or political message, such as *Custer's Revenge*. I concede that some games are genuinely repugnant and lack clear redeeming benefits, yet such games may still help to maintain a general climate of open discourse in which speech is only restricted under exceptional circumstances. The censorship favored by staunch critics of videogames is only warranted in the rare cases where games incite violence or constitute threats of violence in themselves.

Warning: Disturbing Content

As I argued in chapter 2, many critics of videogames mistakenly assume that players passively endorse simulated actions as being morally justified. The discomfort some players report when encountering shocking content is a sign of how misguided this assumption is. In one study, Consalvo, Busch, and Jong find that "players for the most part did not consider game spaces as 'judgment-free zones' for either their own play or that of others, instead freely admitting that feelings of discomfort or shame (or sometimes more) were appropriate for deviant acts they took in-game."[2] This research reveals that offensive content often meets considerable resistance from players—even those who enjoy the game. In other words, players can be upset by a game and still enjoy it. This may seem strange, but it is entirely consistent with games being amoral in themselves while still being able to evoke thoughts of activities that would be immoral if they were real. Simulated violence may be fictional and not morally problematic in itself, but it brings our attention to unpleasant realities that are morally and politically significant.

We feel disgusted and offended at simulated immoral actions because they remind us of real-world analogues that warrant condemnation. We do not witness a real country's descent into chaos in *Far Cry 4*, but it is hard to ignore the game's references to the Maoist insurgency in Nepal or to forget that real people are suffering in civil wars around the world. We do not really torture a suspected terrorist in *Grand Theft Auto V*, but the game forces us to face the reality of torture via simulation and encourages us to give some thought to the detainees who were waterboarded during the War on Terror. Players feel uncomfortable about simulated murder, sexual assault, and child abuse not because they are actually guilty of the actions they simulate or because they lack the ability to distinguish reality from fantasy but because representations of immoral actions reference real-world equivalents that are profoundly uncomfortable.

Of course, not all uncomfortable content is the same. Simulated torture and fictional murder are clearly different from real torture and murder because they do not cause physical and psychological injuries. Condemning videogames for simulating these actions misapplies moral sentiments about real actions to mere reflections of them. Nevertheless, it is possible for acts of aggression to be carried out through communication alone, as in the case of hate speech or incitements to violence. This raises the question of whether some videogames may be immoral by virtue of the messages they present. Patridge thinks that this is possible and attempts to show that amoralists are wrong in thinking that actions performed in videogames lack moral weight (i.e., that a game is "just a game") by looking at simulated violations of social mores. Building on Aristotelian critiques of videogames, she contends that certain simulated actions must be wrong because of what they say about those who participate in the simulations. As she explains, "A virtuous agent would not undertake such an activity for the sake of pleasure, sexual or otherwise. So, it at least makes room for the possibility that our game play, fictionalized as it is, might also be expressive of a flaw in our character."[3]

Patridge is especially concerned by games that have "incorrigible social meanings." As she correctly points out, certain images can be deeply upsetting because of their meaning within a particular context. In her example, Americans are apt to find a cartoon of President Obama eating a watermelon upsetting because this is generally recognized as a racial insult. When it comes to this kind of imagery, Patridge says that "the meaning is incorrigible in that it is exceedingly difficult to overturn, and it is social in that this difficulty is explained by facts about a particular social reality."[4] She extends this reasoning to argue that videogames with racist or sexist messages are morally problematic. She says that *Resident Evil 5* is objectionable because it features a white protagonist who kills black African zombies and is reminiscent of the atrocities of colonization. *Custer's Revenge* is another example, as it ends with a white protagonist raping a Native American woman who is tied to a pole. According to Patridge, players of these games show a moral failing if they think that the imagery is funny, if they do not realize that it is wrong, or if they know that the images are wrong but enjoy the games anyway.

As I explained in chapter 4, there is good reason to doubt the Aristotelian critique of videogames (i.e., the claim that merely simulating immoral actions can damage a person's character). This argument does not fit well with Aristotle's writings about the cathartic effects of tragedy and conflates the performance of simulated actions with the habitual performance of real immoral actions. However, Patridge goes beyond the usual Aristotelian argument that games habituate players to immorality by looking at the social context in which game content appears to be immoral. She makes some insightful points about how games may be harmful in much the same way that hate speech is harmful. That is, even if individual players are unaffected by the racist imagery of *Custer's Revenge*, there could be a social cost to reproducing racial stereotypes. This shows that the moral issues inherent in games are also political issues. The effort to find something wrong with games and with individual players' enjoyment of them turns from individual psychology to how the player is acting in an intersubjective context in which others' thoughts and feelings must be taken into account.

I acknowledge that much of the content that critics of videogames take issue with is insensitive and offensive but argue that to call this content immoral or to impose censorship is usually too strong a response. The reasons for this can be found by drawing on insights from research on free speech rights. Thus far, researchers have not borrowed much from that literature, perhaps because of an aversion to equating games with other media and losing a sense of their uniqueness. However, this perspective has much to offer. Games are usually controversial because of how narrative elements contextualize players' actions. Narratives provide meaning to button clicks. They determine whether players are simulating justified or unjustified violence, consensual sex or rape. They also provide the information to categorize characters by race, gender, sexual orientation, or other attributes that may be used as the basis for discrimination. It is a narrative decision to create enemies that look black rather than white. Because narrative framing is the source of controversial representations, it is helpful to evaluate offensive games by using the same standards of narrative analysis that have been developed to analyze other controversial media, such as films, books, and music.

Drawing an analogy between videogames and other media when it comes to theorizing offensive content holds two advantages. First, it is vital to be as consistent as possible when making moral appraisals of different types of entertainment. Videogames have suffered an undue burden from double standards when critics treat them as having less redeeming value than other media or when they assume that the messages games present are more harmful without adequate evidence to show that this is the case. Adopting the same standards to analyze different types of media is a vital step toward overcoming this bias and making more consistent moral judgments. Second, research on videogames can benefit immensely from the extensive writings on free speech rights, which have already covered many of the same issues that are central to controversies surrounding videogames. It is true that games have distinctive characteristics and that theories of speech may need to be updated in light of their interactivity, yet existing research can at least offer a starting place on which more gaming scholars can build. Of particular importance is the conceptual language that has developed for understanding controversial speech and identifying when it crosses moral boundaries.

There are no settled answers in the struggle to determine when speech acts deserve moral condemnation, but many defenders of expansive free speech rights follow in the tradition of John Stuart Mill by endorsing his harm principle, which states that actions should be permitted so long as they do not harm others. As he puts it, "The only purpose for which power can be rightfully exercised over any member of a civilized community, against his will, is to prevent harm to others."[5] This is a classic statement of political liberalism, which is deployed by free speech advocates who think that speech must be protected because words lack the capacity to injure or kill. Mill's harm principle is often interpreted as meaning that speech should only be restricted in cases of slander and libel, incitement, or threat, when the speech acts inflict some kind of demonstrable damage. Few videogames make erroneous, damaging factual claims about specific people such that they would violate rules against slander and libel. This leaves incitement and threat as the more urgent concerns. The former involves offensive speech that is used to encourage people to commit real acts of violence, such as by producing a book that exhorts readers to attack members of minority groups. Threats directed against specific individuals and groups are likewise not merely offensive but can cause the recipient or recipients severe psychological harm by creating fear of attack. In both cases, the speech goes beyond merely offending to inflicting harm.

Videogames rarely, if ever, encourage players to go out into the real world and commit violent acts in any sense that would qualify as incitement. Just the opposite. Even the most heavily criticized games tend to situate violence within some narrative context in which it is justified, which is to say a context in which it does not count as murder. Players usually battle against terrorists, criminals, zombies, and Nazis. They fight enemies who are supposed to be killed not only based on the logic of the game but who also deserve it in some sense. Games typically penalize players for unjustified violence, such as shooting civilians, or make it impossible, which is often the case with attacks on children. When games simulate murder, such as when players in *Grand Theft Auto* mow down pedestrians, they typically characterize this as being illegal and stop far short of encouraging players to emulate the behavior. Violence is therefore characterized as being permissible only under certain carefully defined circumstances, which usually coincide with broader social mores about justified uses of force in self-defense and during war. Moreover, games do not urge players to re-enact the violence in the real world, and it is doubtful that any major game would ever do such a thing considering the legal repercussions this would have.

In the extraordinary instances where games do present strong calls to use violence in real life, they can be justifiably considered immoral on the grounds that they are attempting to incite players to act wrongly. Such games are not the ones that feature in the popular debate over violent videogames, such as *Manhunt* and *Grand Theft Auto*. Instead, they come from relatively small developers and have had limited commercial success. *Ethnic Cleansing* is one such example. Created in 2002 by the National Alliance, a white nationalist organization, the game simulates a race war in which neo-Nazis and members of the Ku Klux Klan attack minority groups. I would argue that such a game is immoral and that it can be fairly censored. It incites violence, and there is a high risk of that message finding a receptive audience in societies that are plagued by racial discrimination. The game is likewise profoundly threatening because of the developer's long-standing promotion of racialized violence beyond the boundaries of the videogame. It is therefore possible for a videogame to violate Mill's harm principle, but only under exceptional circumstances. In this instance, the harm arises from a fairly credible threat coming from an organization actively promoting real acts of hate and being deployed in a social context where it could reasonably qualify as incitement.

Joel Feinberg expands on the Millian perspective by distinguishing between harm and offense. He says that offensive acts "are harmless in themselves yet so unpleasant that we can rightly demand legal protection from them even at the cost of other persons' liberties."[6] Feinberg conveys this with the help of a thought experiment in which he invites readers to picture themselves as passengers on the worst bus ride imaginable. Fellow passengers arrive to eat disgusting food, engage in unsanitary behavior, and display disturbing messages. For example, in Story 31, he says that "a counter-demonstrator leaves a feminist rally to enter the bus. He carries a banner with an offensive caricature of a female and the message, in large red letters: 'Keep the bitches barefoot and pregnant.'"[7] This sign is akin to Patridge's examples of a picture of Obama eating watermelon or the rape scene in *Custer's Revenge*—a display so profoundly at odds with social mores that it is reasonable to question its morality and legality. Feinberg argues that some types of offensive content should be restricted, and correctly observes that even the most liberal societies impose some limits on expression in the interest of preserving public order. Prohibitions against wandering the streets naked, issuing threats, or shouting fire in a crowded building are examples of this. Including offense alongside harm as grounds for restricting freedom of expression makes Feinberg's offense principle a stronger basis for challenging the upsetting content that appears in games than Mill's harm principle, which has made Feinberg's principle a more appealing standard for commentators who wish to impose stricter regulations on expression. The trouble is deciding exactly where offensive content crosses the line to become immoral or subject to legal restriction.

Offense is a difficult concept to apply in practice as a basis for making moral or legal judgments. It is an unmeasurable psychological or social cost that can only be gauged qualitatively. There is no way of drawing sharp lines between immoral offensive messages and justified offensive messages, or between offensive content that is morally repugnant and offensive content that is excusable because it has redeeming benefits. There are many borderline cases in which there is reasonable debate about whether offensive actions cross the line to become immoral and/or illegal. Worse still, there is an enormous risk of infringing on the rights of marginalized groups by declaring their actions offensive. Restrictions on virtually every type of marginalized group have historically been supported by claims that the members' lifestyle is offensive in ways that warrant a loss of liberty. Around the world, homosexuals continue to face oppression on the grounds that even private same-sex relationships are offensive to social mores. Mistreatment of transgendered people is likewise routinely carried out because their personal choices offend. The frequency with which claims of offense are misused as tools for discrimination should make us reluctant to restrain offensive speech in any but the most extreme cases in which there are demonstrable costs going beyond mere discomfort or disgust. Any judgments about what kinds of speech are permissible must be made on a case-by-case basis, with a high degree of sensitivity to the costs of stifling expression.

Arguments for restricting offensive speech also tend to make special exceptions for art and for politically important messages.[8] The reasoning here is that the good of permitting this type of content and the potential risk of silencing public dialogue outweigh the costs associated with causing offense. This means that identifying immoral content is not just a matter of showing that offense was inflicted but also showing that the content lacks artistic merit or cognitive value. Nude paintings and sculptures are widely permitted because of their cultural significance, despite bothering some conservatives. Flag burning is highly offensive to many people, yet it is permissible in most liberal democratic societies because it constitutes an evocative form of protest. Restricting this kind of upsetting expression would protect delicate sensibilities at the expense of impoverished political discourse. Thus, another test when judging offensive content in videogames is to decide whether the messages being presented have artistic or political merit in themselves or whether the expression helps to maintain a general openness that facilitates political discourse. This judgment is a matter of proportionality. A particular expression is not wrong simply because it offends. Rather, it is wrong only if the offense is intentional and is inflicted without pursuing some worthwhile goal that overrides the harm inflicted by the offense.

Super Columbine Massacre RPG! is a prime example of an upsetting game that is morally permissible because of its political merit. The game was produced by Danny Ledonne in 2005 and re-creates the 1999 attack on Columbine High School in Littleton, Colorado. The decision to transform a national tragedy into a videogame generated backlash from many critics, including some victims' families. The game was all the more shocking for allowing players to become the killers—a perspective some thought might generate empathy for them and even encourage emulation.[9] It is easy to understand the discomfort with an attack being re-enacted against avatars representing real victims of a mass shooting. The game could be fairly described as offensive, and it poses a risk of inflicting emotional trauma on players and victims. There is also a risk associated with delving into the minds of school shooters, especially if this glamorizes them. Nevertheless, there is much to be gained from an attempt to understand what motivated the killers, especially when so much of the blame has been wrongly placed on popular culture and the media. Using a videogame to simulate the attack was especially poignant because of the efforts made to show that videogames were the cause. The game narrative plays an important role in contextualizing events and re-creating them in a way that promotes understanding without glorifying the shooters or encouraging emulation. It is also clear from Ledonne's defense of the game that it reflects an effort to delve into the psychology of the shooters and the causes of school violence rather than merely an effort to offend.[10]

There is no perfect way of handling a topic as delicate as school shootings—no middle ground that will please everyone. A game like *Super Columbine Massacre RPG!* cannot help but cause offense to many people and profoundly disgust those who play it. It is a testament to videogames' inability to truly desensitize players that many veteran gamers professed being deeply disturbed by the content.[11] It is because the game is offensive, that it can provoke discussion of school shootings, the proper way to remember victims, and how to talk about those who commit atrocities without glorifying their actions. These are valuable conversations to have. If the game were not offensive, it would lack this power. In a sense, *Super Columbine Massacre RPG!* is like a virtual flag burning. It is speech taken to an extreme that is deeply offensive but in which the provocation is essential to the act of protest. Audiences are right to be offended by it, but the developer and players are also justified in raising their voices to spark debate about an urgent national security problem. By refusing to glorify the killers or call for more attacks, the game stops short of inciting violence and therefore qualifies as a defensible speech act in which potential benefits outweigh potential harms.

Feinberg recognizes the challenges associated with identifying when it is justifiable to regulate offensive expression. He offers some guidelines and says that the intensity of the offense, the number of people affected, the motive of the speaker, and the ease of avoiding the content should all be taken into consideration. By his account, public demonstrations of hatred designed to reach large audiences and spread fear, such as Nazi rallies, can be justifiably restricted. On the other hand, offensive media, which would include videogames, should generally be protected because they are easy to avoid, have minimal impact beyond the immediate audience, and are usually not designed with malevolent intent. In the end, the decision about what content is morally and/or legally permissible must be made on a case-by-case basis with careful attention to the text in question and the potential risks. I argue that in most cases it is too strong to say that games are morally blameworthy simply because they offend and that the costs associated with stifling expression are so high that censorship is only justified in extreme cases. A game must pose some kind of clear and demonstrable danger based on incitement or threat to warrant moral condemnation or legal restriction, and as I have shown in the preceding chapters, there are virtually no clear cases of games that meet this standard.

We can and should interrogate offensive content in games like *Custer's Revenge*, and there are good grounds for moral condemnation of those who use these games as a way of satisfying malicious fantasies. At the same time, the critiques of upsetting games tend to look less like reasonable inquiries into whether the games are morally permissible and more like attempts to find some way to impugn videogames by looking for extreme content in a handful of cases. Patridge is certainly correct in thinking that much of the perceived wrongness associated with games arises from social circumstances and that games may be morally questionable because of their social meaning. At the same time, this argument for situating games in their social context can be turned on its head. Just as it is appropriate to judge the offensiveness of games based on their context, it is appropriate to determine the extent of acceptable expression based on the prevailing norms related to free expression. Most liberal democratic societies take a permissive attitude toward free speech because of its benefits and the myriad challenges associated with distinguishing justifiable content from unjustifiable content. Restrictions on books, television shows, movies, and other entertainment media are reserved for extreme cases in which there is a relatively clear and specific associated risk. The same general respect for expression should be extended to videogames.

Racism and Sexism

It is helpful to situate the disagreement over offensive representations in terms of the research on how marginalized groups are depicted in games. Most cases of hate speech are directed against marginalized groups, and the games that most plausibly qualify as being immoral target women and/or minorities (as in the case of *Custer's Revenge* and *Ethnic Cleansing*). Moreover, this is one of the most active areas of gaming research, with many commentators accusing video-games of being racist or sexist because of the lack of attention to minorities or because of how minorities are represented.

One line of argument is that marginalized groups are underrepresented in videogames and that this perpetuates exclusion. Underrepresentation consti-tutes a failure to recognize members of marginalized groups and by extension may exacerbate feelings that they are abnormal or inferior. This may also alien-ate players from those groups, excluding them from the entertainment and learning experiences that games offer. Exclusion is a reasonable concern, but once again critics pursuing this argument overstate reasonable concerns and by extension overstate the case for thinking that videogames are morally problem-atic. Marginalized groups are underrepresented and misrepresented in games, but the numbers do not tell the whole story. As in other controversies I have considered, the problem is less with games than with the more fundamental social and political conditions they reflect.

David Leonard is among the most ardent opponents of racial misrepresenta-tions in videogames. He describes videogames as "a White-centered space" because "more than 50% of player-controlled characters are White males; less than 40% of game characters are Black."[12] His argument rests heavily on this claim of underrepresentation, but it is difficult to substantiate. The first prob-lem is with the lack of evidence to support the figure cited. It is difficult to judge what games Leonard bases his conclusion on, as he provides no list to support his estimate. This reflects a general lack of transparency in the statistical data critics of videogames provide. The games Leonard references in his qualitative case studies are all set in the United States, which has a population that is roughly 12.6 percent black.[13] This makes his estimate that 40 percent of video-game characters are black a very high proportion when judged against demo-graphic realities. Without a list of the games included in his estimate, it is impossible to say whether the 40 percent figure is fair. However, it is clear that there is a problem with his claim of underrepresentation within the context of games that attempt to mirror American society, as his figures indicate that black characters are actually overrepresented. This raises a deeper question: what counts as fair representation? Should videogames be expected to mirror the general population's composition, or should games include equal numbers of all groups? As with the other free speech issues I have raised, there are no easy answers. Leonard and others who claim that some groups are underrepresented should attempt to find some guidelines for game developers to follow. Without a clear standard of fairness or evidence of an intent to misrepresent racial minorities, such a critique of games is unproductive and serves to perpetuate a sense of moral outrage at games without offering reasonable solutions.

Claims that women are underrepresented in games are more convincing on the surface, as women are clearly underrepresented compared to their proportion of the overall population. In one of the earliest and most influential of these studies, Tracy Dietz found that in thirty-three Nintendo and Sega Genesis games, 41 percent included no female characters and 28 percent of those that did only showed them as sexual objects.[14] Similarly, in a later study of forty-seven randomly selected videogames, Berrin Beasely and Tracy Standley reported that women only made up 8.54 percent to 27.36 percent of the characters, depending on the type of game.[15] These studies also showed that the number of female characters is linked to the game genre. Women are most common in individual sports games and least common in group sports and fighting games. The unequal distribution of men and women is most noticeable in violent games. These rarely include women, and when they do, the characters are usually in supporting roles.[16] The underrepresentation of female characters goes beyond games themselves. Other media associated with them show the same bias. According to Erica Sharrer, game advertisements are around three times more likely to show male characters than female characters.[17] In an analysis of the way gender appears in game review sites, James Ivory concludes that "in general, female characters were represented in far fewer of the sampled game reviews than male characters,"[18] as only 42 percent of reviews mentioned female characters. The range of these studies, both in a temporal sense and in the variety of game-related media analyzed, indicates the pervasiveness of unequal representation in gaming.

Women's underrepresentation results at least partly from how games are designed to mirror the real world. Many games, including those that studies have flagged as showing the most severe bias, involve roles that restrict women's participation. For example, many of the best-selling action games of the past two decades, including the *Call of Duty*, *Medal of Honor*, and *Battlefield* series, simulate combat in militaries that did not allow women to participate in ground combat. Any attempt to mirror the realities of gender-exclusive historical roles in games will invariably result in unequal numbers of male and female characters. Including female characters among the infantrymen storming the beaches of Normandy in *Call of Duty 4* would be anachronistic and present players with an inaccurate view of World War II. In fact, such a dramatic rewriting of history would leave games open to the criticism that they are attempting to cover up past infringements on women's rights. Women are also excluded from most of the professional leagues that sports videogames are based on, so it should come as no surprise that this genre likewise marginalizes women. Inclusion in games about real professional sports teams would require creating fictional female characters to play alongside male avatars representing real people. The same problem extends to existing franchises borrowed from other media, such as those involving superheroes. These franchises must either retain their existing biases or be substantially reconfigured when they are adapted to videogames.

In Beasely and Standley's study of forty-seven games, at least fourteen are simulations of activities that excluded women within the setting. They depict military ground combat prior to women's inclusion in it and professional sports leagues that are reserved for men.[19] Dietz's influential 1998 study of Nintendo and Sega games included at least seven games based on real activities that exclude women. Seven are based on superhero and television franchises that have few female characters.[20] This means that fourteen of the thirty-three games Dietz investigated could only include women by altering their source material. Videogames are not the root cause of women's underrepresentation. They are only reflecting more fundamental gender inequalities.

Games with few minority characters may likewise do this for the sake of accurately reflecting source material or real-world events that game developers have limited power to alter unless they abandon their goal of representational accuracy. This is the case in games simulating historical periods when racial minorities were excluded from settings or roles that are the game's subject. For example, when judged in terms of representational accuracy, it is fitting that the numerous games about the American military during World War II would include few minority characters because the military was segregated at the time. When it comes to games about historical events or real institutions, it is only when situating games in the context of the real events and places they simulate that it is possible to determine whether their content is fair. When games attempt to mirror the real world, they inevitably copy its inequities. Once again, the fundamental problem of inequality is less with games themselves than with real institutions that have unfairly excluded certain groups.

The failure to distinguish between the different representational contexts of games that attempt to mirror the real world and those that envision alternative realities reveals one of the problems with overreliance on quantitative methods for how games depict marginalized groups. Although quantitative research has yielded a great deal of useful information about patterns in representation of women and other groups, studies too often overlook the underlying reasons for inequality. It is essential to rethink how moral claims about videogames are made and to reorient these claims more effectively. The problem is not simply that certain groups do not have enough presence in videogames but rather that videogames bear a complex relationship with the real world. They may be expected to reflect it accurately or to reconfigure it imaginatively, with different implications in terms of what would constitute fair inclusion. As in the case of offensive games, those that may contain racial or gender bias are often complex texts that must be approached with attention not only to what is being represented but also to the overall context in which meaning takes shape.

Visual images are rarely self-sufficient sources of meaning. Images that appear in isolation or without some sense of context are ambiguous. For example, a picture of a dead body in the newspaper sends a powerful message, but what exactly that message is requires explanation. It could be a murder victim or someone who died of natural causes. If the person died in a war zone, we may not know who was responsible or whether the attack was warranted. The person could be an enemy fighter or a civilian, or perhaps somewhere in between. How we interpret such an image depends on related images and accompanying narrative descriptions provided by the caption.[21] The incompleteness of meaning is a core assumption of semiotic theory. No sign means something in isolation. Meaning is established through networks of relationships. It is only with this interpretive assistance that we can understand what the image actually means. And passing any judgment about the moral or political implications of an image is certainly premature without access to this information. This point must extend to the interpretation of offensive games. A controversial setting, a lack of inclusivity, and sexualization are upsetting, but we may not know what deeper implications these have—we may not really understand what these elements of the game mean—without some sense of the game as a whole. Establishing the context is therefore essential.

Anthony Shiu offers a good example of a contextually grounded critique of underrepresentation.[22] He analyzes the racial inequalities of *Duke Nukem 3D* and *Shadow Warrior* with reference to the context in which the games are set. *Duke Nukem 3D* is set in Los Angeles, an extremely diverse place in which white people are now a minority, but its characters are exclusively white. Any attempt to re-create Los Angeles would require a far more diverse assortment of characters than are included in the game. Shiu even cites demographic figures in support of this point, which help to establish a clear standard for judging inclusiveness. Thus, rather than objecting to underrepresentation without a clear standard of judgment or without acknowledging the forces that may constrain a game's inclusivity, Shiu judges *Duke Nukem 3D* in terms of its own mimetic orientation. He shows that the game fails to reflect the diversity one should find in the game's setting. By forming a sense of what would count as fair representation in the chosen context, it becomes possible to critique the game on its own terms. Its failure to be more inclusive is a representation failure based on the standards the game itself creates by its attempt to model a particular place.

Of course, many games are not based on historical events, existing franchises, or real activities shaped by gender bias. Games set in fantasy worlds, alternative realities, or the future have far more freedom in how they represent characters. Critiques of underrepresentation that focus on these kinds of games have a much stronger basis for uncovering evidence of bias. When games are set in alternative realities, developers can create more egalitarian worlds rather than simply reflecting the inequalities of the real world. In these cases, games often do fall into the pattern of relying heavily on white male characters, especially in leading roles. Whether intentionally or unintentionally, many perpetuate trends of underrepresentation that infect the real world and other types of media. It is here that the critiques of representational biases in videogames can focus most fairly and effectively—on those instances in which games are in a position to subvert these broader trends by producing simulations that are more egalitarian.

Videogames are in a unique position to create convincing new worlds and should take advantage of that power to break free of real-world biases whenever possible. Wark argues that "the beginnings of a critical theory of games—a gamer theory—might lie not in holding games accountable as failed representations of the world, but quite the reverse. The world outside is a gamespace that appears as an imperfect form of a computer game."[23] I do not know exactly what Wark has in mind, but it seems as though this proposal could offer some help when it comes to issues of race and gender. Many games, perhaps even a majority, attempt to mirror the real world or other media. They are models of things that already exist, which cannot help but reproduce existing biases. Mirroring is an inherently conservative enterprise, in the sense that the mirror must reflect the flaws of the original. However, when it comes to race and gender, there is scope for imaginatively creating new worlds that have more progressive content and that offer new perspectives. In this sense, games might go beyond simply re-creating existing biases to construct spaces in which these cease to exist—spaces in which the games provide an aspirational look at what might be achievable. Ironically, games set in dystopian worlds are sometimes the best at doing this precisely because they set out to imagine alternative realities in which existing inequalities need not apply.

When Are Representations Fair?

Fair representation is not simply a matter of numerical equality. How avatars look plays a key role in characterizing groups. As with the quantitative evaluations of underrepresentation, fair criticism of the appearance of minority groups requires sensitivity to the contexts of the game worlds and their overall attitude toward racial issues. Two considerations are particularly important. First, the prevalence of satire in videogames means that characters cannot always be taken at face value. Some characters are potentially upsetting because of their racialized or sexualized appearance, but they should be interpreted within a game's overall context and with attention to what political or artistic point a game is attempting to make. Second, games are polysemic and may support divergent interpretations within the scope of the evidence they present. This does not mean that characters are empty shells that can take on any meaning but rather that any given character may permit a range of plausible interpretations. It is important to avoid assigning characters a fixed, essential identity when their meaning is open to contestation.

Investigations of male minority characters find that they are usually shown as physically powerful, aggressive, and "hypermasculine."[24] Leonard says that this image is especially prominent in sports games and action games, which usually portray black characters as being naturally muscular and athletic. He goes on to argue that, by making the black characters physically powerful, the games keep attention on the black characters' bodies. Thus, games facilitate "the virtual occupation of black bodies" through the hypermasculine display.[25] Susan Jeffords points out that black men and white men are depicted differently.[26] The former are shown as docile and complacent men that are not threatening for white audiences, while white men can be more rebellious and assertive.

Games in the *Grand Theft Auto* series are among those that have most often been accused of reinforcing racial stereotypes that could arguably be classified as hate speech.[27] Many of the factions are formed along racial lines, and groups are shown in unflattering ways. This leads Leonard to claim that *Grand Theft Auto 3* "legitimizes white supremacy and patriarchy and privileges whiteness and maleness, all the while substantiating the necessity of law and order and reactionary social governance."[28] He considers the games' representation of the Other more problematic than the games' violent and sexual messages, saying, "These games don't teach kids how to be violent or how to solicit a prostitute—in fact there is little scholarly evidence that substantiates such a claim—but contributes to an understanding of how to thwart violence through increased policing and state control of the dangerous Other."[29] Leonard thus defuses one critique of the games to make room for a different line of argument based on the racial imagery.

Although the *Grand Theft Auto* series includes unfavorable representations of minorities, as Leonard points out, it does not privilege a particular racial group over others. Each group receives the same type of racialized depiction. The games feature myriad stereotypical ethnic gangs, including Italian, Jewish, Irish, Russian, and Korean mafias, Chinese triads, black, white, Eastern European, and Hispanic street gangs, white biker gangs, and neo-Nazis. There is therefore nothing unique about the stereotyping of certain minorities in the game or about the intimation that the groups' members are involved in crime. The offensive stereotypes and links to crime are universal. More importantly, the game presents its minority characters as parodies rather than as realistic characters. The games are deliberately ironic, satirizing pop culture texts and group stereotypes.[30] The narrative and characters of *Grand Theft Auto* are framed as a parody of contemporary society, implicitly challenging the stereotypes. The contextual evidence therefore indicates that the stereotypes should not be taken literally, as an endorsement of prejudice.

The evidence offered to substantiate claims that the *Grand Theft Auto* series is racist can just as easily support the view that the series is attempting to undermine racial stereotypes through satire. Leonard criticizes the radio broadcasts in San Andreas by saying "the radio not only blasts a spectrum of jams, all of which further reflects the commodification of an imagined Black aesthetic, but a series of reactionary public service announcements, which embody a virtual moral panic and contribute to those efforts outside this virtual urban space."[31] By contrast, Kiri Miller reads these broadcasts as satires of talk radio commentators: "Disrupting gameworld immersion with irony, Rockstar's writers invite the player-ethnographer to join in criticizing the object of their satire: mainstream American commercial media."[32] As Miller's example shows, the radio broadcast seems to be an exaggeration of the racism inherent in the claims that the United States is being corrupted, and not a serious attempt to promote intolerance. The exaggeration of this message, in this broadcast and in others, heightens its ridiculousness and clarifies its racial overtones. The invocations of the freedom of opinion and the influence of sponsors further challenge the racist message by suggesting that it is a matter of personal bias and that it is opportunistically directed at garnering higher ratings. Other radio programs and advertisements are also parodies, making the references to race part of a much larger satire of contemporary culture.

Ben DeVane and Kurt Squire show that when asked about the representation of race in *Grand Theft Auto*: *San Andreas*, players were able to identify the stereotyping as part of the game's pop culture critique, and that many thought the game exposed real social problems: "Participants from socially and economically marginalized groups—African American, working-class, or working poor—used the game as a framework to discuss institutional racism in society."[33] They also find that those who played more games had readings of the game's representation of race that were more nuanced, a result that indicates that gaming experience improves a person's ability to notice the way race appears in games and to think critically about its function.

The representation of female characters is also controversial. Beasely and Standley find that female characters are usually shown in revealing clothing that transforms them into sexual figures. They also have sexual characteristics emphasized. Based on this, the authors conclude that "there is considerable gender role stereotyping in video games."[34] This assessment of female characters as more sexualized than male characters is substantiated by numerous studies that reach the same conclusion.[35] This goes beyond games to other media associated with them, as the sexualized female characters are evident in game art, gaming websites, and game reviews.[36]

The *Tomb Raider* series, which follows the adventures of the thin, large-breasted protagonist Lara Croft, is a favorite target for those who object to sexualized female characters.[37] Arthur Berger argues that Croft gives male players a chance to indulge their fantasies of controlling an attractive woman.[38] Astrid Deuber Mankowsky says that Croft reduces femininity to the body and that she therefore remains a traditional figure.[39] Others disagree with these characterizations and seek to show how Croft can be interpreted in alternative ways. Just as in the many other gaming controversies I have covered, there is no consensus on the meaning of the images. Polysemy leaves enough room for interpretive differences that are driven by different attitudes about which representations are favorable and which are discriminatory. By the standards of second-wave feminism, Croft is an objectifying figure that exploits female sexuality by reproducing it as part of male fantasies. Second-wave feminists generally oppose the sexualization of women in media, on the grounds that such depictions reinforce stereotypes about women and present them as being reducible to physical characteristics. However, by the standards of third-wave feminism, Croft is a potentially empowering character who shows that a woman can be proud of her beauty and sexuality while still defying stereotypes of female passivity.[40] These features can coexist, and may even be complementary. As Helene Shugart, Catherine Egley Waggoner, and D. Lynn O'Brien Hallstein put it, "Third-wavers seek to embrace sexual desire and expression, freeing it from the limits of patriarchy and heterosexuality as well as from what they perceive to be the antisex sensibilities of second-wave feminism."[41]

The narrative of the *Tomb Raider* series lends credence to the third-wave feminist interpretation, as the games present Croft as a powerful figure who is capable of overcoming challenges independently. At times, she must even rescue her male friends, reversing typical gender roles in media representations of women. Croft is not simply a sexualized female character. She defies traditional roles and stereotypes. As Maja Mikula explains, she is a fragmented character but one that seems deliberately constructed to break away from stereotypes of female passivity: "The heroine's constructed identity is no more than an amalgam of values representing all the different faces of empowerment in advanced capitalist societies: class, wealth, appearance, physical fitness, strong will, intelligence and independence."[42] Whether one sees Croft's physical attributes as progressive or sexist, it is clear that the role she performs in the game—the role of a competent protagonist who does not require male assistance—is an improvement over the female characters in earlier video games who, like the Princess in *Super Mario Bros.*, were empty figures to be rescued by male characters.

Lara Croft may share part of the responsibility for the positive changes in how other female characters are depicted. Jeroen Jansz and Raynel Martis find that female characters are more common than they were a few years ago and that their roles are more prominent and active.[43] They call the change the "Lara phenomenon" in honor of the role Lara Croft had in showing that women can make popular videogame protagonists. Therefore, whatever one's opinion of Croft and more recent sexualized female protagonists such as Rayne and Bayonetta, it is important to see the role they play in advancing the medium by introducing women as leading characters. This is again a matter of performing game analysis in a contextually sensitive way. Critiques of the sexualized appearance of female characters are certainly right in arguing that this encourages the objectification of women. However, it is vital to see how some representations of women, though sexualized, mark an improvement in the role they have in videogames.

There is room for reasonable disagreement over whether marginalized groups are underrepresented or misrepresented in videogames. In the interest of fostering inclusivity, it is imperative to evaluate games and critics' objections critically. However, with room for reasonable disagreement over the right proportion of characters and how they should look, it is equally important to be cautious about how these critiques are framed and whether they are fair. It is essential to evaluate games in terms of their representational context and with attention to the range of interpretations they can support. It is likewise important to avoid excessive moralizing when it comes to how developers make choices.

None of this is intended to deny that games can embody sexist and racist content. They certainly can do this, and in many instances they do. It is also undeniable that many players embrace this content and attempt to exclude certain groups from gaming. In one of the darkest chapters in the history of videogames, the Gamergate movement sought to intimidate prominent women in the industry through a campaign of harassment that included death threats and the release of personal information. That movement was later integral to forming the alt right in the United States, with figures like Milo Yiannopoulos and other affiliates of Breitbart News making an easy transition from attacks on women and minorities in the gaming world into attacks on their status in real life.[44] To this day, racist and sexist comments in multiplayer games are shockingly common. Anyone who plays in online multiplayer matches is likely familiar with the persistent use of racist, sexist, and homophobic insults. My goal in looking at the critiques of racism and sexism is not to deny that these are sometimes genuine problems but rather to show that critique is often directed too broadly and at the wrong targets. As I have emphasized throughout the book, games are not unique in their ability to present objectionable and upsetting messages. They are unfairly demonized and credited with having an inordinate power to corrupt. Critics likewise tend to overstate the case against games and to underestimate the importance of protecting offensive content from excessive regulation.

Threats, Incitement, and the Extent of Speech

We should not treat offensiveness as a moral failing in itself. Some games are offensive in pursuit of an artistic or political point. Others may cause offense because they mirror real-world inequalities or engage in satire. We should be critical consumers of games while still being aware of the tendency toward overstating the case against them. Above all, we should approach games with some openness toward the range of meanings they may reasonably support based on the contextual information they offer. What, then, should we make of a case like *Custer's Revenge*? It is useful to return to this example because it falls outside many of the defenses I have set out so far. The game's developer, Mystique, did not seem to have had any redeeming artistic or political goals in mind when simulating violence against Native Americans by a white soldier. There is an element of historical realism to the game insofar as it references atrocities that were actually committed, but there is little evidence in favor of reading the game as a realist text attempting to call attention to genocide. The developer's other titles were sexual simulations, which suggests that *Custer's Revenge* was meant to be a titillating rape fantasy. The title further indicates that the fictional Custer is rewriting history through his sexual triumph. It is possible to imagine a game that looks just like *Custer's Revenge* being developed for satirical purposes. After all, what better metaphor could there be for the conquest of the Americas than that of a white man engaged in rape? However, unlike in *Grand Theft Auto*, there is nothing in the game narrative to support such a reading. The most plausible interpretation is that the game is deliberately offensive, with no higher purpose than making money and appealing to base fantasies.

Custer's Revenge is a proverbial case of the exception that proves the rule. It is a morally dubious game that attracts considerable attention because it is among a small subset of games that are deeply offensive without leaving much room for divergent interpretations. It does not incite violence in the same way as *Ethnic Cleansing*, which I would argue should exempt it from censorship. Nevertheless, the weight of the evidence indicates that moral condemnation of the game is justified. The response to *Custer's Revenge* is evidence of why players deserve more credit for being morally sensitive. The game was widely condemned, not only from the usual lineup of activists promoting censorship but also from a broad range of organizations and individuals concerned with this specific game. Atari reported receiving 1,200 complaint letters every day, dissociated itself from the game, and sued the developers.[45] The game drew attacks from across the political spectrum, especially from groups representing women and Native Americans. To this day, it regularly tops lists of the most offensive games ever produced. It is a reminder that although moral condemnation of games needs to be reined in and framed in more reasonable terms, a critical perspective remains necessary.

Conclusion

A troubling game may cause discomfort and upset our sensibilities, but this does not mean that the game or its players are immoral. This transformation of moral issues associated with gaming into political issues leads back to ongoing disputes about the proper extent of free expression. We must avoid conflating the feelings of offense caused by certain types of simulated content with genuine moral violation. To do otherwise risks hinging our moral intuitions on capricious conditions that change based on the social context and time period. Players who enjoy simulating atrocities such as rape, murder, and pedophilia may cause offense, but this does not necessarily mean that they are acting immorally. Throughout this chapter, I have considered a number of reasons why videogames might justifiably simulate offensive content. The moral indignation at videogames is often driven by feelings of offense rather than by substantive moral considerations. Political commentary and satire are extremely valuable and common in games that attract ire. This kind of content is inherently valuable and should be protected against excessive restrictions. Videogames that lack clear political and social commentary may also engage in unequal representation in their attempt to mirror the real world. Nevertheless, in these cases, the problem is not as much with virtual inequality as with real inequality that is so deeply rooted that it seeps into games about historical events, sports, superheroes, and other topics. Videogames have the capacity to challenge stereotypes and to work toward greater equality, especially when set in the future or in fictional worlds. They should be praised for taking these steps, though at times inclusivity may come with its own challenges associated with how members of those groups are portrayed.

Offensive content should be evaluated with reference to how videogame narratives contextualize the characters and events they represent. Criticism must be tempered by an awareness of whether stereotyping is driven by intolerance or satire, and it should seek to identify offensive content that is excusable because of efforts to make political or artistic points. Games that incite violence or issue threats, such as *Ethnic Cleansing*, can be justifiably considered immoral and be restricted based on the standards of free speech that prevail in most liberal democratic societies. Those like *Custer's Revenge*, which fall short of promoting violence, may escape censorship but still deserve moral condemnation. By contrast, games like *Super Columbine RPG!* have a much stronger claim to being morally permissible and legally protected from censorship if they lack the characteristics of incitement and are offensive for the sake of making political points.

Conclusion

I have covered quite a bit of ground throughout the book, so it is worth revisiting the central theses. My first goal was to show that the moral outrage surrounding videogames is largely misguided, regardless of whether it is framed in terms of concern that games cause behavioral changes in individual players or in terms of the political impact of persuasive games. I have argued that games do have the power to influence players but that any influence is mediated by existing beliefs and values. Players are not blank slates imprinted with videogames' messages, nor are they passive victims of a contagion. Players approach games with existing perspectives that help to determine what the games mean, according to the logic of polysemy. The diversity of player perspectives leads to a diversity of interpretations and of messages to be drawn from games. Efforts to find strong adverse influences in a particular game or across the medium as a whole seriously overstate the extent of videogames' power over players and are inadequately supported by the existing empirical research.

My second goal was to explore the significance of moral issues in games. Simulated moral decisions are fictional and therefore not morally problematic according to deontological, consequentialist, or aretaic theories. Players interacting with avatars in videogames do not intend to inflict real harm or commit real infractions, nor do they cause real adverse effects or rehearse wrongful actions in a way that would plausibly forge bad habits based on Aristotelian virtue ethics. Some players may have real desires to commit wrongful acts that they bring into videogames, such as if they use simulations to imagine killing someone, but the acts they perform within game worlds are nevertheless nonmoral because they are fictional. The moral defects in such players can only be explained in terms of real actions or intentions to perform real actions, which is to say that the moral concerns must be extrinsic to the media used for enacting such depraved fantasies.

Third, I rejected the amoralist argument that games have no moral significance. I drew on the analogy with narrative thought experiments to explain how videogames may help us reflect on moral issues and explore them from various perspectives. Regardless of whether players choose to be good, evil, or neutral, they must decide on an ethical orientation and incorporate that into their gameplay. They must navigate simulations with attention to what moral implications actions have within the game world, and while considering the relationship between the simulated actions and the real world. Games encourage the exploration of moral puzzles by designing these in many different ways that bring fresh perspectives on different aspects of moral reasoning and illustrate different types of dilemmas. Making morality integral to game design helps to ensure that games can simultaneously enlighten and entertain. Players contribute to this by discussing and debating their decisions within fan communities, especially those that form online.

Fourth, I argued in favor of rethinking the strategies for critiquing persuasive games and games with offensive content. Persuasive games warrant critique and should continue to receive careful scrutiny, but they should not be treated as mere attempts to indoctrinate or mislead. Games that are designed to persuade or that have strong ideological undertones reflect real perspectives and interests. They grant insight into how other people see the world, which is especially important when it comes to understanding what motivates those with ideologies different from our own. Rather than dismissing these kinds of games as mere deceptions, I advocate engaging with them and appreciating what they have to show us, while still employing critical methods that do not depend on characterizing the games as simple instances of propaganda. We can employ external critiques based on evaluating how games model the world: what information they include, what they omit, and how the narrative is framed. Such a strategy can expose problems with how a game represents an issue or event without requiring us to assume that the developers are willfully misleading or that their ideology is false. Internal critique is based on evaluating the coherence of the game rules and the ideology that is inherent in the game. Here, consistency takes precedence, and ideologies can be evaluated by their own merits without assuming any particular external perspective.

Finally, I sought to show that although we should be critical consumers, we should refrain from conflating feelings of discomfort with moral concerns. Many videogames are disturbing and offensive, yet the capacity to upset is integral to what makes games useful tools for posing important moral and political questions. It is fair to be upset by the content of games, but we must also remain aware that some disturbing games have redeeming benefits that may be visible from different interpretive vantage points. This is especially clear when offensive content is satirical, when it is excusable within the context of the game narrative, or when it offers social commentary. Some games truly are morally dubious or deserving of censorship based on prevailing standards of permissible speech, but these are rare and have had limited commercial success. This will likely remain true in the future, as the commercial imperatives behind games push against hateful motives that would restrict the size of the potential audience.

My perspective on the morality of games may seem too permissive to many readers. After all, I am arguing that it is reasonable to enjoy deeply disturbing simulations, that we can learn something from games that are often dismissed as propaganda, and that even extremely offensive videogames usually warrant protection from censorship because the medium is so often used for important political and social commentary. As I have emphasized, I do not want to foreclose critical investigation of games. My goal is only to move away from the moral panic framework of critique that has unfairly maligned so many games. I have proposed new approaches to critique that can be employed without demonizing or discrediting games.

The arguments I have made hold lessons for future research on the moral and political significance of videogames. I have sought to refute several lines of critique that fuel a moral panic about games in an effort to show that they and their underlying assumptions must be discarded. These critiques hang like weights around scholarly and popular discussions of videogames, impeding progress toward more sophisticated theories. It is rare to see journalists or politicians talk about games except to blame them for some great problem, and much of the scholarly research is devoted to an endless quest to show what is wrong with games or with a particular game. Critique is valuable and must continue, but critique that is theoretically flawed or empirically groundless is a hindrance. Most importantly of all, we must abandon the sense of contamination that underpins the most problematic critiques and that is the single greatest barrier to research. Players are moral agents who have the power to interpret their experiences. They are not blank slates but instead active participants who interpret, judge, and reflect. Ideas are not imprinted on them but rather are filtered through cognitive schema comprised of existing beliefs and values.

My analogy to thought experiments is meant to highlight games' significance when it comes to modeling moral challenges. Videogames entertain with help from the kinds of scenarios that philosophers use for theory development and explication. Moreover, games can make moral counterfactuals far more complex and include the execution element—that feeling of actually making a decision rather than just thinking about making a decision. The capacity for moral simulation is one of the medium's greatest strengths and should be seen as such.

Games can only present moral challenges if they introduce extreme scenarios involving murder and sexual deviance. They can only force us to confront uncomfortable political and social realities by taking chances and running the risk of causing offense. We need to have a much higher tolerance for upsetting content in games because it is essential for building compelling counterfactuals and encouraging moral reflection.

Acknowledgments

I want to thank my wife, Amanda Carroll, for supporting me throughout this project and being an excellent source of constructive feedback. She always believed that videogame research was worthwhile, and encouraged me to pursue it even at a time when many other scholars told me to focus on more traditional topics. My dogs, Ember, Panda, and Pinaka, gave me emotional support and affection during many long workdays. I am grateful for the feedback I received from Garry Young; it is wonderful to have support from a scholar who has made such important contributions to this field. I am likewise indebted to Christopher Ferguson for providing feedback on my work and offering opportunities to shape policy decisions related to violent videogames. Felix Ciuță, Pat Harrigan, Matt Kirschenbaum, Andrew Elliott, Matthew Kapell, Karolien Peols, and Steven Malliet have helped me immensely with opportunities for research and public engagement related to videogames. I am grateful to the many anonymous reviewers who have critiqued my research on videogames over the years. The debates I have been fortunate to have with reviewers forced me to develop stronger arguments and to find better evidence. My old roommate Brian McKernan deserves credit for getting me interested in videogame scholarship many years ago. Finally, I would like to thank Nicole Solano from Rutgers University Press for believing in this project and seeing it through to the end, as well as everyone else at the press who did the hard work of transforming the manuscript into a book.

Notes

Introduction

1 "Moscow Airport Terror Mirrors Video Game," *Russia Today*, January 25, 2011, https://www.rt.com/news/modern-warfare-execution-airport/.

2 Joel Feinberg, "Voluntary Euthanasia and the Inalienable Right to Life," *Philosophy & Public Affairs* 7, no. 2 (1978): 93–123.

3 Charles Tilly, "Trust and Rule," *Theory and Society* 33, no. 1 (2004): 1–30.

4 Thomas Hobbes, *Leviathan* (New York: Cambridge University Press, 1996).

5 John R. Searle, *Making the Social World: The Structure of Human Civilization* (New York: Oxford University Press, 2010).

6 Craig A. Anderson and Brad J. Bushman, "Effects of Violent Video Games on Aggressive Behavior, Aggressive Cognition, Aggressive Affect, Physiological Arousal, and Prosocial Behavior: A Meta-analytic Review of the Scientific Literature," *Psychological Science* 12, no. 5 (2001): 353–359; Craig Anderson, Douglas A. Gentile, and Katherine E. Buckley, *Violent Video Game Effects on Children and Adolescents: Theory, Research, and Public Policy* (New York: Oxford University Press, 2007).

7 Christopher J. Ferguson, "NRA's Video Game Smacks of Hypocrisy," *CNN*, January 16, 2013, https://www.cnn.com/2013/01/16/opinion/ferguson-nra-video-games/index.html.

8 "Moscow Airport Terror Mirrors Video Game."

9 Roger Stahl, "Have You Played the War on Terror?," *Critical Studies in Media Communication* 23, no. 2 (2006): 112–130.

10 Plato, *Phaedrus* (Cambridge: Cambridge University Press, 1952).

11 Plato, *The Republic* (Cambridge: Cambridge University Press, 2000), 79.

12 Charles de Secondat Montesquieu, *The Spirit of the Laws* (New York: Cambridge University Press, 1989); Jean-Jacques Rousseau, *Émile: Or Treatise on Education* (New York: Prometheus Books, 2003); Alexis de Tocqueville, *Democracy in America* (New York: W. W. Norton, 2007).

13 Garry Young, *Ethics in the Virtual World: The Morality and Psychology of Gaming* (London: Routledge, 2014).

14 Patrick M. Markey and Christopher J. Ferguson, *Moral Combat: Why the War on Violent Video Games Is Wrong* (Dallas: BenBella Books, 2017); Christopher

Ferguson, "Evidence for Publication Bias in Video Game Violence Effects Literature: A Meta-analytic Review," *Aggression and Violent Behavior* 12, no. 1 (2007): 470–482.

Chapter 1   The Conceptual Terrain of Simulation

1 Jesper Juul, *Half-real: Video Games between Real Rules and Fictional Worlds* (Cambridge, MA: MIT press, 2011).
2 Greg Lastowka, *Virtual Justice* (New Haven, CT: Yale University Press, 2010).
3 Jean Baudrillard, *Simulacra and Simulation* (Ann Arbor: University of Michigan Press, 1994).
4 Jean Baudrillard, *The Gulf War Did Not Take Place* (Bloomington: Indiana University Press, 1995).
5 Julian Dibbell, "The Life of the Chinese Gold Farmer," *New York Times Magazine*, June 17, 2007, http://www.nytimes.com/2007/06/17/magazine/17lootfarmers-t.html.
6 McKenzie Wark, *Gamer Theory* (Cambridge, MA: Harvard University Press, 2007), 7.
7 Graeme Kirkpatrick, *Aesthetic Theory and the Video Game* (Manchester: Manchester University Press, 2011), 5.
8 Henry Jenkins, "Game Design as Narrative Architecture," in *First Person: New Media as Story, Performance, Game*, ed. Noah Wardrip-Fruin and Pat Harrigan (Cambridge, MA: MIT Press, 2004).
9 Garry Young, *Ethics in the Virtual World: The Morality and Psychology of Gaming* (London: Routledge, 2014), 72.
10 James Newman, *Videogames* (New York: Routledge, 2004), 63.
11 For examples, see Klaus Mathiak and René Weber, "Toward Brain Correlates of Natural Behavior: fMRI during Violent Video Games," *Human Brain Mapping* 27, no. 12 (2006): 948–956; Nicholas L. Carnagey, Craig A. Anderson, and Brad J. Bushman. "The Effect of Video Game Violence on Physiological Desensitization to Real-Life Violence," *Journal of Experimental Social Psychology* 43, no. 3 (2007): 489–496.
12 Steven Pinker, *The Blank Slate: The Modern Denial of Human Nature* (New York: Penguin, 2003).
13 Jerome H. Barkow, Leda Cosmides, and John Tooby, eds., *The Adapted Mind: Evolutionary Psychology and the Generation of Culture* (New York: Oxford University Press, 1992).
14 Martin Jones and Robert Sugden, "Positive Confirmation Bias in the Acquisition of Information," *Theory and Decision* 50, no. 1 (2001): 59–99; George E. Marcus, John L. Sullivan, Elizabeth Theiss-Morse, and Daniel Stevens, "The Emotional Foundation of Political Cognition: The Impact of Extrinsic Anxiety on the Formation of Political Tolerance Judgments," *Political Psychology* 26, no. 6 (2005): 949–963; Raymond S. Nickerson, "Confirmation Bias: A Ubiquitous Phenomenon in Many Guises," *Review of General Psychology* 2, no. 2 (1998): 175–220; Charles S. Taber, Damon Cann, and Simona Kucsova, "The Motivated Processing of Political Arguments," *Political Behavior* 31, no. 2 (2009): 137–155; George E. Marcus and Michael B. MacKuen, "Anxiety, Enthusiasm, and the Vote: The Emotional Underpinnings of Learning and Involvement during Presidential Campaigns," *American Political Science Review* 87, no. 3 (1993): 672–685.
15 David P. Redlawsk, Andrew J. W. Civettini, and Karen M. Emmerson, "The Affective Tipping Point: Do Motivated Reasoners Ever 'Get It'?," *Political Psychology* 31, no. 4 (2010): 563–593 at 563.

16 John Fiske, *Television Culture* (New York: Routledge, 1987).

17 Henry Jenkins, *Textual Poachers: Television Fans and Participatory Culture* (New York: Routledge, 1992), xxi.

18 Steven E. Jones, *The Meaning of Video Games: Gaming and Textual Strategies* (New York: Routledge, 2008), 9–10. See also Judd Ethan Ruggill and Ken McAllister, *Gaming Matters: Art, Science, Magic and the Computer Game Medium* (Tuscaloosa: University of Alabama Press 2011), 87.

19 Fiske, *Television Culture*, 12.

20 Jones, *The Meaning of Video Games*.

21 Matt McCormick, "Is It Wrong to Play Violent Video Games?," *Ethics and Information Technology* 3, no. 4 (2001): 277–287; Marcus Schulzke, "Defending the Morality of Violent Video Games," *Ethics and Information Technology* 12, no. 2 (2010): 127–138; Garry Young, "Violent Video Games and Morality: A Meta-ethical Approach," *Ethics and Information Technology* 17, no. 4 (2015): 311–321.

22 Julia Driver, *Consequentialism* (London: Routledge, 1993).

23 Immanuel Kant, "Groundwork on the Metaphysics of Morals," in *Practical Philosophy*, ed. Mary J. Gregor (New York: Cambridge University Press, 1999), 73.

24 Kant, "Groundwork on the Metaphysics of Morals," 80.

25 Jeremy Bentham, *An Introduction to the Principles of Morals and Legislation* (Mineola, NY: Dover Publications, 2007).

26 John Stuart Mill, *Utilitarianism* (New York: Bantam Books, 1993).

27 Ren Reynolds, *Playing a "Good" Game: A Philosophical Approach to Understanding the Morality of Games* (Toronto: International Game Developers Association, 2002), 4.

28 Grant Tavinor, *The Art of Videogames* (Malden, MA: Blackwell, 2009).

29 G.E.M. Anscombe, "Modern Moral Philosophy," *Philosophy* 33 (1958): 1–19.

30 Alasdair MacIntyre, *After Virtue: A Study in Moral Theory* (Notre Dame, IN: University of Notre Dame Press, 2007).

31 Aristotle, *Nicomachean Ethics* (Upper Saddle River, NJ: Prentice Hall, 1999).

32 McCormick, "Is It Wrong to Play Violent Video Games?"; Christopher Bartel, "Free Will and Moral Responsibility in Video Games," *Ethics and Information Technology* 17, no. 4 (2015): 285–293; Stephanie Patridge, "The Incorrigible Social Meaning of Video Game Imagery: Making Ethical Sense of Single-Player Video Games," *Ethics and Information Technology* 13, no. 4 (2011): 303–312.

Chapter 2 The Moral Panic Surrounding Videogames

1 Tom Kertscher, "Which Is Higher: The Number of People, or the Number of Guns, in America?," *Politifact*, February 20, 2018, https://www.politifact.com/wisconsin/statements/2018/feb/20/kevin-nicholson/which-higher-number-people-or-number-guns-america/.

2 Monique Wonderly, "A Humean Approach to Assessing the Moral Significance of Ultra-violent Video Games," *Ethics and Information Technology* 10, no. 1 (2007): 1–10; Jeanne B. Funk, Debra D. Buchman, Jennifer Jenks, and Heidi Bechtoldt, "Playing Violent Video Games, Desensitization, and Moral Evaluation in Children," *Applied Developmental Psychology* 24 (2003): 413–436; Craig Alan Anderson, Douglas A. Gentile, and Katherine E. Buckley, *Violent Video Game Effects on Children and Adolescents: Theory, Research, and Public Policy* (New York: Oxford University Press, 2007).

3 https://www.killology.com/bio.

4 Tayr Link, "NRA's 'killology' Expert Calls for More Guns to Fight an 'Assassination Generation,'" *Salon*, May 3, 2017, https://www.salon.com/2017/05/03/nras -killology-expert-calls-for-more-guns-to-fight-an-assassination-generation/.

5 Glenn Beck, *Control: Exposing the Truth about Guns* (New York: Threshold Editions, 2013).

6 Bill O'Reilly, *Culture Warrior* (New York: Broadway Books, 2006).

7 Dave Grossman, *On Killing: The Psychological Cost of Learning to Kill in War and Society* (New York: Back Bay Books, 2009).

8 Dave Grossman and Gloria DeGaetano, *Stop Teaching Our Kids to Kill: A Call to Action against TV, Movie & Video Game Violence* (New York: Crown, 1999), 4.

9 S.L.A. Marshall, *Men against Fire: The Problem of Battle Command* (Norman: University of Oklahoma Press, 2000).

10 Roger J. Spiller, "S.L.A. Marshall and the Ratio of Fire", *RUSI Journal* 133 (Winter 1988): 63–71; John Whiteclay Chambers II, "S. L. A. Marshall's Men against Fire: New Evidence Regarding Fire Ratios," *Parameters* 33, no. 3 (Autumn 2003): 114–121; Fredric Smoler, The Secret of the Soldiers Who Didn't Shoot," *American Heritage* 40, no. 2 (March 1989): 36–45; Evan Thomas, "A Myth of Military History," *Newsweek*, December 11, 2007, https://www.newsweek.com/myth-military-history -94505.

11 Robert C. Engen, "Canadians against Fire: Canada's Soldiers and Marshall's 'Ratio of Fire,' 1944–1945" (MA thesis, Queen's University, 2008).

12 Steven Pinker, *The Better Angels of Our Nature: Why Violence Has Declined* (New York: Viking, 2012).

13 Paul Robinson, Nigel De Lee, and Don Carrick, eds., *Ethics Education in the Military* (Hampshire: Ashgate, 2008); James Connelly, Don Carrick, and Paul Robinson, eds., *Ethics Education for Irregular Warfare* (Burlington, VT: Ashgate, 2009).

14 Robinson, De Lee, and Carrick, *Ethics Education in the Military*; Connelly, Carrick, and Robinson, *Ethics Education for Irregular Warfare*.

15 Michael G. Wessells, *Child Soldiers: From Violence to Protection* (Cambridge, MA: Harvard University Press, 2006).

16 Steven Pinker, *The Blank Slate: The Modern Denial of Human Nature* (New York: Penguin, 2003).

17 https://www.virtra.com/.

18 Amanda Davies, "The Hidden Advantage in Shoot/Don't Shoot Simulation Exercises for Police Recruit Training," *Salus Journal* 3, no. 1 (2015): 16–30.

19 Bobby Ross Jr., "Violence: Who's to Blame?" *The Oklahoman*, December 26, 1999.

20 Lawrence Kutner and Cheryl Olson, *Grand Theft Childhood: The Surprising Truth about Violent Video Games and What Parents Can Do* (New York: Simon and Schuster, 2008).

21 Kutner and Olson, *Grand Theft Childhood*, 140.

22 Pinker, *The Better Angels of Our Nature*, xxv.

23 Mary Ballard and J. Rose Wiest, "Mortal Kombat (tm): The Effects of Violent Videogame Play on Males' Hostility and Cardiovascular Responding 1," *Journal of Applied Social Psychology* 26, no. 8 (1996): 717–730.

24 Nicholas L Carnagey, Craig A. Anderson, and Brad J. Bushman, "The Effect of Violence on Physiological Desensitization to Real-Life Violence," *Journal of Experimental Social Psychology* 43, no. 4 (2007): 489–496.

25 Klaus Mathiak and René Weber, "Toward Brain Correlates of Natural Behavior: fMRI during Violent Video Games," *Human Brain Mapping* 27, no. 12 (2006): 948–956.

26 Douglas A. Gentile, Patrick K. Bender, and Craig A. Anderson, "Violent Video Game Effects on Salivary Cortisol, Arousal, and Aggressive Thoughts in Children," *Computers in Human Behavior* 70 (2017): 39–43 at 41.

27 Michelle P. Warren and Naama W. Constantini, eds., *Sports Endocrinology* (New York: Springer, 2000).

28 Craig Anderson and Karen E. Dill, "Video Games and Aggressive Thoughts, Feelings, and Behaviour in the Laboratory and in Life," *Journal of Personality and Social Psychology* 78, no. 4 (2000): 772–790.

29 For an excellent sustained critique of this article, see Christopher Ferguson, "The Good, the Bad and the Ugly: A Meta-analytic Review of Positive and Negative Effects of Violent Video Games," *Psychiatric Quarterly* 78, no. 4 (2007): 309–316.

30 Christopher J. Ferguson, Stephanie M. Rueda, Amanda M. Cruz, Diana E. Ferguson, Stacey Fritz, and Shawn M. Smith, "Violent Video Games and Aggression: Causal Relationship or Byproduct of Family Violence and Intrinsic Violence Motivation?," *Criminal Justice and Behavior* 35, no. 3 (2008): 311–332.

31 Bruce D. Bartholow and Craig A. Anderson, "Effects of Violent Video Games on Aggressive Behavior: Potential Sex Differences," *Journal of Experimental Social Psychology* 38, no. 3 (2002): 283–290.

32 Craig A. Anderson and Brad J. Bushman, "Effects of Violent Video Games on Aggressive Behavior, Aggressive Cognition, Aggressive Affect, Physiological Arousal, and Prosocial Behavior: A Meta-analytic Review of the Scientific Literature," *Psychological Science* 12, no. 5 (2001): 353–359.

33 For examples, see Glenna L. Read, Mary Ballard, Lisa J. Emery, and Doris G. Bazzini, "Examining Desensitization Using Facial Electromyography: Violent Videogames, Gender, and Affective Responding," *Computers in Human Behavior* 62 (2016): 201–211; Patrick M. Markey and Christopher J. Ferguson, *Moral Combat: Why the War on Violent Video Games Is Wrong* (Dallas: BenBella Books, 2017).

34 Kutner and Olson, *Grand Theft Childhood*.

35 Christopher Ferguson, "Evidence for Publication Bias in Video Game Violence Effects Literature: A Meta-analytic Review," *Aggression and Violent Behavior* 12, no. 1 (2007): 470–482.

36 Pinker, *Better Angels of Our Nature*, 128.

37 Michael R. Ward, "Video Games and Crime," *Contemporary Economic Policy* 29, no. 2 (2011): 261–273.

38 Charlotte Markey, Patrick Markey, and Juliana French, "Violent Video Games and Real-World Violence: Rhetoric versus Data," *Psychology of Popular Media Culture* 4, no. 4 (2015): 277–295 at 291.

39 Ferguson, "The Good, the Bad and the Ugly," 310.

40 Anderson, Gentile, and Buckley, *Violent Video Game Effects on Children and Adolescents*, 52.

41 Anderson and Dill, "Video Games and Aggressive Thoughts, Feelings, and Behaviour in the Laboratory and in Life"; Anderson and Bushman, "Effects of Violent Video Games on Aggressive Behavior."

42 Funk et al., "Playing Violent Video Games, Desensitization, and Moral Evaluation in Children," 416.

43 Grossman and DeGaetano, *Stop Teaching Our Kids to Kill*, 71.

44 Wonderly, "A Humean Approach to Assessing the Moral Significance of Ultra-violent Video Games," 6.

45 Wonderly, "A Humean Approach to Assessing the Moral Significance of Ultra-violent Video Games," 8.

46 Ross G. Menzies and J. Christopher Clarke, "A Comparison of in vivo and Vicarious Exposure in the Treatment of Childhood Water Phobia," *Behaviour Research and Therapy* 31, no. 1 (1993): 9–15; Joseph Wolpe and Janet Abrams, "Post-traumatic Stress Disorder Overcome by Eye-Movement Desensitization: A Case Report," *Journal of Behavior Therapy and Experimental Psychiatry* 22, no. 1 (1991): 39–43.

47 Michael Scharkow, "The Accuracy of Self-Reported Internet Use—a Validation Study Using Client Log Data," *Communication Methods and Measures* 10, no. 1 (2016): 13–27.

48 The ostensible link between gaming and violence is a common topic in the gaming fan community, which often elicits vehement reports that the link is imaginary. For example, see the many Reddit threads related to this topic, such as https://www .reddit.com/r/gaming/comments/81fmtb/i_am_sick_of_hearing_about_how _video_games_cause/.

49 Funk et al., "Playing Violent Video Games, Desensitization, and Moral Evaluation in Children."

50 Dick Couch, *A Tactical Ethic: Moral Conduct in the Insurgent Battlespace* (Annapolis, MD: Naval Institute Press, 2011); Timothy L. Challans, *Awakening Warrior: Revolution in the Ethics of Warfare* (Albany: State University of New York Press, 2007).

51 Andrew Golub, Luther Elliott, Matthew Price, and Alexander Bennett, "More than Just a Game? Combat-Themed Gaming among Recent Veterans with Posttraumatic Stress Disorder," *Games for Health* 4, no. 4 (2015): 271–277.

52 Markey and Ferguson, *Moral Combat*, 156.

53 Amanda Lange, "'You're Just Gonna Be Nice': How Players Engage with Moral Choice Systems," *Journal of Games Criticism* 1, no. 1 (2014), http://gamescriticism .org/articles/lange-1-1/.

54 Tilo Hartmann and Peter Vorderer, "It's Okay to Shoot a Character: Moral Disengagement in Violent Video Games," *Journal of Communication* 60 (2010): 94–119.

55 Hartmann and Vorderer, "It's Okay to Shoot a Character," 96.

56 Hartmann and Vorderer, "It's Okay to Shoot a Character," 96.

57 David I. Waddington, "Locating the Wrongness of Ultra-violent Video Games," *Ethics and Information Technology* 9, no. 2 (2007): 121–128 at 127.

58 Steven L. Kent, *The Ultimate History of Video Games*, vol. 2: *From Pong to Pokemon and Beyond* (New York: Three Rivers Press, 2001).

59 James Newman, *Videogames* (New York: Routledge, 2004), 66.

60 Grossman and DeGaetano, *Stop Teaching Our Kids to Kill*, 3.

61 For example, see Eugene F. Provenzo, "Virtuous War, Simulation and the Militarization of Play," in *Education as Enforcement: The Militarization and Corporatization of Schools*, ed. Kenneth J. Saltman and David Gabbard (New York: Routledge, 2011), 284.

62 Steven E. Jones, *The Meaning of Video Games: Gaming and Textual Strategies* (New York: Routledge, 2008), 16.

63 Jan Van Looy, Cédric Courtois, Melanie De Vocht, and Lieven De Marez, "Player Identification in Online Games: Validation of a Scale for Measuring Identification in MMOGs," *Media Psychology* 15, no. 2 (2012): 197–221; Alistair Soutter and Michael Hitchens, "The Relationship between Character Identification and Flow State within Video Games," *Computers in Human Behavior* 55 (2016): 1030–1038.

64 Waddington, "Locating the Wrongness of Ultra-violent Video Games," 127.

65 Waddington, "Locating the Wrongness of Ultra-violent Video Games."

66 For example, see player responses to the mission at https://www.reddit.com/r
/gaming/comments/2pom7w/remember_no_russian/.

67 Jeanne B. Funk, Heidi Bechtoldt Baldacci, Tracie Pasold, and Jennifer Baumgard-
ner, "Violence Exposure in Real-life, Video Games, Television, Movies, and the
Internet: Is There Desensitization?," *Journal of Adolescence* 27 (2004): 23–39 at 24.

68 Mia Consalvo, "Rule Sets, Cheating, and Magic Circles: Studying Games and
Ethics," *International Review of Information Ethics* 4, no. 12 (2005): 7–12.

69 Lange, "You're Just Gonna Be Nice."

70 Garry Young, "Violent Video Games and Morality: A Meta-ethical Approach,"
Ethics and Information Technology 17, no. 4 (2015): 311–321 at 313.

Chapter 3   Imaginary Transgressions

1 Nicholas Rescher, *Imagining Irreality: A Study of Unreal Possibilities* (Chicago:
Open Court, 2003), 18.

2 Philippa Foot, "The Problem of Abortion and the Doctrine of Double Effect,"
Oxford Review 5 (1967): 5–15.

3 Julian Baggini, *The Pig That Wants to Be Eaten: 100 Experiments for the Armchair
Philosopher* (New York: Plume, 2005), x.

4 https://www.pippinbarr.com/2011/10/07/trolley-problem/.

5 There is disagreement over exactly what qualifies as a thought experiment. One
dispute is about the relationship they should have to empirical research. Nicholas
Rescher interprets the concept of a thought experiment broadly to include almost
any use of counterfactual reasoning to raise theoretical or empirical questions. See
Nicholas Rescher, "Thought Experimentation in Presocratic Philosophy," in
Thought Experiments in Science and Philosophy, ed. Tamara Horowitz and Gerald J.
Massey (Savage, MD: Rowman and Littlefield, 1991), 31–42. By this account, a
thought experiment is just another name for a hypothetical scenario that is used to
explore a problem. This sets a relatively low standard for qualifying as a thought
experiment. Others would draw the boundary around thought experiments more
narrowly. J. N. Mohanty thinks that thought experiments can only be concerned
with things that cannot be performed in real life. See J. N. Mohanty, "Imaginative
Variation in Phenomenology," in Horowitz and Massey, *Thought Experiments in
Science and Philosophy*, 41–72. This would preclude thought experiments involving
empirically testable hypotheses. Such a definition would exclude thought experiments that are potentially testable but that are dangerous, as well as those that
precede empirical testing in an effort to anticipate how to improve the research
design. I would argue that more restrictive definitions are apt to needlessly leave out
some of the most compelling advantages of this sort of experimentation yet on
either extreme do not impose restrictions about what media can be involved in an
experiment. Others have explained thought experiments as a type of modeling that
allows experimenters to work with mental rather than physical manipulations to
produce the experiment. See Michael A. Bishop, "Why Thought Experiments Are
Not Arguments," *Philosophy of Science* 66, no. 4 (1999): 534–541. Such definitions
are certainly right to an extent, just so long as the lack of physicality is not overstated. Thought experiments must stand in for real events as a simulation, yet they
can still use a physical analogue or physical processes as a model. They do not need
to be purely mental. It would be strange to think that Pippin Barr's simulated
Trolley Problem is less of a thought experiment than a narrative statement of the

Trolley Problem. If anything, the simulation is more experimental, by making it easier to control key variables.

6 For discussions of this, see Grant Tavinor, *The Art of Videogames* (Malden, MA: Blackwell, 2009).

7 Eva M. Dadlez, *What's Hecuba to Him? Fictional Events and Actual Emotions* (University Park: Pennsylvania State University Press, 1997), 126.

8 Thomas Wartenberg, *Thinking on Screen: Film as Philosophy* (London: Routledge, 2007).

9 Hilary Putnam, "Meaning and Reference," *Journal of Philosophy* 70 (1973): 699–711.

10 James Robert Brown, *The Laboratory of the Mind: Thought Experiments in the Natural Sciences* (New York: Routledge, 2011).

11 Brian Greene, *The Elegant Universe: Superstrings, Hidden Dimensions, and the Quest for the Ultimate Theory* (New York: W. W. Norton, 1999).

12 Karl Popper, *The Logic of Scientific Discovery* (New York: Harper Torchbooks, 1968).

13 Thomas Kuhn, *The Structure of Scientific Revolutions* (Chicago: University of Chicago Press, 1996), 263.

14 R. M. Sainsbury, *Paradoxes* (Cambridge: Cambridge University Press, 2009), 1.

15 David Edmonds, *Would You Kill the Fat Man? The Trolley Problem and What Your Answer Tells Us about Right and Wrong* (Princeton, NJ: Princeton University Press, 2014), xii.

16 Marcus Schulzke, *Pursuing Moral Warfare* (Washington, DC: Georgetown University Press, 2018).

17 Contrary to critics' claims, such simulations are usually designed to promote ethical awareness and proper use of force, not to promote violence.

18 Bernard Williams, "A Critique of Utilitarianism," in *Utilitarianism: For and Against*, ed. Bernard Williams and J.J.C. Smart (Cambridge: Cambridge University Press, 1973), 77–149.

19 Daniel Dennett, *Elbow Room* (Cambridge, MA: MIT Press, 1984), 18.

20 Gilbert Harman, "Moral Explanations of Natural Facts—Can Moral Claims Be Tested against Moral Reality?," *Southern Journal of Philosophy* 60 (1986): 69–78.

21 George Lind, *How to Teach Morality: Promoting Deliberation and Discussion, Reducing Violence and Deceit* (Berlin: Logos Verlag, 2016).

22 Don MacNiven, *Creative Morality* (London: Routledge, 1993), 6.

23 Jonathan Glover, *What Sort of People Should There Be?* (Harmondsworth: Penguin, 1984), 212.

24 Glover, *What Sort of People Should There Be?*, 212.

25 Baggini, *The Pig That Wants to Be Eaten*, x.

26 Lawrence Kohlberg, "Stage and Sequence," in *Handbook of Socialization Theory and Research*, ed. D. A. Goslin (Chicago: Rand McNally, 1969).

27 Williams, "A Critique of Utilitarianism."

28 Dennett, *Elbow Room*.

29 Roy A. Sorensen, *Thought Experiments* (New York: Oxford University Press, 1992), 246.

30 Sorensen, *Thought Experiments*, 242.

31 Sorensen, *Thought Experiments*, 243.

32 For example, see https://telltale.com/community/discussion/40750/did-you-decide -to-cut-lees-arm-off-or-not.

Chapter 4   Digital Morality

1   Jan Steutel and David Carr, "Virtue Ethics and the Virtue Approach to Moral Education," in *Virtue Ethics and Moral Education*, ed. David Carr and Jan Steutel (New York: Routledge, 1999).

2   Michael Heron and Pauline Belford, "'It's Only a Game'—Ethics, Empathy and Identification in Game Morality Systems," *Computer Games Journal* 3, no. 1 (2014): 34–53.

3   James Paul Gee, "What Video Games Have to Teach Us about Learning and Literacy," *Computers in Entertainment* 1, no.1 (2003).

4   Ken McAllister, *Game Work: Language, Power, and Computer Game Culture* (Tuscaloosa: University of Alabama Press, 2006), 59.

5   Arthur A. Raney, "Expanding Disposition Theory: Reconsidering Character Liking, Moral Evaluations, and Enjoyment," *Communication Theory* 14, no. 4 (2004): 348–369; Arthur A. Raney, Jason K. Smith, and Kaysee Baker, "Adolescents and the Appeal of Video Games," in *Playing Video Games: Motives, Responses, and Consequences*, ed. Peter Vorderer and Jennings Bryant (New York: Routledge, 2006); E. A. Konijn and J. F. Hoorn, "Some Like It Bad: Testing a Model for Perceiving and Experiencing Fictional Characters," *Media Psychology* 7, no. 2 (2005): 107–144.

6   Amanda Lange, "'You're Just Gonna Be Nice': How Players Engage with Moral Choice Systems," *Journal of Games Criticism* 1, no. 1 (2014), http://gamescriticism .org/articles/lange-1-1/.

7   Cass R. Sunstein, *Why Societies Need Dissent* (Cambridge, MA: Harvard University Press, 2003).

8   Lange, "You're Just Gonna Be Nice."

9   A. J. Weaver and N. Lewis, "Mirrored Morality: An Exploration of Moral Choice in Video Games," *Cyberpsychology, Behavior, and Social Networking* 15, no. 11 (2012): 610–614 at 614.

10 Mia Consalvo, Thorsten Busch, and Carolyn Jong, "Playing a Better Me: How Players Rehearse Their Ethos via Moral Choices," *Games and Culture* 14, no. 3 (2016): 216–235 at 221.

11 Roy A. Sorensen, *Thought Experiments* (New York: Oxford University Press, 1992), 243.

12 Consalvo, Busch, and Jong, "Playing a Better Me."

13 Sorensen, *Thought Experiments*, 243.

14 Alex Hern, "Grand Theft Auto 5 under Fire for Graphic Torture Scene," *The Guardian*, September 18, 2013, https://www.theguardian.com/technology/2013/sep /18/grand-theft-auto-5-under-fire-for-graphic-torture-scene.

15 For example, see https://www.youtube.com/watch?v=xjlSmCm1K74.

16 Matt McCormick, "Is It Wrong to Play Violent Video Games?," *Ethics and Information Technology* 3, no. 4 (2001): 277–287 at 284.

17 Christopher Bartel, "Free Will and Moral Responsibility in Video Games," *Ethics and Information Technology* 17, no. 4 (2015): 285–293 at 291.

18 Stephanie Patridge, "The Incorrigible Social Meaning of Video Game Imagery: Making Ethical Sense of Single-Player Video Games," *Ethics and Information Technology* 13, no. 4 (2011): 303–312 at 311.

19 Adam Briggle, "The Ethics of Computer Games: A Character Approach," in *The Philosophy of Computer Games*, ed. J. Sageng, H. Fossheim, and T. Mandt Larsen (Dordrecht: Springer, 2012), 164.

20 Jon Cogburn and Mark Silcox, *Philosophy through Video Games* (New York: Routledge, 2009), 59.

21 Aristotle, *Poetics* (New York: Penguin Classics, 1997).

22 Gunter Gebauer and Christoph Wulf, *Mimesis: Culture Art Society* (Berkeley: University of California Press, 1992), 55.

23 Johan Huizinga, *Homo Ludens: A Study of the Play-Element in Culture* (Boston: Beacon Press, 1955).

24 Alan S. Waterman, "Reconsidering Happiness: A Eudaimonist's Perspective," *Journal of Positive Psychology* 3, no. 4 (2008): 234–252.

25 Morgan Luck, "The Gamer's Dilemma: An Analysis of the Arguments for the Moral Distinction between Virtual Murder and Virtual Paedophilia," *Ethics and Information Technology* 11, no. 1 (2009): 31–36 at 35.

26 Peter Singer, "Video Crime Peril vs. Virtual Pedophilia," *Japan Times*, July 22, 2007.

27 Garry Young, "Enacting Taboos as a Means to an End; but What End? On the Morality of Motivations for Child Murder and Paedophilia within Gamespace," *Ethics and Information Technology* 15, no. 1 (2013): 13–23.

28 Bartel, "Free Will and Moral Responsibility in Video Games."

29 For a contrary perspective on pornography, see Nadine Strossen, *Defending Pornography: Free Speech, Sex, and the Fight for Women's Rights* (New York: NYU Press, 2000).

30 Morgan Luck and Nathan Ellerby, "Has Bartel Resolved the Gamer's Dilemma?," *Ethics and Information Technology* 15, no. 3 (2013): 229–233.

31 Rami Ali, "A New Solution to the Gamer's Dilemma," *Ethics and Information Technology* 17, no. 4 (2015): 267–274.

32 Vladimir Nabokov, *Lolita* (New York: Vintage, 1989).

33 Martha C. Nussbaum, *From Disgust to Humanity: Sexual Orientation and Constitutional Law* (Oxford: Oxford University Press, 2010).

Chapter 5   The Many Faces of Moral Reflection

1 Matt Barton, *Dungeons and Desktops: The History of Computer Role-Playing Games* (Boca Raton, FL: AK Peters/CRC Press, 2008).

2 For example, see https://forums.beamdog.com/discussion/33480/morality-and-alignment-what-do-you-choose-and-why.

3 Miguel Sicart, "The Banality of Simulated Evil: Designing Ethical Gameplay," *Ethics and Information Technology* 11, no. 3 (2009): 191–202, at 191.

4 Michael Heron and Pauline Belford, "'It's Only a Game'—Ethics, Empathy and Identification in Game Morality Systems," *Computer Games Journal* 3, no. 1 (2014): 34–53.

5 Grant Tavinor, "BioShock and the Art of Rapture," *Philosophy and Literature* 33, no. 1 (2009): 91–106 at 99.

6 Judith Jarvis Thomson, "A Defense of Abortion," *Philosophy & Public Affairs* 1, no. 1 (1971): 47–66.

7 Rowan Tulloch, "A Man Chooses, a Slave Obeys: Agency, Interactivity and Freedom in Video Gaming," *Journal of Gaming and Virtual Worlds* 2, no. 1 (2010): 27–38.

8 For examples, see http://fallout.wikia.com/wiki/Forum:Which_faction_is_the_%22good%22_faction%3F; https://www.reddit.com/r/Fallout/comments/6zrsue/fallout_new_vegas_whats_your_favorite_faction_and/.

9   Luis de Miranda, "Life Is Strange and 'Games are Made': A Philosophical Interpretation of a Multiple-Choice Existential Simulator with Copilot Sartre," *Games and Culture* 13, no. 8 (2016): 1–18.

10   Mia Consalvo, Thorsten Busch, and Carolyn Jong, "Playing a Better Me: How Players Rehearse Their Ethos via Moral Choices," *Games and Culture* 14, no. 3 (2016): 216–235.

11   Heron and Belford, "It's Only a Game."

12   Joseph Packer, "The Battle for Galt's Gulch: Bioshock as Critique of Objectivism," *Journal of Gaming and Virtual Worlds* 2, no. 3 (2010): 209–223.

13   Marcus Schulzke, "Bioethics in Digital Dystopias," *International Journal of Technoethics* 4, no. 2 (2013): 46–57.

14   Edward Castronova, *Synthetic Worlds: The Business and Culture of Online Games* (Chicago: University of Chicago Press, 2005).

15   Elizabeth Wicks, *The Right to Life and Conflicting Interests* (Oxford: Oxford University Press, 2010).

16   For example, see https://www.shamusyoung.com/twentysidedtale/?p=2013.

Chapter 6   Persuasive Games and Ideological Manipulation

1   Marcus Schulzke, "The Virtual War on Terror: Counterterrorism Narratives in Video Games," *New Political Science* 35, no. 4 (2013): 586–603.

2   Ed Halter, *From Sun Tzu to XBox: War and Video Games* (New York: Thunder's Mouth Press, 2006).

3   Aaron Delwiche, "From the Green Berets to America's Army: Video Games as a Vehicle for Political Propaganda," in *The Players' Realm: Studies on the Culture of Video Games and Gaming*, ed. Patrick J. Williams and Jonas Heide Smith (Jefferson, NC: McFarland), 95.

4   Marcus Power, "Digitized Virtuosity: Video War Games and Post-9/11 Cyber-Deterrence," *Security Dialogue* 38, no. 2 (2007): 271–288 at 278.

5   Louisa Hearan, "Terrorist Games Linked to Russian Airport Bomb," *Sydney Morning Herald*, January 27, 2011, https://www.smh.com.au/technology/terrorist-games-linked-to-russian-airport-bomb-20110127-1a66i.html.

6   Lori Mezoff, "America's Army: 'Proving Grounds' Launched on Steam," *Recruiter Journal*, October 2, 2015, http://www.therecruiterjournal.com/americarsquos-army-proving-grounds-launched-on-steam.html.

7   Robertson Allen, "The Unreal Enemy of America's Army," *Games and Culture* 6, no. 1 (2011): 38–60.

8   Power, "Digitized Virtuosity," 281.

9   Peter Mantello, "Playing Discreet War in the US: Negotiating Subjecthood and Sovereignty through Special Forces Video Games," *Media, War, & Conflict* 5, no. 3 (2012): 269–283.

10   Mark B. Salter, "The Geographical Imaginations of Video Games: *Diplomacy, Civilization, America's Army* and *Grand Theft Auto IV*," *Geopolitics* 16, no. 2 (2011): 359–388 at 360.

11   Jon R. Anderson, "Taliban Infiltrate 'America's Army'—and Why That's a Good Thing," *Army Times*, September 3, 2013, http://www.armytimes.com/apps/pbcs.dll/article?AID=2013309030017.

12   Paul Tassi, "ISIS Uses 'GTA 5' in New Teen Recruitment Video," *Forbes*, September 20, 2014, http://www.forbes.com/sites/insertcoin/2014/09/20/isis-uses-gta-5-in-new-teen-recruitment-video/.

13 Roger Stahl, *Militainment, Inc.: War, Media, and Popular Culture* (New York: Routledge, 2009).

14 David L. Robb, *Operation Hollywood: How the Pentagon Shapes and Censors the Movies* (New York: Prometheus Books, 2004).

15 Simon Dalby, "Warrior Geopolitics: Gladiator, Black Hawk Down and The Kingdom of Heaven," *Political Geography* 27, no. 4 (2008): 439–455.

16 Dave Thier, "Navy SEALs Reprimanded for Work on Medal of Honor: Warfighter," *Forbes*, November 9, 2012, https://www.forbes.com/sites/davidthier/2012/11/09/navy-seals-reprimanded-for-work-on-medal-of-honor-warfighter/#672ee7ce3499.

17 Robert Sparrow, Rebecca Harrison, Justin Oakley, and Brendan Keogh, "Playing for Fun, Training for War: Can Popular Claims about Recreational Video Gaming and Military Simulations Be Reconciled?," *Games and Culture* 13, no. 2 (2015): 174–192 at 177.

18 Sparrow et al., "Playing for Fun, Training for War," 187.

19 Sparrow et al., "Playing for Fun, Training for War," 182.

20 Jan Thorson and Per-Arne Öberg, "Was There a Suicide Epidemic after Goethe's Werther?," *Archives of Suicide Research* 7, no. 1 (2003): 69–72.

21 Pat Brown, *Killing for Sport: Inside the Minds of Serial Killers* (Beverly Hills, CA: Phoenix Books, 2003), 60.

22 Brendan Nyhan and Jason Reifler, "When Corrections Fail: The Persistence of Political Misperceptions," *Political Behavior* 32, no. 2 (2010): 303–330.

23 Larry M. Bartels, "Beyond the Running Tally: Partisan Bias in Political Perceptions," *Political Behavior* 24, no. 2 (2002): 117–150; Milton Lodge and Charles S. Taber, "Automaticity of Affect for Political Leaders, Groups, and Issues," *Political Psychology* 26, no. 3 (2005): 455–482.

24 Felix Ciută, "Call of Duty: Playing Video Games with IR," *Millennium* 44, no. 2 (2016): 197–215 at 205.

25 Adam J. Berinsky, *In Time of War: Understanding American Public Opinion from World War II to Iraq* (Chicago: University of Chicago Press, 2009); Christopher Gelpi, Peter D. Feaver, and Jason Reifler, *Paying the Human Costs of War: American Public Opinion & Casualties in Military Conflicts* (Princeton, NJ: Princeton University Press, 2009).

26 James Igoe Walsh, "Precision Weapons, Civilian Casualties, and Support for the Use of Force," *Political Psychology* 36, no. 5 (2015): 507–523.

27 Lonna Rae Atkeson and Cherie D. Maestas, *Catastrophic Politics: How Extraordinary Events Redefine Perceptions of Government* (Cambridge: Cambridge University Press, 2012); Nyhan and Reifler, "When Corrections Fail."

28 Philip E. Tetlock and Aaron Belkin, "Counterfactual Thought Experiments in World Politics," in *Counterfactual Thought Experiments in World Politics: Logical, Methodological, and Psychological Experiments*, ed. Philip E. Tetlock and Aaron Belkin (Princeton, NJ: Princeton University Press, 1996), 32.

29 Bob Brecher, *Torture and the Ticking Bomb* (New York: John Wiley & Sons, 2007).

30 Brecher, *Torture and the Ticking Bomb*.

31 "America's Army 3: Frequently Asked Questions (FAQ)," http://aa3.americasarmy.com/documents/AA3_Knowledge_Center_FAQ.pdf.

32 Matthew Thomas Payne, "War Bytes: The Critique of Militainment in *Spec Ops: The Line*," *Critical Studies in Media Communication* 31, no. 4 (2014): 265–282.

33 Michael Freeden, "Ideology and Political Theory," *Journal of Political Ideologies* 11, no. 1 (2006): 3–22 at 20.

34 James N. Druckman, "The Implications of Framing Effects for Citizen Compe-
    tence," *Political Behavior* 23, no. 3 (2001): 225–256 at 235.
35 Ian Bogost, Simon Ferrari, and Bobby Schweizer, *Newsgames: Journalism at Play*
    (Cambridge, MA: MI T Press, 2010).
36 Aaron Hess, "'You Don't Play, You Volunteer': Narrative Public Memory Construc-
    tion in Medal of Honor: Rising Sun," *Critical Studies in Media Communication* 24,
    no. 4 (2007): 339–356 at 341.
37 Bogost, Ferrari, and Schweizer, *Newsgames*, 108.
38 Alexander Galloway, "Social Realism in Gaming," *Game Studies* 4, no. 1 (2004).
39 Colin H. Kahl, "In the Crossfire or the Crosshairs? Norms, Civilian Casualties, and
    U.S. Conduct in Iraq," *International Security* 32, no. 1 (2007): 7–46.
40 Kahl, "In the Crossfire or the Crosshairs?"
41 Ken McAllister, *Game Work: Language, Power, and Computer Game Culture*
    (Tuscaloosa: University of Alabama Press, 2006), 60.

Chapter 7   Speaking through Games

1 Amanda Lange, "'You're Just Gonna Be Nice': How Players Engage with Moral
   Choice Systems," *Journal of Games Criticism* 1, no. 1 (2014), http://gamescriticism
   .org/articles/lange-1-1/.
2 Mia Consalvo, Thorsten Busch, and Carolyn Jong, "Playing a Better Me: How
   Players Rehearse Their Ethos via Moral Choices," *Games and Culture* 14, no. 3
   (2016): 216–235 at 230.
3 Stephanie Patridge, "The Incorrigible Social Meaning of Video Game Imagery:
   Making Ethical Sense of Single-Player Video Games," *Ethics and Information
   Technology* 13, no. 4 (2011): 303–312 at 305.
4 Patridge, "The Incorrigible Social Meaning of Video Game Imagery," 308.
5 John Stuart Mill, *J. S. Mill: "On Liberty" and Other Writings* (Cambridge:
   Cambridge University Press, 1989), 13.
6 Joel Feinberg, *Offense to Others* (Oxford: Oxford University Press, 1985), 10.
7 Feinberg, *Offense to Others*, 13.
8 Marcus Schulzke, "The Social Benefits of Protecting Hate Speech and Exposing
   Sources of Prejudice," *Res Publica* 22, no. 2 (2016): 225–242.
9 Brian L. Ott, "Super Columbine Massacre RPG! The Procedural Rhetoric of
   Critical (Gun) Play," *Cultural Studies, Critical Methodologies* 17, no. 2 (2017):
   125–132.
10 Keith Stuart, "Danny Ledonne on Super Columbine Massacre RPG," *The Guardian*, August 9, 2007, https://www.theguardian.com/technology/gamesblog/2007
   /aug/09/dannyledonneo.
11 For example, see https://www.gamespot.com/forums/games-discussion-1000000
   /has-anyone-heard-of-super-columbine-massacre-rpg-26567231/.
12 David Leonard, "Not a Hater, Just Keepin' It Real," *Games and Culture* 1, no. 1
   (2006): 83–88 at 84.
13 https://www.cia.gov/library/publications/the-world-factbook/geos/us.htm.
14 Tracy L. Dietz, "An Examination of Violence and Gender Role Portrayals in Video
   Games: Implications for Gender Socialization and Aggressive Behavior," *Sex Roles*
   38, nos. 5–6 (1998): 425–442.
15 Berrin Beasely and Tracy Collins Standley, "Shirts vs. Skins: Clothing as an
   Indicator of Gender Role Stereotyping in Video Games," *Mass Communication and
   Society* 5, no. 3 (2002): 279–293 at 287.

16 Justine Cassell and Henry Jenkins, "Chess for Girls? Feminism and Computer Games," in *From Barbie to Mortal Kombat: Gender and Computer Games*, ed. Justine Cassell and Henry Jenkins (Cambridge, MA: MIT Press, 2000), 10.

17 Erica Sharrer, "Virtual Violence: Gender and Aggression in Video Game Advertisements," *Mass Communication and Society* 7, no. 4 (2004): 393–412.

18 James Ivory, "Still a Man's Game: Gender Representation in Online Reviews of Video Games," *Mass Communication and Society* 9, no. 1 (2006): 103–114 at 109.

19 Beasely and Standley, "Shirts vs. Skins," 293.

20 Dietz, "An Examination of Violence and Gender Role Portrayals in Video Games," 434.

21 Ben O'Loughlin, "Images as Weapons of War: Representation, Mediation, and Interpretation," *Review of International Studies* 37, no. 1 (2011): 71–91 at 81.

22 Anthony Sze-Fai Shiu, "What Yellowface Hides: Video Games, Whiteness, and the American Racial Order," *The Journal of Popular Culture* 39, no. 1 (2006): 109–125.

23 McKenzie Wark, *Gamer Theory* (Cambridge, MA: Harvard University Press, 2007), 138.

24 Tanner Higgin, "Blackless Fantasy: The Disappearance of Race in Massively Multiplayer Online Role-Playing Games," *Games and Culture* 4, no. 1 (2009): 3–26; Paul Barrett, "White Thumbs, Black Bodies: Race, Violence, and Neoliberal Fantasies in Grand Theft Auto: San Andreas," *Review of Education, Pedagogy & Cultural Studies* 28, no. 1 (2006): 95–119.

25 David Leonard, "'Live in Your World, Play in Ours': Race, Video Games, and Consuming the Other," *SIMILE: Studies in Media & Information Literacy Education* 3, no. 4 (2003): 1–9 at 3.

26 Susan Jeffords, *Hard Bodies: Hollywood Masculinity in the Reagan Era* (New Brunswick, NJ: Rutgers University Press, 2004), 147.

27 Barrett, "White Thumbs, Black Bodies,"; David Leonard, "Young, Black (& Brown) and Don't Give a Fuck," *Cultural Studies, Critical Methodologies* 9, no. 2 (2009): 248–272; Anna Everett and S. Craig Watkins, "The Power of Play: The Portrayal and Performance of Race in Video Games," in *The Ecology of Games: Connecting Youth, Games, and Learning*, ed. Katie Salen (Cambridge, MA: MIT Press, 2008).

28 Leonard, "Live in Your World, Play in Ours," 3.

29 Leonard, "Young, Black (& Brown) and Don't Give a Fuck," 254.

30 Kiri Miller, "The Accidental Carjack: Ethnography, Gameworld Tourism, and Grand Theft Auto," *Game Studies* 8, no. 1 (2008).

31 Leonard, "Young, Black (& Brown) and Don't Give a Fuck," 266.

32 Miller, "The Accidental Carjack."

33 Ben DeVane and Kurt D. Squire, "The Meaning of Race and Violence in Grand Theft Auto San Andreas," *Games and Culture* 3, nos. 3–4 (2008): 264–285 at 279.

34 Beasely and Standley, "Shirts vs. Skins," 289.

35 Eugene F. Provenso Jr., *Video Kids: Making Sense of Nintendo* (Cambridge, MA: Harvard University Press, 1991); Shirley Matile Ogletree and Ryan Drake, "College Students' Video Game Participation and Perceptions: Gender Differences and Implications," *Sex Roles* 56, nos. 9–10 (2007): 537–542; Melinda C. R. Burgess, Steven Paul Stermer, and Stephen R. Burgess, "Sex, Lies, and Video Games: The Portrayal of Male and Female Characters on Video Game Covers," *Sex Roles* 57, nos. 5–6 (2007): 419–433.

36 James Ivory, "Still a Man's Game: Gender Representation in Online Reviews of Video Games," *Mass Communication and Society* 9, no. 1 (2006): 103–114.

37 Maja Mikula, "Gender and Videogames: The Political Valency of Lara Croft," *Journal of Media & Cultural Studies* 17, no. 1 (2003): 79–87; Jeroen Jansz and Raynel G. Martis, "The Lara Phenomenon: Powerful Female Characters in Video Games," *Sex Roles* 56, nos. 3–4 (2007): 141–148; Arthur Asa Berger, *Video Games: A Popular Culture Phenomenon* (New Brunswick, NJ: Transaction, 2002); Helen W. Kennedy, "Lara Croft: Feminist Icon or Cyberbimbo? On the Limits of Textual Analysis," *Game Studies* 2, no. 2 (2002); Anne-Marie Schleiner, "Does Lara Croft Wear Fake Polygons? Gender and Gender-Role Subversion in Computer Adventure Games," *Leonardo* 34, no. 3 (2001): 221–226; Derek Burrill, *Die Tryin': Videogames, Masculinity, Culture* (New York: Peter Lang, 2008).

38 Berger, *Video Games*, 86.

39 Astrid Deuber Mankowsky, *Lara Croft: Cyber Heroine* (Minneapolis: University of Minnesota Press, 2005).

40 Jon Cogburn and Mark Silcox, *Philosophy through Video Games* (New York: Routledge, 2009), 67–68.

41 Helene Shugart, Catherine Egley Waggoner, and D. Lynn O'Brien Hallstein, "Mediating Third-Wave Feminism: Appropriation as Postmodern Media Practice," *Critical Studies in Media Communication* 18, no. 2 (2001): 194–210 at 195.

42 Mikula, "Gender and Videogames," 83.

43 Jansz and Martis, "The Lara Phenomenon."

44 Matt Lees, "What Gamergate Should Have Taught Us about the 'Alt-Right,'" *The Guardian*, December 1, 2016, https://www.theguardian.com/technology/2016/dec/01/gamergate-alt-right-hate-trump.

45 Dan Mills, "Explicit Sexual Content in Early Console Video Games," in *Rated M for Mature: Sex and Sexuality in Video Games*, ed. Matthew Wysocki and Evan Lauteria (New York: Bloomsbury, 2015), 90.

Index

About the Author

MARCUS SCHULZKE is the author of *The Pursuit of Moral Warfare: Ethical Theory and Practice in Counterinsurgency Operations* (2018); *Combat Drones and Support for the Use of Force*, with James Walsh (2018); *The Politics of New Atheism*, with Stuart McAnulla and Steven Kettell (2018); *Just War Theory and Civilian Casualties* (2017); and *The Morality of Drone Warfare and the Politics of Regulation* (2017).

Printed in the United States
By Bookmasters